Race, Politics, and Pandemic Pedagogy

Race, Politics, and Pandemic Pedagogy

Education in a Time of Crisis

Henry A. Giroux

BLOOMSBURY ACADEMIC

LONDON • NEW YORK • OXFORD • NEW DELHI • SYDNEY

BLOOMSBURY ACADEMIC
Bloomsbury Publishing Plc
50 Bedford Square, London, WC1B 3DP, UK
1385 Broadway, New York, NY 10018, USA

BLOOMSBURY, BLOOMSBURY ACADEMIC and the Diana logo are trademarks
of Bloomsbury Publishing Plc

First published in Great Britain 2021

For legal purposes the Acknowledgments on p. viii constitute an extension
of this copyright page.

Cover design: Charlotte James
Cover image © Isaac Cordal

Bloomsbury Publishing Plc does not have any control over, or responsibility for,
any third-party websites referred to or in this book. All internet addresses given
in this book were correct at the time of going to press. The author and publisher
regret any inconvenience caused if addresses have changed or sites have ceased
to exist, but can accept no responsibility for any such changes.

A catalogue record for this book is available from the British Library.

A catalog record for this book is available from the Library of Congress.

ISBN: HB: 978-1-3501-8442-8
        PB: 978-1-3501-8443-5
        ePDF: 978-1-3501-8444-2
        eBook: 978-1-3501-8445-9

Typeset by Integra Software Services Pvt. Ltd.
Printed and bound in Great Britain

To find out more about our authors and books visit www.bloomsbury.com
and sign up for our newsletters.

Dedication
For Rania who inspired my faith in the spirit of struggle, love, justice, and hope and taught me the real meaning of how to fight monsters

For Brett, Jack, Jeanne
Thanks to Tony, Ray, Donaldo, Ken, Jasmin, and Linda who never lost their moral center and courageous sense of civic courage.

...whether we are happy or unhappy leads us to write in one way or another. When we are happy our imagination is stronger; when we are unhappy our memory works with greater vitality.

Natalia Ginzburg

Contents

Acknowledgments

Writing is always a collective affair. We build on the ideas, support, and the visions of others. I have been extremely fortunate in writing this book to have had Rania Filippakou by my side. She read every paragraph, helped me refine my ideas, and reminded me when I needed to say more or, as she would say, be brave and willing to take risk when you fight the monsters. Her presence in this book is on every page. I also had the support of close friends who never let me down when I needed them. That includes Tony Penna, Donaldo Macedo, Ray Seliwoniuk, Ken Saltman, Maya and Igor Sabados, and Jasmin Habib. I want to thank Maya Sabados and Grace Pollock for their editorial help. I also want to thank McMaster University for giving me a space to think, teach, do research, and refine my attempts in my work and pedagogy to make a difference in the world. I am truly indebted to Alana Price and Maya Schenwar at *Truthout*, Jeffrey St. Clair at *CounterPunch*, Rowan Wolf at *Uncommon Thought*, and Andrew O'Hehir at *Salon* for their incredible support in publishing my work. Bill Moyers has always been supportive of my work and I am grateful and honored. My dear comrade Oscar Zambrano always has an insightful comment on what I publish and I have learned a great deal from his tireless writings. Brad Evans and I have been working together for years; he is an international treasure and I am always learning from him. I am also grateful and fortunate to have Mark Richardson as my editor at Bloomsbury. He encouraged the project right from the beginning and was always there to support the work. I want to thank my friend, the gifted artist, Isaac Cordal, for allowing me to use his work for the cover of my book. I want to thank my sister, Linda, for always being there for me in good and bad times. Thanks to Ben Fortino who helped me start a new and life-giving chapter in my life. I also want to thank those young people who inspire and energize me and from whom I learn what it means to take seriously matters of justice and civic courage.

Preface: State of Crisis

In this book, I examine how politics is mediated through a series of contemporary events, all of which became more visible with the emergence of the Covid-19 crisis. These include not only a crisis of education in which people began to rethink the very nature of politics and power but also the long-standing elements of police violence, systemic racism, social and economic inequalities, and the increasing visibility of an updated version of fascist politics. The period under review begins on January 30, 2020 when the Director General of the World Health Organization declared the outbreak of Covid-19 as a public health emergency of international concern. I examine the period between the emergence of the Covid-19 crisis and the rise in state repression across the globe, including the occupation of cities by military troops in the U.S., and a growing global resistance to such oppression. The book ends with the defeat of Donald Trump's 2020 bid for re-election for the presidency. During this period, institutional racism became evident with murder of George Floyd, Breonna Taylor and a number of other people of color by white police officers. The Covid-19 crisis also signaled an economic collapse that revealed degrees of poverty and mass suffering that were previously hidden beneath the rhetoric of liberal capitalism. Education was, once again, under siege as teachers were being asked to risk their lives and the lives of their students in order to keep the economy functioning, in spite of the warnings of health experts. Millions of people lost their jobs and did not receive the economic aid they needed to be able to fulfill even basic needs.

This period marks a distinctive episode in both American history and across the globe. It produced new political formations that shifted the nature of the debate about confronting state violence and the rise of a fascist politics, especially under the Trump regime. It also exposed the workings of a failed state under neoliberal capitalism. I also look at what such an analysis might mean for developing a vision of the future. The chronology used in the book is dialectical and moves interchangeably at times between events that took place in the past, present, and point to the future. The issue here is to make clear why this period in time is important, what we can learn from it, and how it speaks to history as a repository of insights and lessons that need to be interrogated, reclaimed, and relearned in the interest of building a democratic socialist society. The notions of critical and pandemic pedagogy are central to this book. They are articulated as a set of concepts that are crucial to understanding how agency, knowledge, desire, and values are struggled over. They are also crucial to understanding both the nature of the global crisis and what it means to rethink politics in the interest of developing mass movements of resistance, especially in the face of the rise of a fascist politics, both in the United States and in a number of countries across the globe. While the focus of this study is on the United States, it has serious implications for how we understand and challenge capitalism as it becomes transformed globally into an updated version of fascist politics. This points not only to an economic and political struggle but also an educational struggle of the first order, one that is necessary to rethink critically matters of agency, power, politics, and justice.

A darkness has spread across the globe, driven by a pandemic pestilence that exhibits a dystopian presence at odds with any just, prudent, and equitable notion of the future. America is in a state of crisis. This medical, racial, economic, and educational crisis touches every aspect of public life. We are in a new historical period, one that has inherited a neoliberal legacy in which every aspect of society has been transformed and corrupted by the tools of financialization, deregulation, and austerity. This is an era in which the scourge of neoliberalism merged with the ideologies of racial cleansing, militarism, and a politics of disposability—an age in which economic activity was divorced from social costs, all the while enabling policies of racial sorting, white nationalism, and a militarized culture to become defining features of the public sphere. It is also an age in which the Covid-19 pandemic has revealed with laser-beam clarity how incapable the irrationality of a profit-driven capitalism is in dealing with a global public health crisis that has been as catastrophic as it has been deadly. Global capitalism has blood on its hands given its willingness to subordinate human life to profit-making, which is directly related to its failure to check the spread of infections and deaths, especially in the United States.

We are also in a period in which established modes of governance are in the midst of a legitimation crisis and new political formations are trying to be reborn, to paraphrase the Italian Marxist Antonio Gramsci. Out of this period of uncertainty, new forces for change have appeared evident in the presence of millions across the globe protesting racial injustice and state violence. The Covid-19 plague has produced an age of uncertainty, fragmentation, despair, and a dire foreboding about the future. Certainties have been replaced by shared fears. More troubling is the apprehension that the present crisis has an air of longevity about it, constituting a turning point in history. The stark choice of what the future might look like appears to hang between the forces of despotism and democracy. Yet, as real as this foreboding appears, history is open, but how it unfolds remains in the balance. The pandemic has been a crisis that cannot be allowed to turn into a catastrophe in which all hope is lost. On the contrary, the pandemic that threatens democracy should also offer up the possibility to rethink politics and the habits of critical education, human agency, values, and what life would be like in a democratic socialist society. Amid the devastation produced by neoliberal capitalism and Covid-19, there are also flashes of hope, a chance to move beyond a contemporary resurgence of authoritarianism, especially with the election of Joe Biden as the President of the United States. This suggests rejecting the normalizing ideologies of a poisonous cynicism and a paralyzing conformity endemic to neoliberal capitalism. It also points to the need to reclaim a vision of a radical politics that is more compassionate, equitable, just, and inclusive.

Within a new wave of resistance and rebellion, anti-democratic principles that had been normalized have been questioned with an inspiring sense of collective urgency. This is especially true among people of color and others bearing the burden of economic and political colonialism. The horrors of inequality, compulsory austerity, defunding of public health systems, and the collapse of the economy in 2008 produced by five decades of neoliberalism are finally being acknowledged as the fundamental plague behind the current pandemic. Under capitalism, public health in the United States has been stripped to the bone. As Ed Yong points out in *The Atlantic*, "Today, the U.S. spends just 2.5% of its gigantic health-care budget on public health ... Since the last recession, in 2009, chronically strapped local health departments have lost 55,000 jobs—a quarter of their workforce." The result is a system that has "the lowest life-expectancy rate of comparable countries, the highest rates of chronic disease, and the fewest doctors per person."[1]

Neoliberalism has produced a plague marked by egregious degrees of exploitation, unchecked militarism, and a racialized politics of disposability in which human beings were viewed as expendable, reinforced if not propelled by an ethos of white nationalism and white supremacy. This long residue of unbridled capitalism is inseparable from its deep-rooted institutionalized racism and a pestilence of disposability, updated into a form of neoliberal fascism. The roots of historic fascism have emerged in new forms in the United States as an evolutionary form that "has distinct features specific to the political and culture of each country."[2]

Fascist principles now operate at so many levels of everyday society that it is difficult to recognize them, especially as they have the imprimatur of power at the highest levels of government. Fascist pedagogical ideas, practices, and desires work through diverse social media platforms and mainstream and right-wing cultural apparatuses in multiple ways. This is the space of a pandemic pedagogy, a system of knowledge, ideas, values, and desires that constitute particular identities, relationships, and specific versions of the present and future. These pedagogical practices are produced in the workstations and cultural pathways that function ideologically and politically to objectify people, promote spectacles of violence, endorse consumerism as the only viable way of life, and legitimate a murderous nationalism.

The pandemic pedagogy that has emerged in the midst of this plague makes ignorance, as both the absence of knowledge and the willful refusal to know, a fundamental principle of politics, and in doing so tends to function so as "to erase everything that matters."[3] Pandemic pedagogy works subconsciously as an affective mode of self-sabotage. It legitimates the language of hate in everyday exchanges, degrades people of color, promotes thoughtlessness through the ubiquity of celebrity culture, and produces an endless array of authoritarian pedagogical practices that serve to exploit, dominate, and depoliticize us. In the pandemic fog of social and historical amnesia, moral boundaries disappear, people become more accepting of extreme acts of cruelty, and willingly submit to propaganda machines that disdain notions of truth and view any viable critique of power as "fake news," all the while disconnecting language and policies from their harmful damages. While I speak in the present tense, this is a legacy that will be with us for some time to come regardless of Trumps failure to be re-elected.

This dark plague of neoliberal fascism is just one pestilence among many. This is a pestilence that engulfs U.S. society as memories of caged children disappear into a culture of immediacy, the killing of journalists is forgotten, and the lynching of Black bodies is buried beneath the discourse of a post-racial society. In addition, the terror of a fascist politics evaporates in the affective modalities of pleasure and fear, and a rampant culture of political theater and spectacles. As the driving educative force of fascist politics, pandemic pedagogy has closed down the space of translation, and thrives on a machinery of inscriptions that erases the notion that human beings are not only moral and political agents but also historical subjects capable of both understanding and changing the world. Pandemic pedagogy has made clear that the most important forms of domination are cultural, intellectual, and pedagogical while embracing the tools of belief and persuasion as appropriate weapons in the struggle over meaning, knowledge, values, and identities. This depoliticizing practice is not only a political and ethical issue but also an educational issue that undermines the power of critical understanding to produce the capacity for action, empowerment, and transformation. Pandemic pedagogy functions as a propaganda machine to bury what Foucault once called "the dramaturgy of the real."

On the other hand, critical pedagogy works to establish a symbolic relationship with the world. It highlights the workings of power and the possibility to use the symbolic and pedagogical tools of resistance as weapons in the struggle over power, knowledge, agency, and social relations. This is a pedagogy in which the political becomes more pedagogical by taking on the challenge of using the power of persuasion to change the way people see things and resist those ideas and institutions that thrive on the energies of the political zombies. Critical pedagogy deepens the role of the political by including and emphasizing the importance of the struggle over cultural meanings and identities as well as over crucial political terrains like the workplace, schools, and the state. If pandemic pedagogy fuels multiple forms of domination that accelerate the deaths of the unwanted and makes social death a self-generated practice, critical pedagogy is the partial political antidote to such practices.

As a counterpoint to existing forms of pandemic pedagogy, the relationship among education, historical consciousness and political action points to new possibilities for change. And while historical consciousness can be both informative and emancipatory, it can lead to "malicious interpretations of the present, as well as elements of history that are difficult to accept."[4] The trajectory of history is not innocent and it needs to be interrogated in order to think through how we can build on it through a process of critique and possibility. At the level of critique, as Angela Davis, has suggested, "we need to figure out context within which people can understand the nature of U.S. history and the role that racism and capitalism and heteropatriarchy have played in forging that history."[5]

On the more emancipatory and empowering side, critical pedagogy informed by historical consciousness and moral witnessing can uncover dangerous memories and the narratives of those whose voices have been drowned out by those who have the power to write history to serve their narrow and reactionary interests. The surge of infections and deaths produced by the Covid-19 pandemic were largely the result of a lack of leadership and ignorance by the Trump administration, matched by a surge of violence by paramilitary forces sent to the nations' cities. The essence of fascism is not only the thirst for violence and the offering to the masses the spectacle of uniformed officers purging the nation of undesirables," but also the relentless, manufactured spread of lies, hatred and falsehoods.[6] One of the greatest dangers facing the U.S was and is a pandemic of willful ignorance and the willingness to surrender power, as individual and social agents, to those who write the past and present in the scripts of domination. Education has never been more imperative as a political tool that can offer the resources to challenge the ideological, educational, and militant practices deployed by emerging right-wing and fascist groups. Education is crucial for understanding how power shapes and is reinvented with respect to questions of culture, sexuality, history and political agency.

As a political project, critical pedagogy makes visible the struggle over those public and private spaces in which people's everyday lives are aligned with particular narratives, identities, cultural practices, and political values. As such, pedagogy is the essential scaffolding of social interaction and the foundation of the public sphere. It is a crucial political practice because it takes seriously what it means to understand the relationship between how to learn and how to act as individual and social agents; that is, it is concerned not only with how individuals learn to think critically but also how they come to grips with a sense of individual and social responsibility. At issue here is the political question of what it means to be responsible for one's actions as part of a broader attempt to be an engaged citizen who can expand and deepen the possibilities of democratic public life. Human agency is inseparable from the formative cultures and pedagogical practices that create the possibility of a mobilized citizenry and radical change.

As such, critical understanding is not just a state of mind but an empowering practice. It is the precondition for social change and pedagogy is crucial in shifting the way people view themselves, others, and the larger world. Democracy requires a certain kind of citizen who thinks in terms of broader solidarities and is willing to both translate private troubles into larger systemic considerations and challenge the various threats being mobilized against the ideas of justice, equity, and popular sovereignty. In order to make education central to politics, critical pedagogy should provide the capacities, knowledge and skills that enable people to speak, write and act from a position of agency and empowerment. In addition, it should energize individuals to think differently so they can act differently. For instance, the current mass rebellions against racism, inequality, and injustice have embraced the pedagogical task of recognizing those modes of agency, identity, and values that have been erased from the script of economic, political, and personal rights.

Agency is being rethought within a notion of freedom that expands human rights to the realm of economic rights. The notion of agency is severely limited and political and personal rights are largely invalidated if one is engaged in a constant struggle to survive economically. In addition, individual freedom under neoliberal capitalism falls on the side of undermining the solidarities needed to live in a socially responsible and just society. As Frank Bruni puts it, "along the way, we went from celebrating individual liberty to fetishizing it, so that for too many Americans, all sense of civic obligation and communal good went out the window."[7] Americans have been in the midst of a crisis in which it is crucial for individuals and social movements to learn anew how to take responsibility, to learn how to listen, and to act with vigilance. The pandemics of injustice that are ushering in massive degrees of poverty, exclusion, suffering and death must be resisted with a new understanding of politics and agency. Moreover, the capacities for individual agency must be expanded to a notion of social agency imbued with a sense of collective resistance. In the current historical moment, this points to the necessity to create an international social movement for the defense of public goods and the principles of a democratic socialist society.

The pandemic crisis, even now, is much more than a medical crisis. At its core, it is both a political and an ideological crisis. This is a crisis of agency and politics. If the radical political horizons of a future society are to be brought into fruition, it is crucial to engage those everyday pedagogical spaces where identities are produced, modes of recognition come into play, and critical points of view can be redeemed. The energies of fascism have become less intense, more fragile, and open to challenge as the limits of right-wing and updated fascist populist movements become more visible. As the virus spread, the merchants of misery and hate had no language to explain or address "the ubiquity of death" spreading across the planet.[8]

Fundamental to the pandemic plague is the need to develop a new political language and mode of identification in which the crisis of citizenship is connected to the crisis of education, and the crisis of globalization is situated within the crisis of power. The most important challenge that the pandemic has produced is not simply how to stop the spread of the virus; we must ask what kind of society do we want in the future, how do we want to live, and who will be the agents to address these issues? Under what narrative for justice will various resistance movements both domestically and internationally come together to put an end to the pandemic of poverty, inequality, racism, and militarism, all of which will outlive the Trump presidency?

The relevance of this challenge hinges on reclaiming the relationship between education and democracy and taking seriously the recognition that the force of education operates in multiple social and public spaces and those spaces should be places where individuals can realize themselves as informed and critically engaged citizens. The pandemic that mushroomed under the Trump administration followed a wave of right-wing movements and modes of governing whose aim was to destroy any vestige of a democratic society and to relegate the value of ethical and social responsibility and the question of justice to the wasteland of political thought.

The ugly terror of a fascist abyss that lurked in the background of this pandemic—one that murdered dreams and employed cynicism as common sense—prevented people from claiming any democratic sense of moral and political agency. What this dystopian pandemic has taught us is that democracy is fragile as "a way of life" and that, if it is to survive, critical education and pedagogy must become central to producing citizens who are informed, politically aware, and willing to produce a culture with the habits and sensibilities that keep a democracy alive. If there is a lesson to be learned from the pandemic it is that democracy is only as strong as the people who inhabit it and who are willing to struggle to keep justice, equity, and the principles of a socialist democracy alive. This is the lesson that will help to prevent the dark clouds of fascism from prevailing in the future the United States and throughout the globe.

A Biden presidency should not point to the end of Trumpism or more accurately a toxic form of neoliberal fascism. The end of Trump's presidency does not suggest that the national nightmare has come to an end, it simply means it is no longer at the center of a mode of governance that wears its racism, corporate greed, cruelty, deadly incompetence, and authoritarianism like a badge of honor. Trump's defeat should not erase the notion that the political, economic, and cultural forces that created the conditions for his presidency have disappeared.

The struggle ahead will be to expose the forces that made Trump possible, to examine how both political parties participated in putting in place the conditions that enabled his coming to power. It is also crucial to think big, create a civic vision in which it becomes possible to put in place a notion of democracy that is truly radical in its call for social justice, broad-based political representation, and economic equality. This project is not merely a political task but also an educational necessity.

The millions across the globe that mobilized against state violence in order to build a socialist democracy were fueled and inspired by the struggle to dismantle the death-machine at the core of the empire. In the current historical moment, democracy may be under a severe threat and appear frighteningly vulnerable, but with young people and others who continue to rise up across the globe – inspired, energized and willing to march in the streets – the future of a socialist democracy is waiting to breathe again. The challenge is too critical to ignore since both humanity and the life of the planet are at stake.

Section I

Pandemic Landscapes

Pandemic Politics and Pedagogy in the Age of the Coronavirus

Education is the most powerful weapon which you can use to change the world.

Nelson Mandela

Neoliberalism as a Pandemic Plague

We have been living in a world that resembles a dystopian novel. A world that could only be imagined as a harrowing work of fiction. The American dream as a promise was pushed aside to give prominence to an American nightmare. We were told not to get close to each other, door handles had an air of danger, civil liberties were evaporating, streets were empty, businesses were shuttered, death tolls were climbing, borders were back with a vengeance, and fear and precarity became the new norm. Roughly 95 percent of the American population at some point was under some form of lockdown, voluntary or state-imposed. We were told endlessly by politicians, health experts, and various pundits that we were in the midst of a medical crisis. They were only partly right.

The current coronavirus pandemic was more than a medical crisis; it was also a political and ideological crisis. It was a crisis deeply rooted in years of neglect by neoliberal governments that denied the importance of public health and the public good while defunding institutions that made them possible. At the same time, this crisis could not be separated from the scourge of inequalities in wealth, income, and power that grew relentlessly since the 1970s.[1] Nor could it be separated from a crisis of democratic values, education, and civic literacy.[2] Through the destructive assaults waged by neoliberal capital on the welfare state and ecosystem, the Covid-19 pandemic was deeply interconnected with the politicization of the social order.[3] In addition, neoliberalism could not be disconnected from the spectacle of racism, ultra-nationalism, anti-immigrant sentiment, and bigotry that dominated the national zeitgeist as a means of promoting shared fears rather than shared responsibilities. Neoliberal capitalism created through its destruction of the economy, environment, education, and public health care a petri dish for the virus to wreak havoc and wide-scale destruction.

The ideological virus-plague had as one of its roots a politics of depoliticization rooted in a variety of market-based assumptions and pedagogical practices. And it will be with us for some time. This is a form of pandemic pedagogy that works to attack and undermine those ideas, values, desires, and modes of agency that enable individuals to become critically engaged actors. As a pedagogical practice, it constructs modes of agency and identification that make it easier for individuals to support and participate in a system that concentrates power in the hands of a financial elite. Moreover, it embraces the moral messages of bigotry, weakens the idea of social responsibility, and undermines the public sphere as a site of hope. Pandemic pedagogy reads the world largely through racialized categories, the purification of national cultures, and the language of privatization and commodity consumption. It is enamored of power to benefit the market and the market's need to create modes of agency defined by commercial and financial exchanges. Pandemic pedagogy produces narratives, forms of identification, values, and a notion of the future pumping with nationalistic adrenalin in which the space of militarism and the coercive metrics of war define social relations, with violence always close by.

Pandemic pedagogy is the enemy of critical pedagogy because it is wedded to reproducing a debased civic culture while renouncing democratic social and political relations. It is a pedagogy for which power functions in the cultural sphere to depoliticize people while replacing democratic forms of solidarity with a social order invested in ultra-nationalism, social atomization, hyper-masculinity, a war culture, and an unbridled individualism. All problems are now cast as a matter of individual fate. It has been a central pedagogical principle of neoliberalism that individual accountability is the only way to address social problems, and, consequently, there is no need to address broader systemic issues, hold power accountable, or embrace matters of collective obligation.[4]

As part of the ongoing crisis, politicians borrowed from the neoliberal pandemic playbook by defining the Covid-19 virus as "an intruder that ... entered human society independently from anything even remotely related to neoliberal politics."[5] In this analysis, politics and power disappear, relegating matters of collective care and support for public health and the common good to the status of an afterthought. When issues are defined through the false narrative of a "natural order," matters of self-and social responsibility degenerate into paralyzing forms of indifference or cynicism. All that is left is an alien world that exists beyond the reach of collective actions, poised against an isolated and privatized self.

To paraphrase Jill Lepore, this is a dystopian world that undermines resistance, glories in fake news, embraces despair, and produces "the fiction of helplessness and hopelessness" whose mantra is "despair more," and go shopping.[6] This was not only Donald Trump's world, but the world of neoliberal capitalism. This was a worldview elevated to the level of a fascist politics that worked ceaselessly to produce a formative culture whose goal was to exacerbate the separateness of others through a discourse of fear and hatred. These narratives of ruin are basic neoliberal assumptions and are at odds with matters of agency, power, and education that are a central feature of a substantive democracy. Neoliberalism's emphasis on commercial rather than democratic values, its virulent ideology of extreme individualism, competitiveness, amoral selfishness, and its disdain for matters of ethics, justice, and truth have undermined critical thought and the power of informed judgment. This is a crisis of politics shot through with indignity, cruelty, and injustice. Moreover, as Pankaj Mishra states, "for decades now, de-industrialization, the outsourcing of jobs, and then automation, have deprived many working people of their security and dignity, making the aggrieved ... vulnerable to demagoguery."[7]

This scourge of neoliberalism camouflages itself as a matter of common sense, produced and legitimated through a pandemic pedagogy that sabotages critical modes of agency. As a politics of control, neoliberalism privatizes and individualizes social problems, i.e., wash your hands, do not sit on toilet seats, and practice social distancing, as a way to contain the pandemic. In this instance, we learned how to be safe while being depoliticized, or uninformed about the role that capitalist economies play in producing a range of ideological viruses that gut the social welfare state and public health systems, if not resistance itself. As Mark Fisher has noted in his use of the term "capitalist realism," capitalism "presents the widespread sense that not only is [it] the only viable political and economic system, but also that it is now impossible even to imagine a coherent alternative to it."[8]

As a mode of pandemic pedagogy, neoliberalism presents itself in an almost infinite number of social media platforms, books, classroom courses, and other sources as the only legitimate political and economic system for which there is no alternative. In doing so, "it seeks to contain any real democratic politics; that is to say, a politics based on collective solidarity and equality [because] democratic politics is a threat to the market."[9] Democracy is dangerous to market fundamentalists because it demands social measures to balance the unfettered power of capital and capitalists to generate profits for the minority at the expense of the majority. Market fundamentalism defines citizens as consumers who are not called upon to think, debate, and engage the world critically. Public goods such as education become instrumentalized and education is reduced to training, empty careerism, and market-based discourses of calculation and networking.[10] Or, more recently, educational discourse is dominated by a technocratic rationality obsessed with methodological considerations regarding online teaching and learning. What the latter make clear is that neoliberalism is both a politics and a pedagogy of containment and disappearance. In this view, the mechanisms of oppressive power become invisible, disposable groups are relegated to spaces of social abandonment, and politics is reduced to elections dominated by the ultra-rich and corporate elite.

As such, critical thought becomes a hindrance and the need for a democracy to cultivate critically educated and engaged citizens gives way to the language of self-interest, privatization, and anti-intellectualism, opening the door for demagogues such as Trump to skirt accountability and flood (tweet) the public with an endless series of falsehoods and fabrications, particularly regarding the current pandemic in the United States.[11] In this instance, the need for a critical and public pedagogy gave way to a pandemic pedagogy of lies and racist slandering, along with a glut of conspiracy theories.[12]

Americans live at a time when neoliberalism wages war on the public and inequality is recast as a virtue. The current historical moment supports notions of self-interest that tear up social solidarities in devastating ways. This historical moment puts a premium on competitive attitudes and unchecked individualism, and allows the market to become a template for structuring all social relations. One effect is that the social contract has been all but eliminated while notions of the public good, social obligations, and democratic forms of solidarity are under attack. Ravaged for decades by neoliberal policies, American society is plagued by a series of crises whose deeper roots have intensified stark class and racial divides. The mass uprisings that have taken place over racial violence, racial capitalism, and the calls to defund the police were a reflection, in part, of the legitimation crisis that neoliberal fascism is experiencing.

Such a divide is evident in the "thirty-four million workers who do not have a single day of paid sick leave"; "30 million people in the US [who] do not have health insurance"; and the shameful existence of "550,000 homeless people in the US."[13] Nearly half of Americans have trouble paying their monthly bills and would have trouble paying for an unexpected $400 expense or emergency.[14] What the pandemic revealed is that neoliberalism can no longer utilize or count on making class and racism disappear as a category through the work of the normalizing and depoliticizing conservative media. Covid-19 also humbled us and, in the words of Min Li Chan, "dispelled us of a belief in individual invincibility … [while making clear] that old habits of thought had to change."[15]

Another cruel neoliberal register of the United States as a highly iniquitous society is the rise of the racial carceral state marked by the largest prison population in the world.[16] As the Covid-19 virus accelerated throughout society, it posed a particularly deadly threat to people in jails and prisons. Inmates, largely people of color, faced a death sentence in prisons where thousands of individuals were in close proximity to each other. This danger is amplified by the fact that the US has the highest incarceration rate in the world, with 4 percent of the world's population and 21 percent of the world's incarcerated population. The widespread threat of infection was made clear, in one instance, when officials tested the entire population at the Marion Correctional facility in Ohio. As Judd Legum points out, "The testing revealed 'at least 1,950 inmates—or 78% of the prison population—and at least 154 staff members have COVID-19.'"[17]

This enforced ruthlessness amounts to a form of state terrorism wedded to a machinery of death and fueled by the rise of the punishing state. At work here is a predatory capitalism that speaks in the market-based language of profits, runaway privatization, and commercial exchange. It also legitimates the language of isolation, deprivation, human suffering, and unbounded precarity. Neoliberal capitalism is the underlying pandemic that fed the global shortage of medical supplies, testing, hospital beds, and robust social welfare provisions, and a growing indifference to human life. The market is another type of lethal virus—a prototype of fascist politics—lurking beneath the apocalyptic social, economic, and medical dislocations taking place every day.

The fear and plague of death was everywhere matched only by the continuing instances of denial, incompetence, and failures of the Trump administration. This is not a form of denial born of ignorance, but as Brian Massumi points out, "an extension of the template of climate denialism to the coronavirus."[18] It was also born out of a neoliberal fear of the return of the protective state, stealth socialism, and the nationalization of crucial spheres such as health care.

Death had a new prominence in the midst of the coronavirus and was visible in a lethality marked by deep inequalities. Capitalism's spaces of neglect, injustice, and depravation, such as nursing homes, the assisted care industry, prisons, and hospitals, were overburdened with the infirm. These landscapes of neglect and despair were filled with the homeless, elderly, and poor, who were disproportionally poor black and brown people. Such populations were relegated in a time of crisis to zones of abandonment to be sacrificed on "the altar of the economy."[19] In this scenario, the apostles of neoliberalism believed that catering to the economy was more important than saving human lives, especially those who have always been viewed as expendable. The sheer ruthlessness and pathological amorality of the market came into play in the call to sacrifice the most vulnerable in order to save the economy. Massumi viewed this as bearing an eerie resemblance to the racial cleansing killing machines of the past. He writes:

> The free-market economy must be saved at all costs. We just have to push through. The most vulnerable should be good troopers and prepare to self-sacrifice to save the country from this threat worse than death: a sick economy. The old, the immuno-compromised, the homeless, and all those who tend in the best of times to fall to the bottom of the triage list (the disabled, those with autism, people with Downs, people with dementia, the poor) will be the nation's unsung heroes. Never mind the resemblance to eugenics.[20]

Under such circumstances, the social sphere and its interconnections became an object of either financial exploitation or utter disdain, or both. What was lost in this depoliticizing and dehumanizing discourse of neoliberalism, made visible in the remains of the pandemic, is that lives are indeed interconnected, for better or for worse. The one thing that should be learned from this pandemic, as well as the mass protest against police brutality and systemic racism, is that the only way for humanity to survive in the future is through new and vibrant forms of social solidarity that "benefit public well-being" and enable Americans to discover their "collective selves."[21] The call for solidarity in the midst of these medical, economic, and racial crises had to be extended to a society in which compassion, mutual aid, shared responsibilities, and collective trust in one another became closely linked to the acquisition of agency, justice, and structural transformation of the larger society. The notion of the social with its mutual networks of interconnections, entanglements, and responsibilities must be reclaimed. As Judith Butler observes, there is a need to face "the way in which we are constituted in relationality: implicated, beholden, derived, and sustained by a social world that is beyond us and before us."[22]

There was a certain irony in the White House call for the public to abide by social distancing. This call, relentlessly violated and disparaged by Trump and Vice President Pence, not only mirrored a medically safe practice to slow down the spread of the virus but also occupied and operated in a different political register—a long-standing neoliberal ideological space that disdained social connections and democratic values while promoting forms of social atomization and hyper-individualism. This is where the medical crisis ran head-on into to a long-standing political contradiction. What was touted as a necessary medical position reinforces by default a hyper-individualism that put self-interests above concerns with the health of others. This was and is also the space where politics had become a tool of neoliberalism as the economy and powers of government attacked and eroded the common good and the foundations necessary for a strong democracy.

In a time of crisis, capitalism reveals itself as a disimagination machine whose underlying message is that the market and whiteness provide the only forms of agency left. In this context, political, economic, and cultural apparatuses become the new pedagogical pandemic workstations incessantly promoting the flight from any vestige of social, ethical, and political responsibility, while parading as the new race- and class-based common sense. Neoliberalism as a disimagination machine produces a high threshold of disappearance, which includes the eradication of truth, facts, evidence, critical judgments, and bodies.

Under such circumstances, everyone becomes an island, a paragon of self-interest, disconnected from society's moral index, broader social issues, and political formations.

Like the coronavirus, neoliberalism is a death-saturated apparatus that has no regard for human life. At work here is a society defined by racial exclusions, the exacerbation of class privilege, the widening of the racial divide, a depoliticizing culture of consumerism, and a punishing state that criminalizes social problems and incarcerates those populations it considers disposable. Of course, the price to be paid as a result of such ruthless practices will come back to haunt the U.S. during a pandemic, because it was recognized that the biggest threat for spreading the virus will in fact came from those groups whom a neoliberal social order viewed as excess. These included millions of people in overcrowded prisons and jails, run-down nursing homes, crowded homeless shelters, and one of the most vulnerable groups, the elderly. It also included "people without access to doctors, paid medical leave or decent housing [who] are unable to quarantine themselves."[23] In this context, it is hard to miss that the threat to public health posed by disposable populations put in harm's way can no longer be viewed through the punishing lens of faulty character, moral failure, or individual limitations. These groups are victims of a form of capitalist oppression steeped in a mind-boggling system of inequality, rife with systemic deprivations and targeted denials.

Central to disimagination machines are oppressive forms of public pedagogy whose aim is to replace social categories, civic responsibilities, and power relations with market values. Trump's language during the pandemic crisis repeatedly elevated the rule of capital, the economy, and profits over human life. In the initial stages of the crisis, Trump's press briefings and public remarks functioned as a form of debased public relations, echoing the performances that marked his political rallies. On January 22, 2020, Trump falsely claimed that the crisis was under total control. In February, he stated without evidence that a vaccine would soon be available to everyone, and in March, he played down the crisis stating, "It will go away." Moreover, as Adam Serwer documents, Trump was constantly and "consciously contradicting his administration's own public-health officials" such as Anthony Fauci, the director of the National Institute of Allergy and Infectious Diseases who was warning that "things will get worse than they are right now."[24] By April, the pandemic was raging. Yet, the White House decided to hand off the responsibility to the states for handling the crisis. According to the *New York Times*, the White House "referred to this as 'state authority handoff,' and it was at the heart of what would become at once a catastrophic policy blunder and an attempt to escape blame for a crisis that had engulfed the country—perhaps one of the greatest failures of presidential leadership in generations."[25] By October, Trump continued to ignore what his top health advisors stated was a "coronavirus pandemic that had driven America to its knees amid a disturbing surge" marked by over 7.2 million infected individuals and more than 207,000 deaths. More concerned about his re-election campaign, Trump discounted the viral surge by essentially abandoning the White House pandemic force for two months, which he viewed as being responsible for bad publicity. In the end, Trump used the pandemic crisis as a racist punch line designed to appeal to his hardcore base.[26]

Under neoliberalism in the age of plagues, politics becomes a war machine running overtime to habituate people to the contradictory operations of power while undermining any sense of dissent, resistance, and social justice. Of course, such inexplicable behavior has to be viewed as part of the wider plague of neoliberalism in which the coronavirus pandemic operates. The financial crisis of 2008 made visible the savage cruelty of neoliberal austerity policies that have for decades ravaged the public good and imposed misery and suffering upon the poor and others considered excess, waste, or unproductive. Unfortunately, the economic crisis was not matched by a crisis of recognition, in spite of the large-scale discrediting of the ruling elite; it appears that little was learned.[27] With its merging of brutal austerity policies, financialization of the economy, the concentration of power in few hands, and the language of racial and social cleansing, neoliberalism has morphed into a form of fascist politics. The new political formation is characterized by a distinctive and all-embracing politics of disposability, racial hatred, a massive gutting of the social state, and support for cultural apparatuses that spectacularize violence, fear-mongering, and state terror. Brutal racialized police violence aimed at undocumented immigrants and poor black people has become its most recent public expression.

Under the Trump administration, fear became a central organizing pedagogical principle, functioning as a drug to induce a political and moral coma, one informed by an endless capacity for diversion and malice. Such actions pointed to a disregard for any notion of the social state that expands the meaning and possibilities of the common good and public health. Also treated with disdain was the broader notion of what Michael Sandel called living together in a community in which matters of solidarity and the sacrifices we make function to treat people with compassion, humanity, and dignity.[28] At the core of Trump's disdain for the common good, argues Shai Lavi, was the fear of a mass movement willing to bring together struggles for emancipation, economic justice, and "political community … founded … on the basis of human equality."[29] That fear became more obvious as millions throughout the globe protested against police violence and racial injustice.

The Politics of a Failed State

The brutality of the pandemic of neoliberalism was evident in Trump's hasty plan on March 16, 2020 to "reopen the economy" by Easter. At that time, he would end cautious measures such as social distancing, and let the contagion run its course. Trump initially rationalized this position by repeating a right-wing argument that "the cure is worse than the disease." After being told by medical experts that 2.2 million people could die if the economy opened too early, Trump "announced that the White House would keep its guidelines for social distancing in place through the end of April."[30] Even then, projections made by the departments of Homeland Security and Health and Human Services estimated that if stay-at-home orders were lifted to open the economy, there would be a "dramatic infection spike and death tolls that would rival doing nothing."[31]

As death tolls from the pandemic reached 140,000 in July 2020, Trump put more Americans at risk by downplaying the need for social distancing and wearing masks, reducing funds for testing, and undermining the top infectious disease expert, Dr. Fauci. Not only did he rarely abide by such precautions himself, he encouraged his followers to put pressure on those states engaged in lockdown rules. Even worse, Trump held a rally in Tulsa, Oklahoma, bragging before the event that 1 million people had requested tickets for it. Both the city's top health official and the editorial board of *The Tulsa World* asked Trump not to hold the rally in a 19,000-seat arena, given the direct danger it posed to people attending. Trump's political opportunism was on full display in responding to urgent requests to protect public safety. His response was as revealing as it was inhumane. His campaign issued a statement indicating that Trump supporters sign a waiver ahead of time indicating they "absolve the president's campaign of any liability if they contract Covid-19."[32]

One journalist called the rally "Covidfest 2020," while pointing to "an event that eventually attracted a little over 6000 screaming fans many of whom refused to wear masks or engage in social distancing."[33] There was more at work here than rampant incompetence on the part of the Trump administration and a mixture of unlimited illiteracy and a shameful disregard for public safety on the part of those attending the rally; there was also a snapshot of a country that had become a failed state. Failed state is an appropriate categorization of the United States under Trump. As Pankaj Mishra argues, the United States descended into an abyss of "dingy realities [that include] deindustrialization, low-wage work, underemployment, hyper-incarceration and enfeebled or exclusionary health systems [that] have long been evident ... the state has been AWOL for decades, and the market has been entrusted with the tasks most societies reserve almost exclusively for government: healthcare, pensions, low-income housing, education, social services and incarceration."[34]

As a failed state, people's lives have been sacrificed in the interest of looting the public sector, reducing taxes for the ultra-rich, and weakening social provisions. Trump's disregard for human life mirrors the moral vacuum that drives his thirst for power. For instance, it is one thing for Trump to lie continuously about the pandemic and just about everything else, but it is another issue to put people's lives at stake for the sake of holding large political rallies to boost his prospects for re-election. As journalist Michelle Cottle remarked in the *New York Times*, "For Trump's triumphal return, his campaign ... decided that no social distancing is required. He want[ed] this to be a spectacle, packed with as much noisy adoration as possible," while bearing no concern for people who might fall sick or, for that matter, drop dead.[35]

While there is no question that social distancing and the call to self-isolate to promote the common good were sound medical practices, they could not be viewed as the only way in which we could imagine working together with a sense of shared responsibility. State-enforced isolation, however crucial in staving off the pandemic, could not be "the only possible version of solidarity and recognition of our interdependence."[36] At the same time, it is important to understand that pitting the nation's economy against public health was a false division. In a society in which state power is used to address public welfare, protect its citizens, and use its resources based on human needs, "no one should have [had] to choose between financial annihilation and helping to spread a deadly disease."[37] Yet, Trump not only capitalized on this false division, he actively promoted it. In doing so, he produced not only a failed state but also a criminogenic administration whose lack of central planning, negligence, incompetence, malfeasance, omissions, misinformation, and the withholding of social protections resulted in untold suffering and a skyrocketing number of fatalities.

When thousands of right-wingers demonstrated in Michigan, causing massive traffic jams, in protest of Governor Gretchen Whitmer's measures to limit the spread of the virus, Trump encouraged them to violate the local stay-at-home orders by tweeting "LIBERATE MICHIGAN." He also tweeted a call to "LIBERATE MINNESOTA" and "LIBERATE VIRGINIA and save your great second Amendment. It is under siege!"[38] Trump's politically and morally irresponsible message of implied violence was aimed at Democratic governors and geared to his right-wing base whose views are odds with 66 percent of Americans who support the case for a nationwide stay-at-home order. Aaron Rupar argued rightly that Trump's posts and militarized rhetoric "are among the most dangerous of Trump's tenure [and] appear to have been inspired by a segment he saw on Fox News minutes earlier."[39]

A number of Republican governors disregarded strict stay-at-home orders and eliminated restrictions designed to close down non-essential businesses. Georgia, Tennessee, Ohio, Florida, and South Carolina, among others, all opened against the wishes of public health experts. On April 1, thirty-five states began easing restrictions rather than abandoning them altogether. By the end of May 2020, almost all states had eased their restrictions, in spite of the fact that in some of those states the number of infections and deaths continued unabated. By November, the virus was surging in almost all of these states, many of which were forced to return to lockdown measures. In some cases, the rationale provided by Republican politicians for opening up their respective states was as illiterate as it was criminogenic. Journalist Frank Rich points to one example of the stupidity and flight from reason at work here. He writes: "In Texas, there's the always reliable lieutenant governor, Dan Patrick, whose argument for back-to-business-as-usual is that 'there are more important things than living.'"[40]

The rationale for a mix of eugenics and a politics of disposability can take many forms and the Covid-19 crisis resurrected this morally detestable logic in the name of economic growth. For instance, Texas Lieutenant Governor Dan Patrick, mentioned above by Frank Rich, argued that elderly people "should be willing to sacrifice themselves for the sake of jobs and economic growth."[41] Of course, there are less obvious paths to sacrificing lives for the sake of economic growth. Dr. Anthony Fauci stated that social distancing was the most important tool for containing the virus; yet Trump still refused to issue a national stay-at-home order, especially at a time when nine states did not have one. At a White House press conference on March 5 and later in July,

Trump stated that things would get a lot worse with many more deaths anticipated, as if this justified his lack of leadership. Soon afterwards, Trump reiterated his belief that he would like to see the country open again sooner rather than later, with a particularly dangerous emphasis on opening public schools. Trump continued with this position in spite of the fact that, by the end of July, the death toll due to Covid-19 had reached a staggering 148,000, with more than 4.5 million people infected. Such actions display a shocking level of moral turpitude, making clear that Trump was more concerned about commerce, the stock market, and his re-election than the ensuing rise in the number of deaths. Bad judgment and political opportunism turned into moral and political irresponsibility as Trump followed through on his wish to reboot what he called "the greatest economy in the history of our country" by allowing federal social-distancing guidelines to expire on April 30, 2020.[42]

As journalists Robert Costa and Philip Rucker point out, "Trump … long viewed the stock market as a barometer for his own reelection hopes."[43] The not-so-hidden and terrifying message is that political opportunism, the drive for profits, and the acceptance of a cruel neoliberal ideology were embraced by the Trump administration without apology. Trump appeared to take pleasure in belittling experts and only followed the advice of public health officials when confronted with the direst warnings. He treated the pandemic as a partisan battle, disparaged governors desperately calling for supplies, and refused to implement a coordinated national federal approach to address the crisis.

Without hard evidence or scientific proof, Trump endorsed specific drugs as treatments, falsely claimed that the U.S. was "close to a vaccine," and often relied on the advice of right-wing pundits and media personalities who pushed conspiracy theories. When it came to the choice of saving lives or the economy, Trump appeared more concerned about the fate of Wall Street. Moreover, his often confused and contradictory public remarks were filled with hyperbole and falsehoods and served to mislead the American public while potentially causing unimaginable misery along with the possibility that "tens of thousands, perhaps millions would get sick and die."[44] In this instance, sheer incompetence coupled with an aversion to experts and scientific evidence rose to the status of a public danger and created the conditions for a catastrophic crisis. Combining ignorance with malpractice, Trump turned the pandemic into a national calamity.

The increasing gravity of the pandemic crisis grew exponentially due to the fact that the White House leadership and a number of Republican governors, especially those in Texas, Arizona, and Georgia, were goaded by Trump not to respond in the early stage of the looming pandemic crisis with any sense of urgency and immediacy.[45] A report by the *Washington Post* stated that it took Trump seventy days from first being notified about the grave implications of the coronavirus to treat it "not as a distant threat or harmless flu strain well under control, but as a lethal force that had outflanked America's defenses and was poised to kill tens of thousands of citizens."[46] Of course, the many people who died because of the reckless lack of leadership were those most vulnerable under the reign of neoliberalism. These included the elderly, the destitute, poor people of color, undocumented immigrants, and people with disabilities—not to mention the frontline medical workers and health-care providers who lacked the equipment they needed to be safe as they worked on the frontlines of the pandemic.

There is more at work here than the hardened depravity of an ill-informed, pathologically narcissistic, petty celebrity politician who caused havoc and needless human suffering in a time of crisis. Trump has always had a penchant for thoughtlessness and self-absorption, and takes delight in humiliating others. His racism appeared unchecked, even in a time of massive hardships, suffering, and death disproportionally affecting Blacks and Latinos. Trump was impervious to the mass uprisings against racial injustice engulfing the United States following the murder of a number of Blacks by the police. Though written in a different context, Stephan Greenblatt offers a description that perfectly fits Trump: "There is no deep secret about his cynicism, cruelty, and treacherousness, no glimpse of anything redeemable in him, and no reason to believe that he could ever govern the country effectively."[47]

Pandemic Madness and the Crisis of Leadership

Trump's crudeness, mendacity, disregard for science, and arbitrary rule had led him to ignore previous warnings from experts about the possibility of a looming pandemic. As journalist, Susan B. Glasser notes, "Trump has spent years devaluing and diminishing facts, experts, institutions, and science—the very things upon which we must rely in a crisis—and his default setting during the coronavirus outbreak has been to deny, delay, deflect, and diminish."[48] This willful form of ignorance and sheer effrontery was on display in his earlier refusal and colossal failure to mobilize the power of the federal government to insure, at the very least, that hospitals and medical staff had enough beds, masks, ventilators, and other personal protective equipment for treating people infected with the virus.

Trump not only failed to provide the necessary leadership to address the coronavirus pandemic, he initially railed against governors leading the charge against the pandemic, claimed the crisis was not serious, and failed in the first few weeks of the outbreak to conduct testing, thereby "allowing Covid-19 to spread within communities undetected."[49] As Judd Legum points out, "During these critical weeks, there was no effort to stockpile protective equipment for health care workers or ramp up production of critical medical devices like ventilators … The federal government's response to the Covid-19 epidemic in the United States has been a disaster."[50] Prior to the onset of the crisis, Trump's stripping the government of essential health services was on display when he "dismantled the pandemic response teams at the White House National Security Council and the Department of Homeland Security."[51] He also ousted Rear Admiral Timothy Ziemer, who served as the Senior Director of Global Health Security and was lauded as "one of the most quietly effective leaders in public health."[52] Ziemer was also a member of the National Security Council, where he was responsible for coordinating "responses to global health emergencies and potential pandemics."[53] When a reporter asked about the shredding and shutting down of essential services and offices needed to prepare for a pandemic, Trump, in his usual petulant manner, replied, "I think it is a nasty question."[54]

Under the regime of neoliberalism, public health funding took drastic cuts in the name of reducing the debit and spiraling deficits. For example, as Amy Kapczynski and Gregg Gonsalves point out:

> seventeen states, along with the District of Columbia, have cut their health budgets over the past few years, and 20 percent of all local health departments have done the same. In fact, over 55,000 jobs at local health departments have been lost since 2008 ... Furthermore, CDC's [Centers for Disease Control and Prevention] Public Health Emergency Preparedness (PHEP) program, the key financing mechanism for state and local public health emergency preparedness, has been cut by a third since 2003. To make matters worse, the president's 2021 proposed budget slashes $25 million from the Office of Public Health Preparedness and Response, $18 million from the Hospital Preparedness Program, and $85 million from the Emerging and Zoonotic Infectious Diseases program.[55]

In this instance, Trump's scorn for experts proved to be deadly and created the conditions for the deaths of hundreds of thousands of Covid-19 patients. This is not simply a question of bad judgment or inept leadership on Trump's part. It goes to the heart of Trump's hatred of professionals in government agencies and departments, and illustrates clearly, once again, his disdain for science, evidence, and truth. Frank Bruni rightly observes, "He parted ways with credibility years ago."[56] Trump's political opportunism knew no bounds, even if it resulted in more deaths from Covid-19. He went so far as to wage a disparaging campaign against Dr. Fauci and was repeatedly at war with the CDC because they offered standards that were at odds with Trump's view of dealing with the pandemic. In a move that shocked many health officials, the Trump administration told hospitals to bypass the Centers for Disease Control and Prevention and send all public health data to a database in Washington. He also suppressed evidence regarding the threat the virus posed to young people.

Ed Pilkington and Tom McCarthy reported in the *Guardian* that Trump not only downplayed the threat the virus posed after the first case appeared on January 20, but his actions were "mired in chaos and confusion."[57] Rather than act quickly to avert a national health disaster,

Trump let six weeks go by before his administration took seriously the severity of the threat and the need for mass testing.[58] Pilkington quotes Jeremy Konyndyk, who led the U.S. government's response in 2013–2017 to a number of international disasters. He stated: "We are witnessing in the United States one of the greatest failures of basic governance and basic leadership in modern times."[59] Judd Legum argues that "Trump's response to the coronavirus pandemic is one of the most catastrophic failures in American history."[60] Noam Chomsky goes even further, describing Trump as "the most dangerous criminal in human history."[61]

Trump had a penchant for turning politics into a form of theater and entertainment into a form of cruelty. In a shocking display of pettiness, he publicly told Vice President Mike Pence not to answer the calls of those governors who are not "appreciative" of his efforts to deal with the pandemic.[62] This included Washington Governor Jay Inslee and Michigan Governor Gretchen Whitmer, both of whom made desperate pleas to the federal government for critically needed supplies and other aid to be sent directly to the states. In his response to the initial pleas of many governors for Trump to invoke the Defense Production Act in order to direct U.S. industries to produce more ventilators, Trump responded by stating that the federal government is "'not a shipping clerk' for … potentially life-saving supplies."[63]

Trump's belief in corporate volunteerism barely hid his neoliberal ideology of deregulation, taken right from the late conservative economist Milton Friedman. Friedman believed that government is the problem and that the market must be free of any interference imposed on corporations. While Trump later invoked the Defense Production Act to force General Motors and other companies to produce more ventilators and other much-needed supplies, Bess Levin argues that Trump's reluctance to take full advantage of the act was based on the pressure put on him by major corporations and the U.S. Chamber of Commerce, stating that they did not want the government interfering with the market.[64] Trump's refusal to heed initially the warnings of the governors reveals a level of ignorance, incompetence, and indifference to public policy that is difficult to grasp given the severity of the pandemic.[65] Downplaying the severity of the pandemic and ignoring the advice of scientific and medical communities took a personal turn when in October 2020 the White House announced that Trump and his wife, Melania, tested positive for coronavirus.

Trump's Racialized Culture of Cruelty

After weeks of attacks and taunts against Asian Americans in the United States, Trump used an incendiary, hyper-nationalized, and racist metaphor, calling the coronavirus the "Chinese virus," and later at a Tulsa rally referred to the virus with the racist term "Kung Flu." Trump has repeatedly used this racist language even though it has strained relations with China and contributed to a rise in racist incidents and a surge of violence and hate crimes against Asian Americans who are blamed for "the spread of coronavirus disease."[66] This is a form of political theater used by "the Trump administration and key congressional Republicans … to gin up tensions to distract from their domestic failures."[67] In addition, Trump repeatedly followed the fascist playbook and weaponized political speech by labeling outside groups such as immigrants as diseased, vermin, infested, and carriers of germs.[68] He broadened the application of this racist and fear-mongering language, which fanned the flames of hatred, to Asian Americans. According to journalist Lauren Aratani:

> Across the US, Chinese Americans, and other Asians, are increasingly living in fear as the coronavirus spreads across the country amid racial prejudice that the outbreak is somehow the fault of China. It is a fear grounded in racism, but also promoted from the White House as Donald Trump—and his close advisers—insist on calling it "the Chinese virus."[69]

It is hard to overlook this type of weaponized irresponsibility buttressed by what appears to be a bottomless display of ignorance, especially given the moving pleas by medical professionals who appeared on social media begging for masks, gowns, ventilators, and other crucial protective and life-saving equipment.[70] Doctors from early hotspots such as New York City appeared on social media and mainstream news networks pleading with the federal government for help, stating that the health-care system was in danger of collapsing. This also happened later in states such as Texas, Oklahoma, and Arizona. Many governors complained that the government's lack of a federal plan created something akin of the Wild West—"a system beset by shortages, inefficiencies and disorder."[71] Beyond the politics of denial and solipsism on the part of Trump, there was also what Robert Jay Lifton calls "malignant normality."[72] This refers to behavior that both normalizes and revels in hate, denial, and violence, fueled by what appears to be an immense pleasure in engaging in acts of cruelty. The effective normalizing and prevalence of such behavior is obvious in a contagion of right-wing populism and conspiracy theories which were gaining further strength across the globe, and were emboldened by Trump's like-minded politics. Trump did not even pretend to have any empathy for the rising death toll or for policies aimed at punishing poor people and underserved children. Trump exhibited a sadistic streak that was monstrous in its disregard for human life. As people died in rapidly accelerating numbers in the U.S., he golfed, talked about his ratings, and rarely ever addressed the massive sorrow and human tragedies people were experiencing.

Trump's cruelty was more than personal. It was a political strategy used to shore up his right-wing and white supremacist allies. Trump has insisted that white people are the real victims of racism and made it clear in his first presidential debate with Joe Biden that he would not renounce white supremacy. At the core of Trump's racial politics was a discourse of disposability, a discourse whose endpoint throughout history was a form of genocide. Irish journalist Fintan O'Toole perfectly captures the essence of Trump's cruelty and the implications it had for a fascist politics. He writes:

> As a society the American people are being habituated into accepting cruelty on a wide scale. Americans are being taught by Trump and his administration not to see other people as human beings whose

lives are as important as their own. Once that line has been crossed—and it is not just Trump and the people around him, but many of Trump's supporters as well—then we know where that all leads, what the ultimate destination is. There is no mystery about it. We know what happens when a government and its leaders dehumanize large numbers of people.[73]

As part of an ongoing effort to shift blame away from himself, Trump attacked and attempted to humiliate reporters who asked him critical questions. He even went so far, in the midst of the pandemic, to claim that "hospitals had squandered or done worse with masks and were 'hoarding' ventilators, and that states were requesting equipment despite not needing them."[74] In another shameful display of his racism and his need to push his own political agenda, he called for a fortified border wall as a "solution to containing the disease," suggesting falsely, once again, that undocumented immigrants are carriers of disease.[75] He went on to suggest that much-needed "masks were "going out the back door" of hospitals.[76] Philip Rucker and Robert Costa argued that "In the three weeks after declaring the novel coronavirus outbreak a national emergency, President Trump delivered a dizzying array of rhetorical contortions, sowed confusion and repeatedly sought to cast blame on others ... He ... faulted governors for acting too slowly and ... accused overwhelmed state and hospital officials of complaining too much and of hoarding supplies."[77]

Relying upon a neoliberal discourse that both privatizes the fight against the virus and sets up a competitive model as a way of addressing the crisis, Trump told governors that they were on their own when it came to finding life-saving ventilators, even though this meant that the states had to bid against each other. In the midst of this market-based practice, it was not surprising that price gouging became rampant. For instance, as Robert Reich observed, "New York State [paid] 20 cents for gloves that normally cost less than five cents, $7.50 for masks that normally go for 50 cents, $2,795 for infusion pumps that normally cost half that, $248,841 for a portable X-ray machine that typically sells for $30,000 to $80,000."[78]

With regard to testing failures, not to mention his slow, fumbling response to the crisis, Trump, on March 13, stated at a news conference, "I don't take responsibility at all." Trump was more concerned about his public image than he was with addressing the pandemic. The latter was made worse by Trump's lack of self-reflection, unwillingness to address criticism about his lack of preparedness, and his willingness to shift the blame for the crisis and its unfolding on China, beleaguered governors, medical professionals, and the media. Rucker and Costa have labeled Trump the "commander of confusion."[79] That is only partly true; he also serves as a model of a twenty-first-century authoritarian and right-wing populist who presided over a country in which more and more groups were considered expendable, power was concentrated in the upper echelons of a financial elite, and social death for the most vulnerable became the medium, if not the organizing principle, of an updated form of fascist politics.

How else to explain Trump's decision to roll back Obama-era fuel efficiency standards, a move that was "particularly lethal for people with impaired lung functions," and his decision, in the middle of a pandemic, to bring "construction crews into southern Arizona from all over the country to extend the border wall."[80] Thousands of workers were crowded into motels, rented rooms, and whatever other spaces they could find to live in, all the while subjected to high-risk conditions for infection by the virus.

One of the most disastrous and morally indefensible acts that surfaced due to Trump's politicization of the Covid-19 crisis was evident when the Trump administration sought to strike down the Affordable Care Act. Speaker Nancy Pelosi noted that stripping away the benefits and protections provided by the Affordable Care Act would mean "130 million Americans with pre-existing conditions would lose the ACA's lifesaving protections and 23 million Americans would lose their health coverage entirely."[81] This meant many people who survived Covid-19 but suffered from a number of recurring ailments due to the disease would no longer have guaranteed coverage. Pelosi was right in adding that Trump's actions were nothing short of "act of unfathomable cruelty."[82] Not only was Trump attempting to take away health care in the middle of one of the worst health crises experienced by Americans, he was determined to give billionaires a massive tax cut of $200,000. Trump's actions constituted a war not only on the social contract, public health care, and fundamental human rights but also on the very meaning of a democracy that places human needs over profits.

We have seen echoes of such cruelty in other eras with outcomes that resulted in the death of millions, such as in the lynching of Blacks in the United States and acts of genocide in Nazi Germany. Cruelty is not something that can be simply personalized in the figure of Donald Trump. Neoliberalism produces its own forms of institutional cruelty through its austerity measures, its decimation of the welfare state, and its support for racialized mass incarceration.[83] The irony here is that since the 1970s in the U.S., the United Kingdom, and other countries, the people who have been in the midst of battling against this pandemic for the benefit of society are the ones who suffered terribly under neoliberal governments. It's also "ironic" that the richest and allegedly most democratic countries in the world, since the 1970s, have been most notable among nations for instituting policies that are destroying a large swath of their own citizens. Rachel Malik, writing in the *London Review of Books*, states:

> Many of those who have suffered most under 'austerity' are now identified as key workers: whether they are overstretched doctors or outsourced hospital cleaners, distribution workers on zero-hours contracts, careers on minimum wage, or nurses expected to train without bursaries. Whether or not the government believes they have value, the most important thing it can do now is listen to what they're saying and take their advice.[84]

Politics as Theater in the Age of the Failed State

Trump's obsession with wealth and ratings, and his limitless self-regard, defined him not only as an inept leader and malevolent megalomaniac but also as a dangerous fraud. In the midst of the rapidly rising death toll in the United States, Trump boasted at one of his press media appearances "about the [high] ratings for the White House's coronavirus task force briefings."[85] This was before he discovered that his ratings were actually going down because of his ineptitude at the briefings, which he later suspended and, when they resumed, stopped attending. This form of political theater and pandemic pedagogy weaponized a rising death toll as an element of entertainment. It also spoke to a lack of empathy and a morbid insensitivity to human suffering. The *New York Times* columnist Frank Bruni touched on this issue when he wrote:

> Americans are dying by the thousands, and [Trump] gloats about what a huge, rapt television audience he has. They're confronting financial ruin and not sure how they'll continue to pay for food and shelter, and he reprimands governors for not treating him with adequate adulation ... This is more than a failure of empathy, which is how many observers have described his deficiency. It's more than a failure of decency, which has been my go-to lament. It's a failure of basic humanity.[86]

Trump's incompetence bore tragic results. Hospitals initially on the east coast and later in the south, southwest and west coasts were overcrowded, medical personnel lacking adequate protective equipment were dying, and the governors of many of these states, as I have mentioned earlier, appeared to be in a running feud with Trump. This is worth repeating. Trump appeared more at ease in insulting governors who criticized him for his lack of leadership than in supplying them with much-needed medical equipment. It gets worse. Trump's penchant for extortion resurfaced in the midst of the crisis in his suggestion to Vice President Pence that if the governors criticized his role in handling the crisis and refused to praise him, they would pay a price. Journalist Michelle Goldberg claims such actions went far beyond the implied threat of political favoritism. She writes that Trump

> strongly suggested that if governors speak candidly about his monumental incompetence, he'll penalize them and their states as they struggle to contain the coronavirus. Once again, he's using his control

of vital aid to extort assistance with his re-election ... there's little doubt governors feel life-or-death pressure to flatter the president [and] that criticizing Trump could jeopardize any help they could receive.[87]

Trump and his administration were not alone in pushing a necropolitics that celebrated death over life, capital over human needs, rapacious greed over compassion, exploitation over justice, "spectacular fits of deception" over the truth, and fear over shared responsibilities.[88] How else to explain the chorus of Trump's supporters in the media, corporate boardrooms, and the White House who argued for rationing life-saving care on the basis of age and disability in order to prevent imposing drastic strains on the nation's hospitals and the U.S. economy? How else to explain that long before this pandemic crisis the apostles of neoliberalism have attempted to underfund services such as "state-funded health care, clean water, good public schools, safe workplaces, pensions, and other programs to care for the elderly and disadvantaged"?[89] Trump may have campaigned against the power of the establishment in 2016, but it became clear very quickly that he was an apostle of the harshest form of neoliberalism and aligned himself with the ruling elite. As George Packer observes, "they shared a basic goal: to strip-mine public assets for the benefit of private interests."[90] One result is that "the publicly owned bones of society—roads, bridges, levees, water systems— [will] slip into a state of such disrepair that it [will] take little to push them beyond the breaking point. When you massively cut taxes so that you don't have money to spend on much of anything besides the police and the military, this is what happens."[91]

Revisiting the Plague of Pandemic Pedagogy

What the current pandemic crisis revealed was the underlying plague of neoliberalism that has dominated the global economy since the 1980s. This dystopian economic and political plague was steadily brandished as a badge of honor by authoritarian politicians such as

Trump, Brazilian President Jair Bolsonaro, Indian Prime Minister Narendra Modi, and other right-wing tyrants.

The Covid-19 pandemic was mapped onto inequalities that poisoned American society and hit hardest the vulnerable, poor, and marginalized while producing disastrous social injuries. While no one was immune from the spread of Covid-19, it was far from a great equalizer. Its disproportionate effects on the poor and vulnerable, especially black and brown communities, pointed to the widening chasm between the rich and powerful wealthy few and the vulnerable and precarious majority. The inequities that this crisis revealed made clear how disasters unfold through relations of power, making it easier to challenge the myth that major catastrophes such as pandemics that affect everyone equally; needless to say, this hid the fact that they may affect everyone, but not in the same way.[92] For instance, ruling-class corruption and its virus of inequality were readily visible in a Covid-19 bailout package in which, as Rob Urie observes, amounted to "bailouts for the rich, the virus for the rest of us."[93]

As pointed out in an edition of *Le Monde Diplomatique*, market mechanisms cannot protect us against the global threats of an environmental disaster or nuclear war. At the same time, neoliberal structures and values undermine a ranges of goods and services "that should be placed beyond the laws of the market." The article states further that "delegating our food, our protection, our capacity to take care of our living conditions to others is folly. We need to take back control."[94] In the midst of this pandemic, ruling-class power and oppression were at the center of the political, ideological, and medical crisis.

As I have mentioned earlier, another plague is the scourge of a pandemic pedagogy. This is a pedagogy produced by right-wing cultural apparatuses such as Fox News, Sinclair Broadcast Group, and Breitbart Media in which the truth is treated with scorn, science is viewed as a hindrance, and critical thought is maligned as fake news. For instance, the Sinclair Broadcast Group had planned to air a program in which "an anti-vaccine activist, said she believed that Fauci manufactured the coronavirus that causes Covid-19 and shipped it to China."[95] This stuff is hard to make up, given the discredited and potentially dangerous falsehoods Sinclair Broadcast Group was willing to circulate in the middle of pandemic that killed hundreds of thousands of people, especially at a time when it was crucial to follow the advice of public health experts and gather the best scientific evidence available to defeat the virus. What Fox News, the Sinclair Broadcast Group, and Breitbart Media revealed in all of their lies and distortions was that capitalism is the enemy of justice, equality, and the truth.

Pandemic pedagogies circulate plagues of willful ignorance, propaganda, and state-sanctioned lies.[96] Such ignorance displays what the filmmaker Raoul Peck calls an "extraordinary capacity for denial in this country, even when confronted with evidence and logic."[97] Under such circumstances, language, at the center of political power and among powerful conservative cultural apparatuses, operates as a marker of refusal, lies, and symbolic violence. These corporate-controlled, right-wing online ecosystems, along with sympathetic political pundits, relentlessly promote conspiracy theories such as the claim that the pandemic was a product of the "deep state" designed to prevent Trump from being re-elected; a hoax created by the Democratic Party; or a virus that it was no less dangerous than the common flu. Right-wing conspiracy theories do more than spread lies, misrepresentations, and propaganda. As the editors at *New Frame* noted: "These pernicious rumors fuel[ed] racism and xenophobia, and lull[ed] people into a false sense of complacency about taking measures to prevent the disease from spreading."[98]

Adam Serwer argues that Trump's authoritarian ideology, with its emphasis on loyalty and sycophantic praise rather than truth, was on full display with the servile conservative media that amplified his messages and legitimized those politicians and pundits who spread conspiracy theories. He writes:

> The conservative radio host Rush Limbaugh, to whom Trump recently gave the Presidential Medal of Freedom, told his listeners "this virus is the common cold." The Fox News host Sean Hannity proclaimed that the president's critics were attempting to "bludgeon Trump with this new hoax," while his colleague Pete Hegseth told viewers, "I feel

like the more I learn about this, the less there is to worry about." The network aired a parade of medical experts offering bogus health advice about the coronavirus, including the claim that the "worst-case scenario" is that "it could be the flu." Republican legislators appeared on the network urging Americans to defy federal health officials' advice to avoid large public gatherings and work from home if possible, with Representative Devin Nunes of California telling Fox News on March 15, "It's a great time to just go out, go to a local restaurant," or "go to your local pub."[99]

In addition to the lies and misrepresentations,[100] Trump's propaganda apparatus with its flood of pandemic pedagogy also relentlessly insisted that all social problems were a matter of individual answerability, so as to depoliticize the public while making them indifferent to a form of neoliberal fascist politics that asserted that the government has no obligation to care for its citizens or that society should not be organized around mutual respect, care, social rights, and economic equality. The price paid here in suggesting that the pandemic was just another "liberal hoax" along with a host of other spectacularized claims was that such messages were at odds with public health warnings and had the potential to cause massive suffering, and even death, among many of their followers.

The Covid-19 crisis was part of a historical moment defined by a pedagogical catastrophe of indifference and a flight from any viable sense of social and moral responsibility. This was and is an age marked by a contempt for weakness, as well as rampant racism, the elevation of emotion over reason, the collapse of civic culture, and an obsession with wealth and self-interest. Under such circumstances, we continue to be in the midst of not simply a political crisis but also an educational crisis in which matters of power, governance, knowledge, and a contempt for scientific evidence have wreaked havoc on the truth and endangered both millions of people and the planet itself. This is a politics fueled by a disimagination machine whose political and cultural workstations make the truth, justice, ethics, and, most of all, bodies, disappear into the abyss of authoritarianism.

At the center of this pandemic was not only a crisis of politics but also a crisis of ideas in which one could not be addressed without the other. While the political crisis laid bare the failure of a brutal capitalism, how people responded to this crisis offered no guarantees. It was only through a critical understanding and shift in consciousness about the need for a radical transformation of society that any viable notion of change could take hold. Gregg Gonsalves and Amy Kapczynski writing in the *Boston Review* were right in stating that "This pandemic … functioned as an X-ray of empire, and we can see clearly now what lies below late twentieth-century U.S. neoliberalism and the new robber-baron capitalism of the twenty-first. It is an architecture of brutality, pitched to produce forms of death and destruction from which none of us will emerge untouched."[101] Their diagnosis is irrefutable, but how Americans continue to respond in light of this enduring crisis politically as an act of resistance remains to be seen.

Towards a Comprehensive Politics

For the conditions to end that brought the plague into existence, it is necessary pedagogically to address how the ideologies of neoliberal fascism prevent people from translating private troubles into broader systemic issues. It is also crucial to wage a pedagogical struggle in order to convince the public to move beyond the culture of privatization and atomization that propels a consumer society and reinforces a single-issue politics detached from broader considerations. Covid-19 produced a political and public health crisis, which can be rightly regarded as one of the most dangerous of modern times. This crisis can only be grasped as a crisis of the social totality, one in which a range of "democratic ills formed the specifically political strand of a general crisis that engulfed the social order in its entirety."[102] The legacy of the viral pandemic must be grasped as part of a broader crisis. Nancy Fraser is instructive here, suggesting, though in a different context, such an approach. She writes, "Neither freestanding nor merely sectoral, today's democratic ills form the specifically political strand of a general crisis that is engulfing our social order in its entirety."[103]

We live in a moment in which it is becoming more credible to acknowledge that the endpoint of capitalism is not only virulent inequality, systemic racism, exploitation, and human suffering but also a brutal machinery of death in which humanity is one step closer to the edge of extinction. This suggests that a crisis can have multiple outcomes resulting in either a surge of authoritarianism and repression or a resurgence of resistance movements at numerous levels willing to fight for a more just and equitable society, one that rejects what Brad Evans has called an age of multiple exclusions, mass terror, increasing expulsions, and the hollowing out of the social state.

The coronavirus pandemic pulled back the curtain to reveal the power of a brutal neoliberalism—and its global financial markets—in all of its cruelty. The political and economic pandemic not only eroded the democratic ideals of equality and popular sovereignty but also created modes of governance that deracinated the social safety net and the public health system. This inequality-generating economic system makes it difficult for the state to protect its citizens in the face of future catastrophic pandemics.[104] Years of neoliberal austerity measures have gutted the social state and made it very difficult to fight the Covid-19 pandemic in 2020–21. A market-driven system that celebrates profit over human needs left behind a hollowed-out government unable to provide an effective response to the most serious challenges posed by the pandemic. As Alfredo Saad-Fiho observes:

> The pandemic hit after four decades of neoliberalism had depleted state capacities in the name of the "superior efficiency" of the market, fostered deindustrialization through the "globalization" of production, and built fragile financial structures secured only by the state, all in the name of short-term profitability. The disintegration of the global economy left the most uncompromisingly neoliberal economies, especially the UK and the USA, exposed as being unable to produce enough face masks and personal protective equipment for their health personnel, not to speak of ventilators to keep their hospitalized population alive.[105]

A glaring example is obvious in the presence of a predatory for-profit health-care system that focuses on profits rather than quality care for all.[106] Another example can be seen in the presence of big pharma, which represent nothing less than "private tyrannies called corporations [that are] unaccountable to the public"[107] and exploit the sick and gouge the public with the high costs of much-needed drugs.[108] There is also the case of pharmaceutical companies planning to make big profits from the pandemic through the development of potential vaccines and the production of overpriced testing kits. If this seems unlikely, it is useful to examine the role of big pharma in producing the opioid crisis in the United States, which points to how dangerous these private corporations can be in their drive for more and more profits.[109]

One of the most obvious and debilitating examples can be found in the horrors of a private health insurance industry that punishes the poor and "constantly seems to produce more byzantine rules to exploit and extract more surplus from the sick."[110] The result was a crippled market-driven system that put a severe strain on medical workers, doctors, and hospitals by failing to deliver ventilators and other essential equipment to treat patients and limit the number of deaths caused by the virus. This public health failure went far beyond Trump's incompetence and market-driven fundamentalism, it also highlighted a central tenet of neoliberal politics, which is to "deny public responsibility and elevate private power and market goods over public goods."[111]

The claim that Trump may be delusional was bolstered by his irresponsible, if not dangerous, assertion at one of his press conferences in which he endorsed two possible cures for the coronavirus. One suggestion was for people to inject themselves with disinfectants and the second was that they expose themselves to ultraviolet rays or a powerful light. Public health officials and some spokespersons for the cleaning agents reacted with both disbelief and a series of warnings about the dangers of ingesting disinfectants.[112] These utterly reckless suggestions were another example of pandemic pedagogy and its roots in Trump's disregard for science, evidence, medical knowledge, and his willingness to repeat the pedagogical arguments of pseudoscience groups preaching false cures who inhabit the right-wing media ecosphere.

The coronavirus pandemic pointed to a moment in the current historical conjuncture in which the space between the passing of one period and the beginning of a new age offered the possibility for not only a new social safety net and national health-care system but also a global movement for radical democracy. In addition, the era of using the government to protect its citizens returned, at least momentarily, in the midst of a horrifying public health crisis. Americans have started to recognize, as Kenneth W. Mack observes, "that government can actually do things to help the lives of citizens."[113]

The legacy of the viral pandemic cannot be discussed outside of the crisis of politics, power, and education.[114] This theoretical approach suggests possibilities for a new democratic vision in which matters of civic literacy, civic values, and ethical duty become central to the rebuilding of a democratic social order. The move from a neoliberal society of individuals and an ethos of shark-like competition to one of social solidarity and collective obligation is crucial to overcome individualized fears and anxieties that undermine social unity. How we live together as a community shaped by the principles of social justice, economic equality, and popular sovereignty are more important now than ever. Democracy needs a polity that is not only informed and knowledgeable, but is also willingly inhabits a linked fate and sense of shared responsibility. This is a space in which our different experiences, identities, and ways of living share a collective fate of solidarity, care, and justice. Masha Gessen rightly states that we need to do more than engage in social distancing and wash our hands, we need to treat this pandemic as both a "political problem and a political opportunity." She writes:

> The real question, though, is: How do we handle this as a society, as communities? What are the opportunities for mutual aid and care, even amid calls for social distancing? What is the response that creates, on the other side of this epidemic, not a collection of atomized individuals who survived a plague but a polity whose members helped one another live? The political leaders who can inspire and inform such a conversation—and such a response—are also the ones who can lead us out of Trumpism.[115]

Thinking Big Through a Language of Critique and Hope

The current and future medical, political, economic, ecological, and racial plagues must be confronted with a language of informed critique and a mobilizing and energizing discourse of concrete possibilities. Critique makes power visible and militant hope creates the individual and collective energy to address the real problems people are encountering in their daily lives. In doing so, it translates passion, emotion, and desires into new forms of understanding and the ongoing democratization of knowledge tied to informed action.[116] It is crucial to develop pedagogical practices that address the underlying causes of poverty, class domination, environmental destruction, white supremacy, and a resurgent racism. It is essential to develop a discourse that extends the possibilities of critique to a wide variety of issues in order to analyze the threads that weave through all of them. We need to extend the political, economic, cultural, and social analyses of the specific problems we face to the wider threats, for instance, of nuclear war and ecological collapse. In the words of Amartya Sen, we need "to think big about society."[117] In spite of the overwhelming nature of the current crisis, there is a need to think beyond being isolated, overwhelmed, and powerless. This suggests not only a revolution in values but also a political project aimed at radical reconstruction, one that has its sights on the creation of a new political and economic social order.

As we have seen in a number of countries such as Hungary, Egypt, the Philippines, China, Thailand, and Israel, the pandemic crisis created extraordinary circumstances for restricting civil liberties, free speech, and human rights while intensifying the possibilities of an emerging authoritarianism.[118] Yet, the brutal reality of neoliberal fascism and its multiple crises can be questioned, and resisted. The pandemic crisis widened the net of people affected by the contagion who, because of poverty, lack of social provisions, and a host of other deprivations endemic to capitalist society, hopefully will be more open to imagining a new and more democratic vision of the future.

There is no doubt that the Covid-19 crisis will continue to test the limits of democracy worldwide. Right-wing movements, neo-Nazis, authoritarian politicians, religious fundamentalists, and a host of other extremists were energized by what Slavoj Zizek called the "ideological viruses ... [lying] dormant in our societies."[119] These included closing borders, the quarantining of so-called enemies, the claim that undocumented immigrants spread the virus, the demand for increased police power, and the rush by religious fundamentalists to relegate women to the home to assume their "traditional" gendered role. Edward Snowden argued that the pandemic posed serious questions about the issues of civil liberties and the right to privacy and the emergence of what he calls the "architecture of oppression."[120]

Conservatives were delighted with the growth of home schooling, especially those versions that rejected evolution, sex education, and harbored a deep scorn for women's rights and LGBT people. At the same time, right-wingers of various slants were energized in their opposition to "sudden and sweeping restrictions on democratic freedoms"[121] that extended from banning public gatherings to the mandating of wearing a mask in a public place.[122]

At the same time, the magnitude of the crisis offered new possibilities in which people could rethink what kind of society, world, and future they wanted to inhabit. What we do not want to do is to go back to a system that equates democracy and capitalism. Nor do we want to limit our vision to isolated issues such as a universal living wage, Medicare for all, a Green new deal, and expanding workers' rights, however crucial these reforms. All of these forms need to come together as part of a more comprehensive call for transformative change. Such actions are especially relevant at a time when the key elements of an anti-capitalist political coalition took center stage during the Covid-19 crisis. These included the struggle for a living wage, the fight against runaway privatization, the critique of surveillance capitalism, the demand for social justice, the necessity for quality health care for all, and the fight for climate justice, economic equality, and a viable welfare state.

Any viable resistance movement must move beyond modifying the system, because such crises have deeper political and economic roots and demand a complete restructuring of society. The urgency of the fight for a democratic socialist society must be seized upon. Once the pandemic is brought under control, the struggle over democracy itself may prove far more important at every level than the former and ongoing struggle against the pandemic. Radical times deserve radical measures in the fight against fascism and the struggle for a socialist democracy. The problems authoritarian and neoliberal societies are facing around the globe demand a new language, one that embraces a revolutionary vision and radical action. David Harvey is right in arguing that "The fundamental problems are actually so deep right now that there is no way that we are going to go anywhere without a very strong anti-capitalist movement."[123] This is as much a pedagogical issue as it is a political consideration. Only with a change in consciousness and values produced to benefit a knowledgeable and educated public can such a movement materialize.

What the pandemic has taught is that it is time to choose between a society that addresses either human needs or becomes one in which a survival-of-the fittest ethos and war-of-all against-all becomes the only organizing principle of society. Arundhati Roy is insightful in warning us that this pandemic emerged at a time when a number of countries are controlled by authoritarians who normalized elements of the fascist state under the guise of addressing the pandemic. Her warning is stark: "Are we going to sleepwalk into this fascist surveillance state that everyone has in store for us?"[124] The historian Yuval Noah Harari adds another register to this warning, suggesting that under the current crisis there are two possible outcomes. He writes:

> the first is between totalitarian vigilance and citizen empowerment; the second is between nationalist isolation and global solidarity. [In a more optimistic note, he further states] a well-informed and self-motivated population is usually more powerful and effective than an ignorant people guarded by the police.[125]

The murder of George Floyd offered up a mirror to the long legacy of racism, state violence, and capitalist injustice that has undermined the promise of a socialist democracy in the United States. It has also challenged those narratives that separate economic justice from political and personal right. The ruthless and criminal murders of Ahmaud Arbery, Breonna Taylor, Eric Garner, Trayvon Martin, and Philando Castile, among others, made clear the need to fight not only for human rights but also for democratic socialism, because in its vision there is the central belief that society should benefit all people, not just the rich and privileged. The ugliness of American capitalism and its embrace of racism, violence, inequality, and a politics of disposability can no longer hide in the shadows. It is time for new visions, a politics of economic justice, and for the kinds of protest, actions, new political formations, and mass displays of civic courage necessary for a new and more humane, equal, and just society to be born.

Militarized Pandemics and the Language of War

War doesn't determine who's right, it determines who's left.

Bertrand Russell

The Language of War

We live at a time when the terrors of life suggest the world has descended into darkness. The Covid-19 crisis created a dystopian nightmare which flooded our screens and media with images nurtured by rampant fear, anxiety, and uncertainty. Bodies, doorknobs, cardboard packages, plastic bags, the breath we exhale, and anything else that offered the virus a resting place was comparable to a ticking bomb ready to explode at any given moment, resulting in massive suffering and untold deaths. We were fearful of shaking hands, embracing our friends, using public transportation, sitting in a coffee shop, or walking down the street. We are told by politicians, media pundits, and others that everyday life has taken on the character of a war zone.

The metaphor of war has a deep sense of urgency and a long and complicated rhetorical history in times of crisis.[1] Militarization has become a central feature of the pandemic age and points to the dominance of warlike values in society. The mass uprisings that engulfed the U.S. in opposition to systemic racism and police violence were but one expression of the growing resistance against militarization and its influence in shaping everyday life. Michael Geyer defines militarization as the "contradictory and tense social process in which civil society organizes itself for the production of violence."[2] Geyer was writing about the militarization of Europe between 1914 and 1945, but his description seems even more relevant today. This is particularly obvious in the way right-wing politicians such as Trump promoted the increasing militarization of language, public spaces, the police, and bodies. Terms such as "war footing," "mounting an assault," and "rallying the troops" were normalized in the face of the pandemic crisis. At the same time, the language of war privileged the proliferation of surveillance capitalism, the closing of borders, and the suspension of civil liberties.[3] On a more authoritarian level, war culture ran the risk of functioning as an element of fascist politics. Trump crossed this line many times during his presidency both in his assaults on peaceful protesters and undocumented workers, and his threats to politicians who have criticized him. It was also been evident in his use of the language of violence in encouraging his followers to beat up members of the oppositional press and his encouraging the police to rough up individuals when they put them into police cars. His refusal to denounce white supremacy, His authoritarian impulses were never far from the surface. At one point, he even suggested postponing the presidential election of 2020, because he was so far behind in the polls.

As the Covid-19 virus brought the engines of capitalism to a halt, the discourse of war took on a new significance as a medical term that highlighted struggles to grapple with underfunded health-care systems, the lack of resources for testing, the surge towards downward mobility, expanding unemployment, the lack of paid sick leave for too many workers, and the ongoing, heart-wrenching, failed efforts to provide protective essentials for frontline and emergency workers. In this rhetoric of urgency, war as a metaphor harbored an element of critique in its attempts to take on a series of social problems that undermine public safety and the common good. At the heart of the adoption of a militarized cultural symbol was a growing political struggle to reverse and amend decades of assaults waged by neoliberal capitalism against the welfare state, essential social provisions, public goods, public health services, and the social contract. The legacy of such assaults has been made strikingly visible in the devastation and havoc that emerged in the midst of the virus. As Arundhati Roy observes:

> the stories of overwhelmed hospitals in the US, of underpaid, overworked nurses having to make masks out of garbage bin liners and old raincoats, risking everything to bring succor to the sick. About states being forced to bid against each other for ventilators, about doctors' dilemmas over which patient should get one and which left to die.[4]

In the halls of dominant power, war has a different resonance and is part of the vocabulary of diversion and command. The language of war is used by the mandarins of power to both underemphasize the economic and social outcomes of the viral pandemic that have brought capitalism to its knees and to reinforce and expand the political formations and global financial systems that are incapable of dealing with the pandemic. Rather than using anger, outrage, emotion, and fear to sharpen our understanding of the conditions that abetted the global plague and what it meant to address it and prevent it in the future, the ruling elite in a number of right-wing countries such as the U.S. and Brazil used the discourse of war either to remove feelings of anxiety from public debate or dismissed them as acts of bad faith in a time of crisis. When used by the ruling elite, war is tied to a politics of disappearance and displaces the violence waged by the state and neoliberal fascism against a range of individual and groups considered disposable because of their class, race, religion, age, and ethnicity. Under such circumstances, politics as an extension of war becomes, in part, a pedagogical tool transformed into a form of pandemic pedagogy in which critical thought is derailed, dissent suppressed, surveillance normalized, and ignorance elevated to a virtue. Amartya Sen is right in arguing that "Overcoming a pandemic may look like fighting a war, but the real need is far from that."[5]

In a moment of mass uprisings and catastrophic change, the language and pedagogy of war reverberated in an echo chamber produced in the highest circles of political power, the defense industries, and right-wing cultural apparatuses. All of which served to turn mass anguish, trauma, exhaustion, and mourning into a fog of conspiracy theories, state repression, and a deepening abyss of darkness that "serves the ends of those in power."[6] The lockdown imposed under the threat of the pandemic meant that over 1 billion young people and adults were spending more time online, prone to the spreading of propaganda by terrorist groups, white supremacists, and extremist groups engaging in a kind of "vigilantism" against Asians, Black Lives Matter dissenters, and state officials imposing public health restrictions.[7] Conspiracy theorists and racists spread a host of lies, attempting to strip marginalized groups of their freedoms. In Trump's case, power was concentrated and used, in the face of massive rebellions, with the tools of repression. For Trump, power and domination mutually informed each other. As Masha Gessen states:

> Donald Trump thinks power looks like masked men in combat uniforms lined up in front of the marble columns of the Lincoln Memorial ... Trump thinks power ... sounds like the word "dominate," repeated over and over on a leaked call with governors. It sounds like the silence of the men in uniform when they are asked who they are ... Donald Trump thinks power looks like masked men in combat uniforms lined up in front of the marble columns of the Lincoln Memorial ... Trump is now performing his idea of power as he imagines it. In his intuition, power is autocratic; it affirms the superiority of one nation and one race; it asserts total domination; and it mercilessly suppresses all opposition. Whether or not he is capable of grasping the concept, Trump is performing fascism.[8]

Under Trump, the scourge of militarization and its legitimating feral pandemic pedagogy of "law and order" included, among other things: sending unmarked federal law enforcement shock troops into American cities to confront/abduct protesters; using these troops to tear gas and shoot rubber bullets at a wall of moms, white moms no less; tear gassing the Mayor of Portland; refusing to rename military bases named after Confederate leaders; and sending messages of fear to his critics.

It is crucial to remember that after Trump was acquitted on both impeachment articles on February 5, 2020 by the House of Representatives,[9] he embarked on a campaign of revenge by firing a number of officials who testified against him. For example, he fired Lt. Col. Alexander Vindman from the National Security Council because of his testimony in the impeachment inquiry. Trump's political loyalties were not on the side of individuals who exhibited integrity and civic courage, and who exercised social responsibility. Trump rewarded just the opposite of these values. This was particularly obvious in his appointment of Stephen Miller, a white nationalist, to serve as a senior policy advisor.[10] He also sent a clear signal to his white supremacists supporters in his debate with former Vice President Joe Biden. He not only refused to condemn a violent white supremacist group, the Proud Boys, he also legitimated and enabled future violent acts by the group.[11]

Militarizing Incompetence

As they lost their jobs in record numbers, Americans had to cut back on food and other essentials. Making matters worse, they received paltry income support from the Trump administration. For instance, large sums of money that were supposed to go to small business through the CARES Act ended up largely in the hands of the big businesses and giant, publicly held companies. As Jonathan Cook observes, Trump and his corrupt band of political sycophants, incompetents, lobbyists, and relatives helped to shape policies that transferred millions of dollars to the corporate sector. He writes:

> huge sums of public money [went] to the biggest corporations. Politicians controlled by big business and media owned by big business are pushing through this corporate robbery without scrutiny—and for reasons that should be self-explanatory. They know our attention is too overwhelmed by the virus for us to assess intentionally mystifying arguments about the supposed economic benefits, about yet more illusory trickle-down.[12]

The zeal to save the economy translated into efforts to further the coffers of the rich. Such policies constituted and were inextricably bound to a politics of "opportunistic authoritarianism," already in play in a number of countries that under the cover of enforcing public health measures were enforcing a range of anti-democratic policies in a wave of repression. As I mentioned in Chapter 1, the Covid-19 pandemic removed from the shadows the notion that market mechanisms could not address the depth and scope of the Covid-19 crisis. This failure of neoliberalism revealed a profound sense of despair and moral void integral to casino capitalism. In addition, the economic crisis illustrated that the spell of neoliberalism was broken and ushered in a legitimation crisis.

The Covid-19 pandemic made visible the false and dangerous neoliberal notion that all problems fall on the shoulders of isolated individuals. In doing so, the pandemic shattered the myth that each of us is defined exclusively by our self-interest and as individuals are solely responsible for the problems we face. Both myths completely broke down as it became obvious that, as the pandemic unfolded, shortages in crucial medical equipment, ventilators, masks, and vital protective equipment were largely due to austerity measures and regressive tax policies that drained resources from public health, public goods, and other vital social institutions. The pandemic tore away the cover of a neoliberal economic system, revealing what Thomas Piketty called "the violence of social inequality."[13] The mythic claim that there is no alternative to neoliberal capitalism and its central ideological contention that government is the problem, or even worse, enemy of the people have been shattered, as have its false assumptions about the value of unchecked production, consumption, deregulation, individual entrepreneurship, and wanton individualism.[14]

The relentless and cruel celebration of markets, profits, and the financialization of everything produced an administration that pitched unproven drugs, exhibited a scandalous complacency, produced endless falsehoods, and abdicated "muscular federal guidance for the states [and fails] to sketch out a detailed long-range strategy for containing the coronavirus."[15] Ed Yong, writing in *The Atlantic*, provides a scathing denunciation of Trump's politics and his failure to contain the virus. He is worth quoting at length:

> No one should be shocked that a liar who has made almost 20,000 false or misleading claims during his presidency would lie about whether the U.S. had the pandemic under control; that a racist who gave birth to birtherism would do little to stop a virus that was disproportionately killing Black people; that a xenophobe who presided over the creation of new immigrant-detention centers would order meatpacking plants with a substantial immigrant workforce to remain open; that a cruel man devoid of empathy would fail to calm fearful citizens; that a narcissist who cannot stand to be upstaged would refuse to tap the deep well of experts at his disposal; that a scion of nepotism would hand control of a shadow coronavirus task force to his unqualified son-in-law; that an armchair polymath would claim to have a 'natural ability' at medicine and display it by wondering out loud about the curative potential of injecting disinfectant; that an egotist incapable of admitting failure would try to distract from his greatest one by blaming China, defunding the WHO, and promoting miracle drugs; or that a president who has been shielded by his party from any shred of accountability would say, when asked about the lack of testing, "I don't take any responsibility at all."[16]

More concerned about his ratings, the stock market, and getting re-elected, Trump exhibited a degree of incompetence so monumental in addressing the pandemic that some critics, such as the journalist Ajamu Baraka, have labeled him a war criminal.[17] This monumental exhibition of incompetence was on full display the same day that NBC News reported 50,000 new cases in 24 hours. As the infections ballooned in numbers and the deaths reached alarming proportions, Trump exhibited neither empathy for the suffering and dead nor any concern about how to contain the escalating crisis. In fact, speaking to Fox Business's Blake Burman on July 1, the president speculated that the virus would magically disappear. Trump stated, "I think we're going to be very good with the coronavirus. I think that, at some point, that's going to sort of disappear, I hope."[18] Ann Jones chronicles Trump's disturbing lack of leadership in confronting the pandemic, especially when it first appeared, providing substance to the charge that Trump committed what amounts to a war crime. She writes:

> As president, he was ... informed of a viral outbreak in Wuhan, China, in early January of this year, but he ignored the message. As has been widely reported, he wasted at least two months in self-serving fantasies, claiming the pandemic would disappear of its own accord or was fake news or a "new hoax" by Democrats plotting his downfall. By March, his conduct had become increasingly erratic, obtuse, combative, and often just flat-out nasty. In April, he abandoned altogether his most pressing presidential duty, first claiming "total power" as president and then shifting the job of testing and protecting the people from an unrestrained pandemic onto state governors already struggling to find basic medical supplies for frontline health care personnel in their own states.[19]

Incompetence, lies, and a disregard for human life appeared to run in the Trump family. As the death toll in the United States reached over 58,000 and the number of infections hit one million, Jared Kushner, Trump's first son-in-law and "pallid nonentity,"[20] claimed that the federal government response to the crisis amounted to "a great success story."[21] Trump appeared to take him at face value and soon afterwards announced he was winding down the pandemic task force as the Covid-19 virus was ravaging the country with astronomical infections and deaths. Trump later changed his mind, saying he didn't realize how popular it was, as if in the midst of such death and suffering its most important attribute was its popularity ratings.[22]

Vice President Mike Pence channeled Kushner's false statement in June 2020 when the pandemic task force met for a public briefing after a two months' absence. Pence announced that the Trump administration had produced "remarkable progress" in dealing with Covid-19, despite a number of surging cases in the south and west. Pence's mind-boggling response came as the death rate from the virus reached more than 125,000 and confirmed infections soared past 2.6 million. Blinded by a massive case of denial amplified by his sycophantic devotion to a president who is a pathological liar, Pence appeared to have conveniently suppressed the fact that, while the U.S. had only 4 percent of the world's population, it had 25 percent of the world's infections and deaths. And, of course, he completely ignored the devastating consequences of this administration's failure to develop a federal strategic response to address the Covid-19 pandemic.

Pence also defended Trump's decision to hold political campaign rallies in the midst of an out-of-control pandemic, despite endless warnings from health officials that such mass events be cancelled. Pence argued that freedom of speech gave people the right to refuse to wear masks and the president the right to put the lives of thousands at risk of infection and death in the name of political opportunism.[23] This is political opportunism functioning as a death-machine. Pence's complicity with policies that could kill thousands was hard to miss. When Pence was asked by a reporter to "recommend that all Americans wear masks as public health officials advise," he declined, and instead urged "people to listen to their local health officials and pray."[24] It is hard to make this stuff up.

Trump's response to the Covid-19 crisis represents a study in the workings of a failed state and the mindset of a deeply disturbed authoritarian egomaniac. For instance, instead of addressing the various crises caused by the pandemic he blamed China for the outbreak, and sent out endless tweets attacking Obamacare. Moreover, as implied above, Trump had blood on his hands. This is evident not only in his well-documented late response to the pandemic but also because of his failure one week before the pandemic started to multiply to impose a lockdown and social-distancing restrictions, which a Columbia University Study stated would have saved 36,000 lives.[25] Trump dismissed the criticism by calling Columbia University a "liberal, disgraceful institution."[26] One wonders how many lives could have been saved if Trump had paid attention to reputable scientific studies and public health experts and had quickly put in place a coordinated federal plan to deal with the virus instead of disdaining scientific evidence and prioritizing the needs of the economy over human life. As the infections rose and the death toll increased, one epidemiologist stated that Trump's lack of a national plan and his endless undermining of public health officials constituted "genocide by default—what else do you call mass death by public policy?"[27]

Unsurprisingly, Pulitzer Prize winner Laurie Garrett sums up Trump's failure in the midst of a crisis that has killed more individuals than every war since the start of the Korean War, combined with the observation that Trump is "the most incompetent, foolhardy buffoon imaginable."[28] While this is difficult to dispute, it is important not to forget that Trump is the most obvious symptom of a systemic form of capitalist oppression marked by endlessly visible structural problems such as massive inequality, endemic political corruption, environmental devastation, and an economic model that has morphed into an updated form of authoritarianism, not to mention what Lacino Hamilton calls "a war against Black bodies."[29] Moreover, the Covid-19 crisis was only one of many existing crises, extending from massive inequality and mass poverty to climate devastation and the threat of nuclear war, though it was the most egregious at the time in terms of its effects on the global economy and the massive death toll it took. What needed to be recognized was that America was in the midst of a tsunami of crises that included, as Arundhati Roy puts it, "a hunger crisis ... a hatred crisis. And ... a health crisis apart from COVID."[30]

Militarizing Repression

One after-effect of the failed neoliberal state is an uptake in levels of oppression in order to prevent the emergence of massive protest movements and radical forms of collective resistance. The suspension of civil rights, repression of dissent, upending of constitutional liberties, and the massive use of state surveillance to serve anti-democratic ends has become normalized. What cannot be over-emphasized is that many of the countries driven by austerity policies and a long-standing culture of cruelty used the pandemic crisis as a way to shape their modes of governance by drawing from what activist Ejeris Dixon calls elements of a "fascist emergency playbook." Dixon is worth repeating at length:

> Use the emergency to restrict civil liberties—particularly rights regarding movement, protest, freedom of the press, a right to a trial and freedom to gather. Use the emergency to suspend governmental institutions, consolidate power, reduce institutional checks and balances, and reduce access to elections and other forms of participatory governance. Promote a sense of fear and individual helplessness, particularly in relationship to the state, to reduce outcry and to create a culture where people consent to the power of the fascist state. Replace democratic institutions with autocratic institutions using the emergency as justification. Create scapegoats for the emergency, such as immigrants, people of color, disabled people, ethnic and religious minorities, to distract public attention away from the failures of the state and the loss of civil liberties.[31]

The evidence for the spread of this ideological virus and its apparatuses and policies of repression are no longer simply the random expressions of fears by individuals and groups concerned by the rise of authoritarian movements and modes of governance.[32] The machineries of fascism in the midst of the pandemic crisis had found a firm footing in a number of countries. For instance, Viktor Orbán, Hungary's prime minister, passed a bill that gave him "sweeping emergency powers for an indefinite period of time … The measures were invoked as part of the government's response to the global pandemic."[33] What became obvious is that the pandemic crisis produced mass anxiety that enabled governments to turn a medical crisis into a political opportunity for leaders across the globe to push through dictatorial powers and use repressive force with little resistance.

Selam Gebrekidan observes that "In Britain, ministers have what one critic called 'eye-watering' power to detain people and close borders. Israel's prime minister shut down courts and began an intrusive surveillance of citizens. Chile sent the military to public squares once occupied by protesters. Bolivia postponed elections."[34]

In the Philippines, President Rodrigo Duterte, who has flagrantly violated civil rights in the past, in the midst of the pandemic was given emergency powers by the congress. Under the cloak of invoking public health measures because of the threat posed by the coronavirus plague, China broke up protests in Hong Kong and arrested many of its leaders. It also passed a new security law, which endangers, if not puts to an end, the right to protest peacefully. In Russia, President Vladimir Putin initiated a "referendum" that enabled him to stay in office until 2036.[35]

South Africa passed a law that criminalized what it called disinformation about Covid-19. In India, Prime Minister Modi used the power of his office to encourage "news outlets to publish inspiring and positive stories about the government's response to the pandemic, citing a need to push back on 'rumour' and 'negativity.'"[36] Egypt expelled reporters critical of its handling of the Covid-19 crisis.[37]

In the United States, Trump's Justice Department asked Congress "for the ability to ask chief judges to detain people indefinitely without trial during emergencies—part of a push for new powers that comes as the coronavirus spreads through the United States."[38] As the leader of the most powerful nation on the planet, Trump emboldened leaders from Egypt and Turkey to the United Kingdom and South Africa to use the pandemic as an excuse to suppress critical and independent journalism. Trump's embrace of fascist principles was on full display, when he "reportedly said China's decision to detain Uighur Muslims in concentration camps was 'exactly the right thing to do' and encouraged Chinese leader Xi Jinping to 'go ahead with building the camps,' according to a book excerpt published Wednesday by John Bolton, Trump's former national security adviser."[39] Clearly, Trump's adoration of dictators went far beyond their amassing of power and extended to their disregard for human rights.

In the U.S., Trump blamed the media for spreading fake news about the virus, attacked reporters who ask critical questions, packed the courts with federal sycophants, dehumanized undocumented immigrants by labeling them as carriers of the virus, and claimed that he had "total authority" to reopen the economy, however dangerous the policy, and however fast Covid-19 was spreading in the U.S. As the pandemic worsened, the economy deteriorated, and mass protesters filled the streets, Trump promoted fear to endorse elements of white supremacy, ultra-nationalism, censorship, and social cleansing while unleashing the storm clouds of fascism on dissenters.

As the pandemic reached record numbers in terms of both infections and deaths, Trump offered no clear and consistent message or federal plan "to mount a successful public health response to a viral outbreak."[40] With respect to mass mobilizations against police violence, he called protesters thugs and terrorists, portrayed himself as the law and order president, and attacked demonstrators with federal troops. He repeatedly criticized and attempted to humiliate reporters who ask him critical questions. He supported voter suppression and had publicly stated that making it easier to vote for many Americans such as blacks and other minorities of color would mean "you would never have a Republican elected in this country again."[41]

In the midst of economic hardships and widespread suffering due to the raging pandemic, Trump tapped into a combination of fear, racism, and a cathartic cruelty, while emboldening a savage lawlessness aimed at the most vulnerable populations. How else to explain his calling the coronavirus the "Chinese virus," or the "Kung Flu virus," regardless of the violence it elicited by right-wingers against Asian Americans. Trump amplified his racist and xenophobic remarks when talking to his base. He took a pathological delight in stoking racism. His cruelty and lack of empathy seeped into most of his policies and speeches, and was most obvious in his call to reopen the economy, knowing that doing so too hastily meant that thousands could die as a result, mostly the elderly, poor, and other vulnerable individuals.[42] Beneath Trump's moral apathy lay the fantasy of white supremacy, ignorance, and the workings of a moral monster.

As I noted earlier, how else to explain his reluctance to provide much-needed aid to those states run by Democratic governors, while suggesting that the problems they faced were due to their lack of political talent? This is a particularly vicious and racist form of partisan politics given that, as the journalist Giovanni Russonello has pointed out in *The New York Times*, "The coronavirus ... spread most quickly in high-density urban settings, and it has been particularly vicious among people of color, many of whom were already at an elevated risk because of pre-existing conditions and a relative lack of quality health care. It just so happens that those populations also tend to vote Democratic."[43]

Trump's efforts to relax social distancing by urging states to reopen their economies defied logic in light of projected death totals moving upward from 125,900 as of June 28 to more than 215,000 by October 1.[44] In spite of the surreal misery and death caused by this pandemic, the failure of leadership appeared to be spiraling out of control. Such conclusions seem unmistakable, given the dire warnings that appeared daily by noted public health professionals, often in contradiction to the Trump's downplaying of the seriousness of the pandemic. For instance, Dr. Anthony Fauci, the nation's most renowned infectious disease expert, warned in a Senate hearing on June 30, 2020 that "the number of new infections in the United States could more than double to 100,000 a day if the country fails to contain the surge that is now underway in many states ... putting the entire country at risk."[45]

Given these figures, it is morally irresponsible and politically inconceivable that the Trump administration would urge a full-fledged reopening of the economy and fail to learn from past mistakes such as using "the power of the state to force workers to report to work at meat processing plants that were inundated with Covid-19 infections."[46] Ajamu Baraka, writing in *The Black Agenda Report*, argues that "These policies not only represented a cruel and inhumane disregard for the health and lives of workers but are international crimes."[47] Some liberal writers, such as Paul Krugman, called such actions irresponsible when, in effect, Trump's policies came closer to constituting a war crime, given how many people were projected to die in what the *New York Times* called "a steady, unrelenting march of deaths and infections."[48]

Trump considered himself "a wartime president," but the lives that are often sacrificed in war are for a larger cause and do not apply in Trump's case. This is evident, given Trump's publicly admitted willingness to put thousands of American lives at risk largely to pump up the economy in order to further his re-election efforts. As Trump stated, "Will some people be affected badly, Yes. But we have to get our country open, and we have to get it open soon."[49] Not only "some people" died, but as many as 10,000 daily or more, and they were mostly African Americans, the elderly, first responders, and those who worked at the epicenter of the crisis. Trump's callousness amounted to more than ignorance, indifference, and his living in a moral vacuum.

Militarizing the Media

In a time of crisis, the relationship between language and politics becomes more vivid, if not urgent. This was particularly true for the Trump administration, which used language to downplay apocalyptic suffering and massive numbers of deaths while encouraging lawlessness, if not the threat of right-wing violence. There were no demilitarized spaces in Trump's America. Evasion and political opportunism have replaced truth and justice, while the language of mystification legitimated a tsunami of ignorance that furthered the collapse of morality, solidarity, and civic courage.

The militarization of language as a mode of diversion was on full display in Trump's claim that the American public were the new warriors enlisted in the battle to fight the coronavirus pandemic. More specifically, this militarized language was used by Trump to legitimate his shameful comment that a cure, referring to the stay-at-home orders and the shutting of the economy, was potentially "worse than the problem itself." For Trump, saving the economy was more important than saving lives. As "warriors," the American public were told to support this new battlefield strategy, while it was suggested that everyone was responsible for addressing the pandemic crisis, which mostly meant reopening the economy in spite of its potential sacrifice of lives. After all, wars are always accompanied by a mix of sacrifice and death. This tactic diffused Trump's own obligation to lead the country forward with a plan while normalizing the possibility of a pandemic that, as of July 21, 2020, has infected nearly 63,000 people daily. And, once again, let us not forget that such deaths disproportionately affected Black people, the poor, and the elderly. This is especially true for poor people of color. According to science writer Ed Yong,

> As of early July, one in every 1,450 Black Americans had died from COVID-19—a rate more than twice that of white Americans. That figure is both tragic and wholly expected given the mountain of medical disadvantages that Black people face. Compared with white people, they die three years younger. Three times as many Black mothers die during pregnancy. Black people have higher rates of chronic illnesses that predispose them to fatal cases of COVID-19. When they go to hospitals, they're less likely to be treated. The care they do receive tends to be poorer.[50]

Trump's warrior rhetoric attempted to hide the White House's decision to prioritize saving the economy over the concerns of the medical community to save lives. Instead Trump focused on his "law and order" theme, exaggerated stories about mail in ballots, and attacked the legitimacy of the upcoming election. Downplaying the threat of the coronavirus was more than ethically irresponsible, more than another attempt on the part of the Trump administration to divert attention away from his administration's failure to take account of early warnings about the pandemic and provide adequate levels of testing, medical supplies, ventilators, masks, and a national plan to contain and stop it. It was also about normalizing false choices, sacrificing lives to support what the super patriots call the "American way of life." Or as anthropologists Catherine Lutz and Anne Lutz Fernandez put it: "That it's okay for 'Grandma' to die, along with the other members of society, who in former Fox News host Bill O'Reilly's crass terms, 'were on their last legs anyway.'"[51]

The choice between saving the economy and staying home at the risk of going hungry, lacking medicine, and fulfilling basic human needs was a false choice. It was a brutal trade-off. Not only did it devalue human life in general, it provided a rationale for saying that some lives were more valuable than others, and this took place largely in racial terms. In this case, the elderly, poor people of color and class, and those with predisposed conditions were defined as disposable. Normalizing this position not only legitimated a script for social Darwinism, it also jettisoned morality and social responsibility from the dangerous assumption that some lives can be prioritized over others in the interest of economic wellbeing. In a country defined by endless wars, massive inequality, punishing levels of poverty, and the concentration of wealth, income and power in relatively few hands, Trump's notion that what was good for the economy was also good for society and the American public was both false and misleading. In this discourse, the toxic notion that money drives politics disappeared, along with iniquitous relations of power.

Normalizing a cruel pragmatism through the language of militarization that pits sacrificing lives against saving jobs is more than a false dilemma, it is a script that echoes a history in which those who were once considered disposable were sacrificed in the interest of racial, political, and social cleansing. Governments with a reverence for life should be able to protect their citizens through a massive expansion of social benefits, universal health care, and financial subsidies for small and large business until it is safe for people to go back to work and resume their daily lives. By normalizing death in the name of economic and political expediency, Trump opened the door to legitimating an indifference to public health, the pandemic of inequality, and a sustained attack on the welfare state and the health of democracy itself. On the issue of whether the economy should have been opened, Dr. Tom Frieden, the former director of the Centers for Disease Control and Prevention under President Barack Obama, rightly argued that the way the pandemic has

> been handled has obscured the messy truths of reality and created false dichotomies. It's just not about closed versus open. It's about how to open safer and how to do it carefully so we don't have to close again … And it's not about health versus the economy. Protecting health is not getting in the way of economic recovery. It is the route to economic recovery.[52]

In the age of the Covid-19 pandemic, culture was militarized. Donald Trump and the right-wing media in the United States both politicized and weaponized the coronavirus pandemic. They weaponized it by using a de facto state of emergency to promote Trump's political attacks on critics, the press, journalists, and politicians who questioned his bungling response to the pandemic crisis. They politicized it by introducing a series of policies under the rubric of a state of exception. These included diverting bailout money to the ruling elite and defense contractors, militarizing public space, increasing the power of the police, waging attacks on undocumented immigrants as a public health threat, and promoting voter suppression. In addition, Trump further strengthened the surveillance state, fired public servants for participating in the impeachment process, and initially claimed that the virus was a hoax perpetuated by the media and Democrats who were trying to undermine Trump's re-election. Trump also repeatedly claimed that the Democratic Party was a party of traitors, who were unpatriotic and wanted to destroy the country. After losing the presidency, he claimed falsely that he had won the election by a lot. He attempted to bolster this lie insisting that the election was stolen from him through large-scale fraud and the stealing of votes. Once the press named Biden the winner, Trump refused to concede.

Militarizing the Police

The call by those demonstrating against racial violence to defund the police grew out of a collective rage and awareness of how deeply embedded racism was in the culture of policing. What was often missed is that the nation's increasing militarized police forces cannot be separated from the endless amounts of surplus military equipment provided through the 1033 Program set up by the Department of Defense in 1997. Commenting on the importance of taking on the militarization of the police, Andrew Bacevich laid out the connection between the arms industry and the militarized approach to law enforcement. He writes:

> in 1997, the Department of Defense set up the 1033 program as part
> of the National Defense Authorization Act to provide thousands

of domestic police forces with "surplus" equipment of almost every imaginable militarized kind. Since then, thanks to your tax dollars, it has given away $7.4 billion of such equipment, some of it directly off the battlefields of this country's forlorn "forever wars." For items like grenade launchers, mine-resistant armored vehicles, military rifles, bayonets, body armor, night-vision goggles, and helicopters, all that police departments have to fork over is the price of delivery. The Pentagon has, in fact, been so eager to become the Macy's of militarized hardware that, in 2017, it was even willing to "give $1.2 million worth of rifles, pipe bombs, and night vision goggles to a fake police department," no questions asked.[53]

Another underlying example of systemic militarization at work in the Covid-19 pandemic centered around the White House initiating the "largest spending binge in history" on the military and the U.S. national security state. As Mandy Smithberger points out, Trump allocated billions for "weaponry and other military expenses," all the while funding arms dealers and diverting much- needed funds for health-care costs.[54] Rather than divert billions into the public health sector and social safety net, Trump took $7.2 billion from a highly inflated military budget of $738 billion in order to build a "great, great wall" on the southern border. Instead of allocating millions for testing, shoring up a budget for the Centers for Disease Control, and providing support and equipment for essential workers on the front lines fighting Covid-19, Trump bought more F-35 Joint Strike Fighters than the Pentagon requested and created a sixth branch of the military called Space Force. This was a program designed to militarize space as the world's newest war-fighting domain.[55] Trump allocated $1.4 trillion towards its development.

There is more at stake here than wasted military investments, there is also the refusal to take funds allocated for military spending and use them to build much-needed infrastructures that would give people work, provide universal health care, put more money into public and higher education, enact a universal wage, and put millions into programs to eliminate homelessness, poverty, and food and housing deprivations.

Medea Benjamin and Zoltán Grossman point to the dreadful, wasteful consequences of investing in the military dreadnought at the expense of financing valuable social programs:

> The 2020 military budget of $738 billion is larger than those of the next 10 countries combined. *The Washington Post* reported that if the U.S. spent the same proportion of its GDP on its military as most European countries do, it "could fund a universal child-care policy, extend health insurance to the approximately 30 million Americans who lack it, or provide substantial investments in repairing the nation's infrastructure." Closing the 800-plus overseas military bases alone would save $100 billion a year … Even President Dwight Eisenhower described military spending in 1953 as "a theft from those who hunger and are not fed."[56]

The crises facing the United States and many other countries are interrelated and cannot be abstracted from the mutually dependent forces of capitalism, racism, militarism, and authoritarianism. What is crucial to remember is that no call for change will work if its focus and strategies are linked to isolated issues such as defunding the police. For instance, defunding the police cannot be removed from the equally related call to defund the military. As Benjamin and Grossman observe, "Prioritizing the police and military means deprioritizing resources for community needs."[57] The root cause of oppression in the United States is the systemic oppression and violence waged by neoliberal capitalism as it works through the different registers of class, race, ethnicity, gender, sexual orientation, and the destruction of the environment. While the role of the police in producing racial violence and state terrorism cannot be overlooked, the root of such violence goes much deeper and must address the larger economic and political structures of injustice.[58] Rev. William Barber goes to the heart of the necessity to understand police violence within a broader political context, referring to what he calls the "death measurement." He writes:

> every regressive policy has what I call a DM on the DL—that is, a death measurement on the down low. When we talk about, for instance, the

death of George Floyd, which we have to, and police violence, but police violence is only one part of racism that kills and classism that kills. For every 500,000 people that are denied healthcare, 2,800 people die. Seven hundred people die every day from poverty, even before COVID. And we know we're headed toward poverty going probably plus-50% in this economic downturn. Every regressive policy has a death measurement on the down low. And we've got to bring those things out. We even have to show people that racist voter suppression has a death measurement, because when people are allowed to get elected through racist voter suppression, and then, once they get elected, they block healthcare, they block living wages, they block reparations, they in fact are blocking policies that could cause people to live. And in blocking them, people die.[59]

Redirecting money into valued social programs also needs to be addressed as part of a comprehensive politics regarding the underlying causes of violence in neoliberal society. In part, this means taking seriously what it means to take money from the military, the ultra-rich, the financial sector, and big corporations.[60] This calls for a radical transformation, not creeping reforms, and is essential in order to fund social services, and the most basic needs, such as economic rights, all of which provide the conditions for individuals to have a sense of dignity and empowerment. Bacevich rightly argues that, while the mass antiracism protest was urgently necessary and honorable, it fell short of addressing the diverse register of violence produced by America as a failed state. He writes that what also needs to be addressed is a militarism that produces "the American propensity for war," "the bloated size of the Pentagon budget," and "the dubious habit of [the U.S.] maintaining a sprawling network of military bases across much of the plant."[61] The politics of militarization is also present in neoliberal capitalism's war on the planet and must be included in any viable call for real change. Militarization and inequality provide the devastating framework that intensifies institutional racism, systemic poverty, ecological devastation, a war culture that increases the propensity for nuclear war, and crisis of public health.

Trump's language of dehumanization coupled with his appalling ignorance and unlimited incompetence appeared as a perfect fit for the media spectacle that he made a central feature of his presidency. Trump's "anti-intellectualism had been simmering in the United States for decades and fully boiled over" during his presidency. When incorporated as a central feature of the right-wing social media, Trump's promotion of civic illiteracy and charged emotional rhetoric became "a tremendously successful tool of hegemonic control, manipulation, and false consciousness."[62] Trump's apocalyptic rhetoric appeared to match the tenor of the moment as there was a surge in right-wing extremism, anti-Semitism, deadly racism, and a culture of lies, dehumanization, and cruelty. At the same time, his language exhibited a mounting compulsion and hyper-immediacy that flattened out and vulgarized any viable notion of communication. What we witnessed as the pandemic intensified in the United States, and in some other countries across the globe, was the increasing threat of authoritarian regimes to both use the media to normalize their actions and to wage war against dissidents and others struggling to preserve democratic ideas and principles.

Trump's ignorance on numerous issues has made him the laughing stock of millions across the globe, especially his suggestion that drinking or injecting disinfectant or bleach was a possible cure for Covid-19. But, more importantly, it undermined America's role as a world leader and elevated Trump to the role of a narcissistic buffoon.

Trump may be the world's most celebrated buffoon, but he is also one of the most dangerous politicians alive. Under the Trump administration, the notion of war expanded to include alleged "internal enemies" such as the press, which he called "the enemy of the people,"[63] and he argued that Democrats involved in the impeachment process, such as Adam Schiff, be arrested for treason.[64] In his presidential bid against former Vice President Joe Biden, Trump called him a member of the radical left who wants to "let terrorists roam free," "Abolish Police, Abolish ICE, Abolish Bail, Abolish Suburbs, Abolish the 2nd Amendment—and Abolish the American Way of Life."[65] This is a language used by demagogues, authoritarians, and fascists. He consistently appeared as a politician who was unhinged, filled with hate, and willing to do anything to win re-election. Trump relentlessly weaponized his language when talking about undocumented immigrants, as did his media sycophants. Fox News talking heads such as Tucker Carlson, media pundits such as Ann Coulter, and conservative talk show celebrities such as Rush Limbaugh used the discourse of "invasion" in referring to immigrants trying to make their way to the United States.[66] Trump went further and once recommended electrifying the border wall "with spikes on top that could pierce human flesh."[67] He also retweeted, and thus endorsed, news footage of a white St. Louis couple pointing guns at peaceful protesters "marching for police reform."[68] He later complained about their being possibly charged with a crime.

Trump's dangerous pandemic pedagogy thrived in a culture addicted to performance and spectacle. Given his experience in the realms of reality TV and celebrity culture, Trump was driven by mutually reinforcing registers of spectacular fits of self-promotion, a near pathological use of Orwellian doublespeak, and an obsession with the ratings his media coverage receives.[69] One of the insults he threw out at reporters in his coronavirus briefings was that their networks had low ratings, as if that were a measure of the relevance of the question being asked. Unlike any other president, Trump used the mainstream media and social media to mobilize his followers, attack his enemies, and produce a Twitter universe of misinformation, lies, and civic illiteracy. He used the media to fan the flames of racism, underplayed police brutality, remained silent about the disproportionate numbers of African Americans dying from Covid-19, and produced misinformation about scientific evidence concerning the origins, spread, and safety measures necessary to contain the virus. Instead of addressing the pandemics of racism and poverty and the surge of Covid-19 cases, Trump militarized the police force, used the conservative media to label protesters as thugs, and portrayed himself as a president willing to use "substantial dominant force." Using the right-wing mediascape to channel his authoritarian and bigoted messages, Trump both produced and legitimated the conditions that drove thousands into the streets protesting systemic racism, the militarization of the police, endemic poverty, and further cover-ups of "the vast scope and scale of the racial challenge we all face."[70]

On July 3, 2020, Trump used the backdrop of Mount Rushmore to address a large group of supporters, ignoring the warning of public health officials fearing large crowds would spread the virus. Trump used the holiday, which had all the signs of a Nuremberg rally of the 1930s, to deliver a dark, hateful, and divisive speech, against the added stagecraft of American military might in the form of flyovers conducted by the South Dakota Army, Air National Guards, and the US Air Force. Trump portrayed protesters against racism and police violence as "part of a new left fascism" who were waging a "merciless campaign to wipe out our history, defame our heroes, erase our values, and indoctrinate our children."[71] Without evidence, he shamelessly denigrated urban schools and accused teachers of teaching students to "hate our country." Making clear the ideological poison behind previous racist comments in which "he called the words Black Lives Matter a 'symbol of hate', [he has also] threatened to veto a must-pass defense policy bill because it include[d] an amendment that called for the removal of the names of the Confederate leaders from all military assets within three years."[72] Downplaying the legacy he pushed for "patriotic education," a term often associated with authoritarian regimes.

Trump's weaponized attacks mark a dangerous shift in both language and politics itself. He has emptied words of their meaning and turned them into their opposite. In one instance, he distorted the meaning of fascism by labeling people protesting against racial violence as fascists, and expanded his notion of "enemies" to include not only immigrants, but all those "liberal Americans who, he believed, constituted a direct threat to the standing of his conservative base."[73] Measured arguments and facts disappeared in Trump's discourse to be replaced by a despotic contempt for reason, unchecked ignorance, and a resurgent nationalism. We have seen how this language as a medium of hate and violence has an endpoint in homicidal extremes. Trump pushed a poisonous mix of historical ignorance, hate, and anti-intellectualism to a new level of danger. Trump employed a pandemic pedagogy in which language became unmoored from critical reason, informed debate, and the weight of scientific evidence. Instead, it was tied to pageantry, political theater, and the consolidation of power, as well as the dictates of violence.

For Trump, language became a form of cruel performance that functioned to lull people into acquiescence through an appeal to a rancid populism and galloping authoritarianism. This is the language of militarism, white supremacy, and fascism. We have seen this type of violence before. Pinochet in Argentina, Hitler in Germany, and Mussolini in Italy shared the gruesome practice of turning ideas into ashes; books were burned, and the alleged "enemies of the state" disappeared. There is more at work here than what Ariel Dorfman calls a "frightening felonious stupidity."[74] There is also the disappearance of those spaces where individuals can embrace the principles of justice, equality, and the grammar of ethics. Trump destroys everything that makes politics and democracy possible.

In spite of mass protests over racialized police violence, Trump doubled down on his race-fear-baiting tactics, and had the support of the wealthiest media moguls in the United States. For instance, Trump had the backing of the hedge-fund billionaire Robert Mercer and his family, who have given millions to conservative media groups such as Breitbart News, the right-wing Media Research Center, and a number of ultra-conservative groups, and is a major force in the new era of media propaganda. He used his wealth and media galaxy to correct what he called "liberal bias," such as the call for climate change, and, as Carole Cadwalladr reports in the *Guardian*, is a major force waging war on the mainstream media.[75] Mercer provided enormous financial support for Trump's election in 2016. Not surprisingly, Trump was a firm believer in Mercer's notion of "platform capitalism" and has championed the right-wing media by both echoing their positions on a number of issues and using them to air his own. The diverse forms of conservative media have been enormously complicit in justifying Trump's call for the Justice Department to dig up dirt on his political rivals, including the impeachable offense of extorting the Ukrainian government through the promise to withhold military aid if they did not launch an investigation into his political rival, Joe Biden. Moreover, they supported his instigation of armed rebellions via his tweets urging his followers to liberate Minnesota, Michigan, and Virginia, all of whom have Democratic governors, by refusing to comply with stay-at-home orders and social-distancing restrictions.[76] Ironically, he urged and supported anti-social-distancing protests that violate his own federal guidelines for containing the virus.

Trump used the police powers of the state, especially ICE, to round up children and separate them from their parents at the border. In a flagrant display of militarized lawlessness, Trump sent unmarked and unaccountable federal officers to a number of cities. Numerous social media showed them beating up protesters, firing rubber bullets into crowds, and launching stun grenades into streets filled with demonstrators. In response to Trump's claims that he was sending federal agents to Chicago, among other cities, Chicago Mayor Lori Lightfoot stated bluntly, "We do not welcome dictatorship. We do not welcome authoritarianism, and we do not welcome unconstitutional arrest and detainment of our residents."[77] Philadelphia District Attorney Larry Krasner got more personal and called Trump a "Wannabe Fascist."[78]

Placing loyalty above expertise, he surrounded himself with incompetent sycophants, and made policy decisions from his gut, often in opposition to the advice of public health experts. All of this was echoed and supported by the conservative and right-wing eco-system, especially Fox News, Breitbart News, and what appeared to be a legion of right-wing commentators such as Laura Ingraham, who deceitfully compared Covid-19 to the flu and in one of her more zealous moments claimed the lockdowns were equivalent to living under Saddam Hussein. Fox News not only produced conspiracy theories such as the claim that the virus was the product of the "deep state" and was being used by Democrats to prevent Trump from being re-elected, it also produced misinformation about the virus and represented what seventy-four journalism professors and leading journalists described as "a danger to public health."[79]

Like most authoritarians, Trump did everything to control the truth by flooding the media with lies, denouncing scientific evidence and critical judgment as fake news. The latter is a direct attack on the free press, critical journalists, and the notion that the search for the truth is crucial to any valid and shared notion of citizenship. Moreover, in the midst of the coronavirus pandemic, the right-wing pandemic misinformation machine spread false information that put people's lives at risk, especially their audience, whose median age was 65—one of the most vulnerable age groups at risk for dying from the virus. Commenting on the larger significance of Trump's relentless lies, Juan Cole writes:

> Authoritarian regimes breed lies like rotting meat breeds maggots, and as Trump marches the United States into an imperial presidency beyond accountability, his rate of lying has become astronomical. If I just read ten a day, it would take me five and a half years just to read all 20,000 of the lies Trump has told since his election … Trump wishes away stubborn facts that he finds inconvenient. He castigated the climate emergency as a "Chinese hoax" … Nancy Pelosi gets the award for the bon mot of the day. She said "if Trump wants to see a hoax he should look in the mirror."[80]

Trump's systemic lying functioned as more than a tsunami of misinformation and propaganda, it also operated as a mode of pandemic pedagogy whose function was to militarize the culture and the media in order to legitimate its governing principles as a state of exception, emergency, and war. Under such circumstances, the relationship between civil liberties and democracy, politics and law, and justice and injustice was lost. Consequently, a number of plagues overtook American society and its most prominent response was to celebrate war as a source of pride rather than alarm, enact repressive measures, and militarize its linguistic repositories.[81]

Conclusion

Under the Trump regime, politics was used as a weapon of (mis) education and power, and was waged primarily through the militarization of language, the media, and other cultural sites such as sports events. This constitutes a form of pandemic pedagogy—a pedagogical virus that erodes modes of critical agency, democratic values, and civic institutions central to a robust democracy.

Trump cultivated a taste for savagery and defined the world in the image of his own self-interest and war. He revived the architecture of fascism by mainstreaming its emotionally charged anger while mobilizing primitive impulses and affective dogmas. He called people animals, his rallies had all the earmarks of the Nuremberg spectacles of the 1930s; he referred to the oppositional media as fake news, not unlike the appropriation of Hitler's and the Nazis' use of the controlled media, as a way to discredit the oppositional media and journalists who held him accountable; he rounded up the children of undocumented brown people and put them in cages; he made racial cleansing a governing principle of his administration; he normalized lying, making it the basic rhetorical experience of his time in office; he amplified the militarized discourse of fear and numbed the culture with his pervasive anti-intellectualism and control of the right-wing media as unadulterated propaganda machines. He shaped his foreign policy in the discourse of ultra-nationalism. He hired white supremacists and acted like the grifter-in-chief in the White House. All of this pointed to alarming echoes of the past and the need for the American public to learn from history rather than deny it. The elements pointing to the rise of fascism in the United States were on full display, and without apology.

Rejecting the Trump-Nazi comparison made it easier to believe that we had nothing to learn from history and to take comfort in the assumption that it could not happen once again. Democracy cannot survive if it ignores the lessons of the past, reduces education to mass conformity, celebrates civic illiteracy, and makes consumerism the only obligation of citizenship. Max Horkheimer added a more specific register to the relationship between fascism and capitalism in his comment, "If you don't want to talk about capitalism then you had better keep quiet about fascism."[82]

The lessons to be learned from the pandemic crisis must go further than making visible the lies, misinformation, and corruption at the core of the Trump regime. Such an approach fails to address the most serious of Trump's crimes. Moreover, it neglects to examine a number of political threads that together constitute elements common to a global crisis in the age of the pandemic. What also cannot be ignored is the toxic soil from which Trump emerged. Trump, like the Covid-19 crisis itself, was symptomatic of much larger political and economic issues. Similarly, the global response to the pandemic crisis by a number of authoritarian states needs to be viewed as part of a broader crisis of democracy. That is, it needs to be analyzed by connecting the ideological, economic, and cultural threads that weave through often isolated issues. In the United States these would include: white nationalism; the rise of a political party dominated by right-wing extremists; policies aimed at racial cleansing; the suppression of dissent; the collapse of the two-party system; and the ascent of a corporate-controlled media as a disimagination machine and the proliferation of corrosive systems of power and dehumanization.

Crucial to any politics of resistance is the necessity to take seriously the notion that education is central to politics itself, and that social problems must be critically understood before people can act as a force for empowerment and liberation. This suggests analyzing Trump's use of politics as a militarized spectacle, not in isolation from the larger social totality—as simply one of incompetence, for instance—but as part of a more comprehensive political project in which updated forms of authoritarianism and contemporary versions of fascism are being mobilized and gaining traction both in the United States and across the globe. In a society in which ignorance is a virtue and civic literacy and education are viewed as a liability, the ghost of fascism is always nearby. Under such circumstances, pandemic pedagogy is constructed through a language that demobilizes people, leaving them to believe that their oppression is a direct result of their individual deficits or the deficits of people who have a different skin color, don't fit into the alleged universalized white public sphere, and threaten civilization as it is constructed to uphold oppressive racial and class terms.

The pandemic crisis should be a rallying cry to create massive collective resistance against both the Republican and Democratic Parties and the naked brutality of the political and economic system they have supported since the 1970s. That is, the criminogenic response to the crisis on the part of the Trump administration should become a call to arms, if not a model on a global level, for a massive international protest movement that moves beyond the ritual of trying Trump and other authoritarian politicians for an abuse of power, however justified. Instead, such a movement should become a call to put on trial neoliberal capitalism while fighting for structural and ideological changes that will usher in a radical and socialist democracy worthy of the struggle. Capitalism is the virus and it is only "by imagining emancipated futures that we will be driven to set ourselves free from the capitalist parasite."[83]

Hannah Arendt rightly reminds us that we need to retell the story of fascism so that it may never happen again. She writes:

> Not only because these facts have changed and poisoned the very air we breathe, not only because they now inhabit our dreams at night and permeate our thoughts during the day—but also because they have become the basic experience and the basic misery of our times. Only from this foundation, on which a new knowledge … will rest, can our new insights, our new memories, our new deeds, take their point of departure.[84]

Section II

Populism and the Crisis of Education

The Ugly Terror of a Fascist Abyss and the Politics of Depoliticization

The demagogue is one who preaches doctrines he knows to be untrue to men he knows to be idiots.

H.L. Mencken

Fascist Politics and the Crisis of Neoliberalism

Just as the 2008 global economic crisis revealed the failure of liberal democracy and the scourge of neoliberalism, the pandemic crisis of 2020 has revealed how institutions meant to serve the public interest and offer support for a progressive politics can be transformed to serve authoritarian ideologies and a ruling elite. Both view democracy as the enemy of market-based freedoms, ultra-nationalism, and the dictates of white supremacy. As the twenty-first century unfolds, liberal democracy has tipped over into the abyss of a fascist politics.

What was not learned from the 2008 financial calamity is that an economic crisis neither unites those most affected in favor of a progressive politics nor does it offer any political guarantees regarding the direction of social change. Instead, the emotions that fueled massive public anger towards elites and globalization gave rise to a fascist politics with its celebration of populist demagogues and their production of a right-wing tsunami of misdirected anger, hate, and violence towards minority groups such as undocumented immigrants, refugees, Muslims, and people of color.

The 2008 financial crisis wreaked havoc in multiple ways, but the strain it put on the economic system was not as severe as the hardships it caused to thousands of Americans who lost their jobs and homes. The coronavirus pandemic was of a different scale in terms of both lives lost and an egregious lack of state planning. The pandemic has killed thousands of people, including a disproportionate number of people of color, while revealing how the market failed to prepare for the crisis by defunding the public health system and failing to provide the medical tools and resources necessary to fight it. In both instances, the priority of short-term profits over human needs not only depleted state capacities in the name of the alleged superior efficiency of the market but also revealed the dreadful mutilations fostered by deindustrialization, the fragility of financial structures, the privatization of everything, and the dismantling of the welfare state, however hollowed out.[1]

Yet there was another crisis that received little attention, a crisis of agency. This crisis centered around matters of identity, self-determination, and collective resistance, which were undermined in profound ways, giving rise to and legitimating the emergence of authoritarian populist movements in many parts of the Western world both during the 2008 financial crisis and in the wake of the Covid-19 pandemic. In the aftermath of these crises, there was a profound shift in public consciousness in both the United States and in a number of other authoritarian countries. In what follows, I want to focus on the rise of right-wing populism, the conditions that made it possible, and the underlying political forces that revealed the neoliberal response to the pandemic, particularly in the U.S., a catastrophic example of a failed state.

Central to this political and ideological crisis was the declining belief in the legitimacy of both liberal democracy and its pledges about trickle-down wealth, economic security, and broadening equal opportunities preached by the apostles of neoliberalism. In many ways, public faith in the welfare state, quality employment opportunities, institutional possibilities, and a secure future for each generation collapsed. In part, this was a product of the post-war economic boom giving way to massive degrees of inequality, the off-shoring of wealth and power, the enactment of cruel austerity measures, an expanding regime of precarity, and a cut-throat economic and social environment in which individual and corporate interests prevailed over any consideration of the common good. As liberalism aligned itself with corporate and political power, both the Democratic and Republican Parties embraced financial reforms that increased the wealth of the bankers and corporate elite while doing little to prevent people from losing their homes, being strapped with chronic debt, seeing their pensions disappear, and facing a future of uncertainty with no long-term prospects or guarantees.

As noted by Pankaj Mishra, in an age of economic anxiety, existential insecurity, and a growing culture of fear, liberalism's overheated emphasis on individual liberties "made human beings subordinate to the market, replacing social bonds with market relations and sanctifying greed."[2] In this instance, neoliberalism became an incubator for a growing authoritarian populism fed largely by economic inequality and the resurgence of virulent racism. The latter was the outcome of a growing cultural and political polarization that made "it possible for haters to come out from the margins, form larger groups and make political trouble."[3] This tyrannical polarization and surge of fascist politics produced by casino capitalism was accentuated with the growth of fascist groups that shared a skepticism of international organizations, supported a militant right-wing nationalism, and championed a surge of anti-immigrant, anti-Muslim, anti-Black, and anti-democratic values.

This apocalyptic populism was rooted in a profound discontent for the empty promises of a neoliberal ideology that made capitalism and democracy synonymous, while celebrating markets as the model for all social relations. Yet the increase in capitalist barbarism was not due entirely to the takeover of the government by extremists in the Republican Party giving way to the conditions that produced the Trump presidency. The Democratic Party proponents of neoliberalism, such as Bill Clinton and Barack Obama, participated in the dismantling of the social contract, widening economic inequality, and expanding burgeoning landscapes of joblessness, misery, anger, and despair.

Above all, they enacted policies that dismantled civic culture and undermined a wide range of democratic institutions that extended from the media to public goods such as public and higher education. Under such circumstances, democratic narratives, values, and modes of solidarity, which traded in shared responsibilities and shared hopes, were replaced by a market-based focus on a regressive notion of hyper-individualism, ego-centered values, and a view of individuality that eviscerated any broader notion of social, systemic, and corporate problems and accountability. Ways of imagining society through a collective ethos were disparaged, and a comprehensive understanding of politics as inclusive and participatory morphed into an anti-politics marked by an over-, if not exclusive, investment in the language of individual rights, individual choice [missing any notion of economic constraints], and the power of rights-bearing individuals.

Under the reign of neoliberalism, language became thinner and more individualistic, detached from history, and more self-oriented, all the while undermining viable democratic social spheres as spaces where politics brings people together as collective agents and critically engaged citizens. Neoliberal language is written in the discourse of economics and market values, not ethics. This is a market-based language that manipulates public opinion and is immersed in a "pornography of power and a bogus fantasy of machismo."[4] Under such circumstances, shallowness becomes an asset rather than a liability.

More and more, the watered-down language of liberal democracy, with its over-emphasis on individual rights and its neoliberal coddling of the financial elite, gave way to a regressive notion of the social marked by rising authoritarian tendencies, unchecked nativism, unapologetic expressions of bigotry, misdirected anger, and the language of resentment-filled revolt. Liberal democracies across the globe not only appeared out of touch with the misery and suffering caused by neoliberal policies, they also produced an insular and arrogant group of politicians who regarded themselves as an enlightened political formation that worked "on behalf of an ignorant public."[5] The ultimate consequence was to produce what Wolfgang Merkel describes as "a rebellion of the disenfranchised."[6] A series of political uprisings made it clear that neoliberalism was suffering from a crisis of legitimacy further accentuated by the Brexit vote in the United Kingdom, the election of Donald Trump, support for the National Front in France, and the emergence of powerful right-wing populist movements across the globe, especially in Brazil, Hungary, and India.[7]

As a regime of affective management, neoliberalism created a culture in which everyone was trapped in his or her own feelings, emotions, and orbits of privatization. One result was that legitimate political claims could only be pursued by individuals and families rather than social groups. In this instance, power was removed from the social sphere and placed almost entirely in the hands of corporate and political demagogues who used it to enrich themselves for their own personal gain. Power was now used to produce muscular authority in order "to secure order, boundaries, and to divert the growing anger of a declining middle and working-class. Both classes to an increasing extent came to blame their economic and political conditions that produced their misery and ravaged ways of life on 'others': immigrants, minority races, 'external' predators and attackers ranging from terrorists to refugees."[8] Liberal-individualistic views lost their legitimacy as they refused to indict the underlying structures of capitalism and its winner-take-all ethos.

Functioning largely as a ruthless form of social Darwinism, economic activity was removed from any sense of social responsibility and the grammar of ethics, only to be replaced by a culture of cruelty and resentment that disdained any notion of compassion or ethical concern for those deemed as "other" because of their class, race, ethnicity, sexual orientation, or religion. This is a culture marked by gigantic hypocrisies, "the gloomy tabulation of unspeakable violent events," widespread viciousness, "great concentrations of wealth," "surveillance overkill," and the "unceasing despoliation of biospheres for profit."[9]

In the neoliberal worldview, those who are unemployed, poor consumers, or outside of the reach of a market in search of insatiable profits are considered disposable. Increasingly viewed as anti-human, unknowable, faceless, and symbols of fear and pathology. This includes undocumented immigrants in the United States and refugees in Europe as well as those who are considered of no value to a market society, and thus eligible to be deprived of the most basic rights and subject to the terrors of state violence.

Marking selected groups as disposable in both symbolic and material forms, neoliberal politics was transformed into a machinery of political and social death—producing spaces where undesirable members are abused, put in cages, separated from their children, and subject to a massive violation of their human rights. Under a neoliberal politics of exclusion people live in spaces of ever-present danger and risk where nothing is certain, human beings considered excess are denied a social function, and relegated to what Étienne Balibar calls the "death zones of humanity."[10] These are the twenty-first-century workstations designed for the creation and process of elimination, a death-haunted mode of production rooted in the "absolute triumph of irrationality."[11]

Within this new political formation, older forms of exploitation are now matched, if not exceeded, by a politics of racial and social cleansing as entire populations are removed from ethical assessments producing zones of social abandonment. In this new world, there is a merging of finance capital and a war culture that speaks to a moral and political collapse in which the welfare state is replaced by forms of economic nationalism and a burgeoning carceral state.[12] Furthermore, elements of this crisis can be seen in the ongoing militarization of everyday life as more and more institutions take on the model of the prison. Additionally, there is also the increased arming of the police, the criminalization of a wide range of behaviors related to social problems, the rise of the surveillance state, and the ongoing war on youth, undocumented immigrants, Muslims, and others deemed enemies of the state. As I spelled out in Chapter 2, under the presidency of Donald Trump, the language of war and violence became the primary rhetorical tools in both shaping policies and attacking and dehumanizing almost anyone who criticized his leadership and mode of governance.

Under the aegis of a neoliberal war culture, we have witnessed increasing immiseration for the working and middle classes, massive tax cuts for the rich, the outsourcing of public services, a full-fledged attack on unions, the defunding of public goods, and the privatization of public services extending from health and education to roads and prisons. This ongoing transfer of public resources and services to the rich, hedge-fund managers, and corporate elite was matched by the corporate takeover of the commanding institutions of culture, including the digital, print, and broadcast media. What has been vastly underestimated in the rise of right-wing populism is the capture of the media by authoritarian populists and its flipside which amounts to a full-fledged political attack on independent digital, online, and oppositional journalists.

While it is generally recognized that neoliberalism was responsible for the worldwide economic crisis of 2008, what is less acknowledged is that the structural crisis produced by a capitalism on steroids was not matched by a subjective crisis in the popular imagination and consequently gave rise to a surge of reactionary political populist movements. As the economic collapse became visceral, people's lives were upended and sometimes destroyed. Moreover, as the social contract was shredded along with the need for socially constructed roles, norms, and public goods, the "social" no longer occupied a thick and important pedagogical space of solidarity, dialogue, political expression, dissent, and politics.

As shared responsibilities gave way to shared fears, right-wing populism engaged in a politics of divisiveness and a pedagogy of hate. As Nathan J. Robinson observes, this was a populism that favored "reactionary cultural traditions, militarized borders, bigotry, and rabid nationalism ... involves scapegoating foreigners for social problems ... and is racist, sexist, xenophobic."[13] This is the politics of right-wing authoritarians such as Trump, Bolsonaro, Erdogan, Putin, and other fascist politicians.

As public spheres disappeared, communal bonds were weakened, and social provisions withered, tribalism with its communities of exclusion, homage to ultra-nationalism, and regressive notion of the citizens as producers and consumers of goods gained in momentum, offering the myth of unity at the expense of democratic values, equity, and social justice.[14] Under neoliberalism, the social sphere regressed into a privatized society of shoppers in which individuals were atomized, alienated, and steadily removed from the variety of social connections and communal bonds that give meaning to the degree to which societies are good and just.[15]

People became isolated, segregated, and unable "to negotiate democratic dilemmas in a democratic way" as power become more abstract and removed from public participation and accountability.[16] As the neoliberal net of privilege was cast wider, without apology, for the rich and to the exclusion of others, it became more obvious to growing elements of the public that appeals to liberal democracy had failed to keep its promise of a better life for all. It could no longer demand, without qualification, that working people should work harder for less, and that democratic participation is exclusively about elections. It had become more difficult to hide from many disenfranchised groups what Adam Tooze describes as "a disastrous slide from the hypocrisies and compromises of the previous status quo into something even [more dangerous]."[17]

This disavowal of the promises of liberal democracy was amplified in the summer of 2020 as America's slide into authoritarianism became more clear when millions joined peaceful protests throughout the United States in the wake of an increasing number of acts of racially marked acts of police violence. The abyss of fascism loomed larger as Trump responded to the call to end police violence and systemic racism by brandishing his mix of racism, angry nationalism, and yearning for "near-total autocratic power." In a pair of Fourth of July speeches, Trump labeled the demonstrators as "angry mobs" whose purpose was to "unleash a wave of violent crimes in our cities." Combining hyperbole, lies, and threats, he claimed that the country was under siege by what he called "a new far-left fascism that demands absolute allegiance."

As the global crisis has intensified since 2008, particularly as a result of the Covid-19 pandemic, elements of a political and moral collapse central to authoritarian regimes became more obvious and found their most transparent expression of ruthlessness, greed, and unchecked power in the rule of Donald Trump.

Up until the mass demonstrations against police brutality and institutional racism that erupted after the murder of George Floyd by the police, the slide into authoritarianism was made all the easier by the absence of a broad-based left mass movement in the United States. The absence of such a group was evident in the failure of the left as a diverse and fractured political formation to provide both a comprehensive vision of change and an alignment of single-issue groups and smaller movements into one mass movement. Nancy Fraser rightly observes that, following the Occupy Movement, "potential links between labour and new social movements were left to languish. Split off from one another, those indispensable poles of a viable left were miles apart, waiting to be counterposed as antithetical."[18] It remains to be seen if the outburst of anger against police violence across the globe will be eventually transformed into a mass, organized intersectional international movement, one capable of producing a new language, vision, disruptive tactics, pedagogical relations, and critical sources of cultural knowledge. What cannot be ignored, however, is that one of the challenges facing this insurrection is a moment of reckoning that connects what Cornell West calls diverse seeds of violence externally and internally. West connects the mass rebellions over racial violence and police barbarism to part of a wider and more comprehensive understanding of politics. He writes:

> The catalyst was certainly Brother George Floyd's public lynching, but the failures of the predatory capitalist economy to provide the satisfaction of the basic needs of food and healthcare and quality education, jobs with a decent wage, at the same time the collapse of your political class, the collapse of your professional class. Their legitimacy has been radically called into question, and that's

multiracial. It's the neofascist dimension in Trump. It's the neoliberal dimension in Biden and Obama and the Clintons and so forth. And it includes much of the media. It includes many of the professors in universities. The young people are saying, "You all have been hypocritical. You haven't been concerned about our suffering, our misery. And we no longer believe in your legitimacy." And it spills over into violent explosion.[19]

Since the 1970s, there has been a profound backlash by economic, financial, political, and religious fundamentalists and their allied media establishments against labor, an oppositional press, people of color, and others who have attempted to extend the workings of democracy and equality. As the narrative of class and class struggle disappeared along with the absence of a vibrant socialist movement, the call for democracy no longer provided a unifying narrative to bring different oppressed groups together. Instead, economic and cultural nationalism has become a rallying cry to create the conditions for merging a regressive neoliberalism and populism into a war machine. Under such circumstances, politics is imagined as a form of war, repelling immigrants and refugees who are described by President Trump as "invaders," "vermin," and "rapists."

The emergence of neoliberalism as a war machine was evident in the reign of the Republican Party under the Trump administration, which waged assaults on anything that did not mimic the values of the market or bow to Trump's relentless acts of lawlessness. Such assaults take the form of labeling and fixing whole categories of people as disposable, enemies, and force them into conditions of extreme precarity and, as time unfolds, in more conditions of danger. Neoliberal capitalism radiates violence, evident in its endless instances of mass shootings such as those that took place in 2019 in El Paso, Texas and Dayton, Ohio. Violence appears to be rooted in capitalism's DNA and has spread to public schools and neighborhoods marked by extreme poverty, and has shaped the culture of policing. Violence has become an organizing principle of sports and entertainment. Its presence is ubiquitous, a fundamental feature of politics, economics, culture, and everyday life, and works through a society that measures power by the speed to which it removes itself from any sense of ethical and social responsibility. As Beatrix Campbell puts it:

> The richest society on the planet is armed. And it invests in one of the largest prison systems in the world. Violence circulates between state and citizen. Drilled to kill, doomed to die: mastery and martyrdom is the heartbreaking dialectic of the manufacture of militarized, violent masculinity ... The making and maintaining of militarized masculinities is vital to these new modes of armed conflict that are proliferating across the flexible frontiers of globalized capitalism, between and within states.[20]

What has become more and more evident is that the neoliberal agenda has been a spectacular failure. It has destabilized the key institutions of democracy by lowering taxes on the rich, deregulating controls on corporations, imposing financial controls on markets, and cutting social programs.[21] Moreover, it has mobilized on a global level the violent, political, social, racial, and economic energies of a resurgent fascist politics. Across the globe, right-wing modes of governance are appearing in which the line collapses between "outside foreign enemies" such as refugees and undocumented immigrants, on the one hand, and on the other, inside "dangerous" or "treasonous" classes such as critical journalists, educators, and dissidents.

As neoliberal economies more and more resort to violence and repression, Trump's bellicose tirades and discourse of violence and nativism replace any sense of shared responsibilities. In this context, violence is not only elevated to an organizing principle of society but also expands its network of extreme cruelty. Imagining politics as a war machine, more and more groups are treated as excess and inscribed in an order of power as disposable, enemies, and forced into conditions of extreme precarity. This is a particularly vicious form of state violence which undermines and constrains agency and subjects individuals to zones of abandonment evident in the growth of immigrant jails and an expanding carceral complex in the United States and other countries such as Hungary and Brazil.

As neoliberalism's promise of social mobility and expanding economic progress collapsed, it gave way to an authoritarian right-wing populism. Given neoliberalism's lack of vision for the future, the search for narratives on which to pin the hatred of governing elites took an anti-democratic turn. What might have been a progressive revolt against those who "capped health and welfare spending, [imposed] punitive benefit withdraws [that] forced ... many families to rely on food banks [and] withdraw sickness and disability benefits from one million former workers below retirement age"[22] was channeled into a tsunami of violent racial, economic, and political energies that mobilized a fascist politics.

Across the globe, a series of uprisings appeared that signaled new anti-democratic political formations that rejected the notion that there was no alternative to neoliberal hegemony. This was evident not only with the election of Donald Trump in the U.S. and Boris Johnson in the United Kingdom but also with the election of Jair Bolsonaro in Brazil, and growing support for popular movements such as the National Front in France and the Alternative für Deutschland party in Germany. "Establishment politics has lost its legitimacy as voters rejected the conditions produced by financialized capitalism."[23] Unfortunately, what started out as a revolt against privileged elites turned into a movement seething with forms of resentment that were militantly anti-utopian and all too willing to support a wave of reactionary populist leaders in the United States and across Europe.

As Chantal Mouffe observes, in a number of European countries, populist aspirations for autonomy, freedom, and self-determination have "been captured by right-wing populist parties that have managed to construct the people through a xenophobic discourse that excludes immigrants, considered as a threat to national prosperity."[24] At the same time, with the erosion of democratic ideals such as economic and social equality, freedom, and justice, popular resistance has taken a dark turn by reinforcing rather than challenging the widespread forces of exploitation, discrimination, exclusion, and repression.

In the United States both major political parties were more than willing to turn the economy over to the bankers and hedge-fund managers, and produced policies that shaped radical forms of industrial and social restructuring, all of which caused massive pain, suffering, and rage among large segments of the working class and other disenfranchised groups. Right-wing populist leaders across the globe recognized that national economies were in the hands of foreign investors, a mobile financial elite, and transnational capital. In a masterful act of political diversion, populist leaders attacked all vestiges of liberal capitalism while refusing to name neoliberal inequities in wealth and power as a basic threat to their societies. Instead of calling for an acceleration of the democratic ideals of popular sovereignty and economic equality, right-wing populist leaders such as Trump, Bolsonaro, and Orbán defined democracy as the enemy of order and economic progress.

They also diverted genuine popular anger into the abyss of cultural chauvinism, anti-immigrant hatred, a contempt of Muslims, and a targeted attack on the environment, health care, education, public institutions, social provisions, and other basic life resources. As Arjun Padurai observes, such authoritarian leaders hate democracy, capture the political emotions of those treated as disposable, and do everything they can to hide the deep contradictions of neoliberal capitalism.[25] How else to explain that in the midst of a pandemic that killed more than 151,000 Americans and infected over 4 million by July 2020, Trump waged a culture war against civil disobedience, admonished NASCAR for banning the Confederate flag at all events and properties, and attacked NASCAR's only Black driver Bubba Wallace for falsely reporting a hate crime, which he personally did not report. All these interventions were simply code for throwing meat to Trump's white supremacist base.[26] Trump's disregard for the soaring death toll due to the virus appears inconsequential to him, especially since he wrongly thought it would serve to bolster his re-election efforts.

In this scenario, there exists the resurgence of a fascist politics that capitalizes on the immiseration, fears, and anxieties produced by neoliberalism without naming the underlying conditions that create and legitimate its policies and social costs. While such right-wing populist movements may comment critically on certain elements of neoliberalism such as globalization, they largely embrace those ideological and economic elements that concentrate power and wealth in the hands of a political, corporate, and financial elite, thus reinforcing in the end an extreme form of capitalism. Moreover, right-wing populists may condemn globalization, but they do so by blaming those considered outside the inclusive boundaries of a white homeland even though the same forces victimize them.[27] At the same time, such leaders mobilize passions that deny critical understanding, while simultaneously creating desires and affects that produce nativist, ultra-nationalist, and hyper-masculine forms of identification.

In this instance, education functions as an oppressive form of politics, used as a tool of power in the struggle over power, identity, and agency.[28] All pedagogies are contextual, and in this historical moment, a pandemic pedagogy has emerged that is crucial in producing a neoliberal fascism that combines the savagery of the market with an overt form of racial cleansing. What is at stake here is not simply a struggle between authoritarian ideas and democratic ideals, but a fierce battle on the part of demagogues to destroy the institutions and conditions that make critical thought and oppositional accounts of power possible. This was evident, for instance, in Trump's constant attacks on the critical media, often referring to them as "'the enemy of the people' pushing Radical Left Democrat views,'" even as journalists were subject to expulsion, mass jailings, and assassinations across the world by some of Trump's allies.[29] What must be remembered, as Hannah Arendt observed in *The Origins of Totalitarianism*, is that authoritarian movements are contingent upon the unconditional loyalty of "the slumbering majorities" who felt abandoned by elites and governments whom they perceived as "equally stupid and fraudulent."[30]

There is also the problematic use of "the people" in populist discourse. The people is an abstract category that functions as an imagined community, one that erases the deep differences among individuals and diverse political groups. As Joan Pedro-Caranana observes:

> The populist discourse homogenizes what is materially heterogeneous. This means that populism strangles the multiple voices of resistance

and change. The populist synecdoche buries the specific demands and interests of social movements through generalization … In reality, when populists refer to "the people" they mean only those who support (or will support) them. Those who do not support them are excluded from the people and this easily ignites animosity on the side of the excluded. They are treated as non-people. Thus, populist discourse is based on a fiction that it calls people that can never be realized as there will always be a part of society that is not represented by populists and which will be represented by others.[31]

In the face of a looming global recession, it is crucial to understand the connection between the rise of right-wing populism and neoliberalism, which emerged in the late 1970s as a commanding ideology fueling a punitive form of globalization. This historical moment is marked by unique ideological, economic, and political formations produced by ever-increasing brutal forms of capitalism, however diverse.

Neoliberalism's unprecedented concentration of economic and political power has produced a failed state modeled after the models of finance and unchecked market forces. As I have mentioned throughout this book, the effects have become familiar and include cruel austerity measures, adulation of self-regulating markets, the liberating of capital from any constraints, deregulation, privatization of public goods, the commodification of everyday life, and the gutting of environmental, health, and safety laws. Such policies have produced massive inequities in wealth, power, and income, while further accelerating mass misery, human suffering, the rise of state-sanctioned violence and ever-expanding sites of terminal exclusion in the forms of walls, detention centers, and an expanding carceral state.

The economic downturn produced by the Covid-19 pandemic accentuated the antagonisms, instabilities, and crisis produced by the long history and reach of neoliberal ideologies and policies. At a time when 38.1 million Americans lived in poverty, including 20.5 percent of Blacks, inequality amounted to a death trap, as could be seen in the fact that Black and Latinos were three times more likely to be infected by the virus and two times more likely to die from it. Moreover, the economic catastrophe produced by the pandemic contained the seeds to fuel further forces of repression and strengthened the forces of white supremacy, Islamophobia, nativism, and misogyny.

Waging war on democracy and the institutions that produce it, neoliberalism has tapped into a combination of fear and widespread racism that has once again unleashed the mobilizing passions of fascism, especially the historically distinct registers of extreme nationalism, xenophobia, nativism, white supremacy, racial and ethnic cleansing, voter suppression, and an attack on a civic culture of critique and resistance. The result is a new political formation that I have called neoliberal fascism in which the principles and practices of a fascist past and neoliberal present have merged, connecting the worst dimensions and excesses of gangster capitalism with the fascist ideals of white nationalism and racial supremacy associated with the horrors of authoritarian states. Neoliberal fascism hollows out democracy from within, breaks down the separation of power while increasing the power of the presidency, and saturates cultural and social life with its ideology of self-interest, a survival-of-the-fittest ethos, and regressive notions of freedom. What needs to be acknowledged is that neoliberalism as an extreme form of capitalism has produced the conditions for a fascist politics that is updated to serve the interest of a concentrated class of financial elite and a rising tide of political demagogues across the globe.

What warrants repeating is that the mass anger fueling neoliberal fascism is a diversion of genuine resistance into what amounts to a pathology, which empties politics of any democratic substance. This is evident also in the right-wing attack on immigrants and refugees as dangerous outsiders. This hardened version of racism and nativism serves to bury class politics as a major factor in producing a range of oppressive conditions. Moreover, it camouflages its own authoritarian ruling-class interests and relentless attacks on social welfare, labor unions, public goods, women's reproductive rights, and quality health care for all.[32] Mike Lofgren is right in arguing that "If authoritarian populism is the wave of the future, its midwife is neoliberal economics turned punitive and illiberal."[33]

A number of theorists such as Noam Chomsky, John Bellamy Foster, Neil Faulkner, and Federico Finchelstein see similarities between an earlier fascism and the current state of global politics. What they have not fully acknowledged is how neoliberalism has put in motion a distinctive and powerful politics of depoliticization that has undermined viable forms of individual and collective agency capable of resisting neoliberal capitalism and its emerging fascist politics. In this sense, neoliberal fascism is not only about the crisis of economics, historical memory, civic literacy, and politics, it is also about the crisis of agency, or what I call the crisis of depoliticization.

The Politics of Depoliticization

In the current era, politics is no longer about the language of public interest, but about how to survive in a world without social provisions, support, community, and a faith in collective struggle. This is a language that operates as a medium of violence, and marks, as Bill Dixon insists, "a terrifying new horizon for human political experience."[34] This is a language that is horrifying for producing, if not mirroring, without apology for what the end of politics, if not humanity itself, might look like. Under such circumstances, democracy is not merely under siege, but is close to being erased.

Examples of a failed and cruel state abound under the presidency of Donald Trump, who promised to cut in his budget over a trillion dollars in support of Medicare and Medicaid while cutting $4.5 billion from federal spending on food stamps. Moreover, the Trump administration continued to endanger the planet by reducing emissions standards for commercial vehicles and rolling back clean-water protections in the midst of the pandemic.[35] The latter is particularly egregious in that it reversed laws "that placed limits on polluting chemicals that could be used near streams, wetlands and other bodies of water."[36]

Other examples include the White House asking the Supreme Court to end DACA, the Deferred Action for Childhood Arrivals Program, which provides immigration protections for over 700,000 young people brought illegally to the United States as children. A Supreme Court decision rejected Trump's attempt, but left open the possibility for Trump to attempt to end it again.[37] The Trump administration responded to the decision by asserting that it would reject new applications for the program and "limit the renewal term for current DACA recipients to one year instead of the usual two."[38] There was also a Supreme Court ruling allowing the United States to "deny asylum to anyone who passes through another country on their way to the US, blocking most Central American migrants fleeing violence and poverty who arrive at the southern border."[39]

In this unapologetic authoritarian regime, the language of violence, cruelty, and hatred reached new levels. For instance, *The New York Times* reported that Trump suggested shooting immigrants in the legs in order to prevent them from crossing the southern border.[40] It gets worse. Trump also ordered ending the "medical deferred action" program which allows immigrants who are seriously ill to extend their stay in the U.S. by two years in order to receive much-needed medical treatment. Massachusetts Senator Ed Markey captured the barbarism of such a policy in his statement that the Trump administration was now "literally deporting kids with cancer" and that this policy would "terrorize sick kids who are literally fighting for their lives."[41] Trump and his allies appeared to delight in asserting power through acts of barbarity that threaten, disrupt, and condemn entire populations to a politics of disposability and spheres of social atomization. Among the many instances of this type of cruelty is Trump's deportation of 200,000 Salvadorian immigrants as part of his policy of ending the humanitarian program known as the Temporary Protected Status policy. Under this policy, "Salvadorans [had] been allowed to live and work legally in the United States since a pair of devastating earthquakes struck their country in 2001."[42]

This suggests more than a fascist politics of disappearance and racial cleansing. There is also an attack on modes of critical agency and on the educational and cultural institutions that create the conditions where citizens can be educated and informed in order to make democracy possible. As the endpoint of a depoliticizing process, agency becomes susceptible to modes that embrace shared fears, the loss of autonomy, and rancid hatreds rather than collective values and obligations. As a mode of failed sociality, market fundamentalism has turned the principles of democracy against itself, twisting the language of autonomy, solidarity, freedom, and justice that make economic and social equality a viable idea and political goal. Neoliberalism produces a notion of individualism and anti-intellectualism that harbors a pathological disdain for community and, in doing so, reinforces the notion that all social bonds and their respective ethos of social responsibility are untrustworthy. Unchecked notions of self-interest and a regressive withdrawal from a substantive oppositional politics now replace notions of the common good and engaged citizenship, just as "existing political institutions have long since ceased to represent anyone but the wealthy."[43] Under the reign of a market fundamentalism, social atomization becomes comparable to the death of an inclusive and just democracy.

Closely related to the depoliticizing practices of neoliberalism, the politics of social atomization, and a failed sociality is the existence of a survival-of the-fittest ethos that drives oppressive narratives used to define both agency and our relationship to others. Mimicking the logic of a war culture, neoliberal pandemic pedagogy creates a predatory culture in which the demand of hyper-competitiveness pits individuals against each other through a market-based logic in which compassion and caring for the other is replaced by a culture of winners and losers, with the former assuming the status of a national sport, if not religion. As Herbert Rosa observes, under neoliberalism,

> people perceive the world around them, the world they encounter, as a combat zone to be viewed at best with indifference but more often with hostility—a world in which their own position was always precarious anyway—they see the vital, the foreign, the strange that confront them as a danger and a threat. Indeed, their own very real experience has led them to associate change above all with decadence and decline.[44]

The language of aggression replaces matters of concern for those deemed "other" by virtue of their class, ethnicity, religion, or race and their inability or refusal to participate in a consumer society. Underlying this neoliberal worldview is a warrior mentality that replicates a reality TV's mantra of a "war of all against all," which brings home the lesson that punishment is the norm and compassion the exception. Yet, this rhetoric of command does more than pit individuals against each other in an endless loop of competitiveness and a world in which there are only individual winners; it also weakens public values and reinforces a hardening of the culture, one in which a self-righteous coldness takes delight in the suffering of others.

How else to explain Trump's racist comments and cruel policies aimed at undocumented immigrants trying to escape from poverty, violence, gangs, and rogue societies? How else to explain Trump's suggestion that migrants be slowed down by electrifying the wall on the southern border with spikes and a moat filled with alligators and snakes?[45] How else to explain separating children from their parents at the border and then jailing them in wired cages? How else to explain Trump's use of military storm troopers to attack peaceful protesters? The predatory and hyper-masculine culture of extreme competitiveness produces a weakening of democratic values, pressures, and ideals and in doing so creates a culture in which expressions of violence and cruelty replace the ability to act politically, responsibly, and with civic courage. This predatory culture furthers the process of depoliticization by making it difficult for individuals to identify with any sense of shared obligation, meaningful forms of solidarity, and viable notion of the common good. Under such circumstances, politics was no longer about the language of public interest, but about how to survive in a world without social provisions, support, community, and a faith in collective struggle. Or, much worse, how to channel one's fears and anxieties into a hatred of those others marginalized by race, ethnicity, religion, and class.

Potentially democratic public spheres such as the oppositional media, schools, and other public institutions are disappearing under the noxious policies of austerity and privatization, thus reinforcing a hyper-individualized, masculine, and militarized culture that destroys notions of engaged and critical citizenship, along with any viable sense of individual and social agency. Operating under the false assumption that there are only individual solutions to socially produced problems, neoliberal pedagogy reinforces depoliticizing states of individual alienation and isolation, which more and more are normalized, rendering human beings numb and fearful, immune to the demands of economic and social justice, and largely divorced from matters of politics, ethics, and civic courage. This amounts to a form of depoliticization in which individuals develop a propensity to descend into a moral stupor, a deadening cynicism, all the while becoming more susceptible to political shocks, and the seductive pleasure of the manufactured spectacle.

In this instance, the political becomes relentlessly personal, rendering difficult any notion of social agency and collective resistance. More is at stake here than a freezing of the capacity for the development of modes of critical agency; there is also the emergence and signs of widespread apathy as more and more people refuse even the most elementary appeals to participate in elections or educate themselves about politics.[46] Meanwhile, there is the slow deterioration of public spheres that once offered at least the glimmer of progressive ideas, enlightened social policies, non-commodified values and critical exchanges. As public institutions and values are undermined, matters of class and power begin to disappear along with the social movements and public spaces that support them. Unions are weakened, working people lose their jobs with no tools to prevent such losses from happening, and increasingly all that is left is a culture of unfocused anger, despair, immediacy, and entertainment, which infantilizes everything it touches.

As the connections between democracy and education wither, hope becomes the enemy of agency, and agency is reduced to learning how to survive rather than working to improve the conditions that bear down on one's life and society in general. Dealing with life's problems becomes a solitary affair, reducing matters of social responsibility to a regressive and depoliticized notion of individual choice. As the social sphere is emptied of democratic institutions and ideals, apocalyptic visions of fear and fatalism reinforce the normalized assumption that there are no alternatives to existing political logics and the tyranny of a neoliberal global economy. Under neoliberalism, shared notions of solidarity are erased along with institutions that nurture an engaged and critical sensibility. This type of depoliticizing erasure raises the question: can a democratic conception of politics emerge, how does it happen, and what agents of change are available to take up the task of mass and collective resistance? Within contemporary neoliberal populist political formations, language functions to repress any sense of moral decency and connection to others; as a result, individual communication rooted in democratic values and dialogue loses all meaning. Leo Lowenthal argues that individuals are pressured more and more to act as "ruthless seekers after their own survival, psychological pawns and puppets of a system that knows no other purpose than to keep itself in power."[47] Critical agency is now viewed as dangerous and undermined by the ongoing neoliberal pedagogical machineries of power and a culture of manufactured ignorance that works to produce a form of political repression, on the one hand, and political regression and infantilism on the other.[48]

Depoliticization turns ignorance into a virtue, making it all the more difficult for individuals to balance reason and affect, distinguish between fact and fiction, and make critical and informed judgments. To an increasing extent, education both in schools and in the wider cultural apparatuses, such as the mainstream and conservative media, becomes a tool of repression and serves to promote and legitimate neoliberal fascist propaganda. As such, the never-ending task of critique gives way to the failure of conscience, while succumbing to simplistic views of the world defined through an irrationality that is fundamental to a fascist politics. Reason and informed judgment, once a precondition for creating informed citizens, gives way to a culture of shouting, emotional overdrive, and shortened attention spans. New digital technologies and platforms controlled by monopolies trade in consumerism, speed, and brevity and conspire to make thoughtfulness, if not thinking itself, difficult. Knowledge is no longer troubling; instead, it is pre-packaged in the 24/7 news cycle, reduced to babbling one-liners and commercial smart bombs.[49]

As neoliberal ideology works its way through the vast reach of the mainstream and conservative media, it operates as a disimagination machine that attempts both to control history and erase moments of resistance and oppression. History as an act of dangerous memory is whitewashed, purged of utopian ideals and replaced by apocalyptic fantasies. These include narratives of decline, fear, insecurity, and anxiety, and visions of imminent danger, often expressed in the language of invasion, dangerous hordes, criminal and disease-infected others. As public vocabularies and transcripts disappear, it is difficult for individuals to understand historically the multiple wars waged on democratic ideals. Everything appears to lack any antecedents, making the poisonous vitriol and policies of neoliberal fascism more energizing, fresh and free of a repressive history.

Rather than revealing humanity's legacy of repression and violence, or its heroic moments of resistance, memory is trapped in the present. The politics of depoliticization—with its refiguring of the social sphere, collective identity, historical memory, and critical thinking—now begins to take the form of an acute indifference, withdrawal from public life, and a disdain for politics that amounts to a political catastrophe. The move from crisis, which implies the possibility of change, to catastrophe in which politics dissolves into cynicism and despair ends up producing what Richard Rodriquez calls "an astonishing vacancy."[50] In a society steadily marked by a flight from the common good, the ethical duty to care for the other vanishes or is viewed with contempt. In short, matters of self-fulfillment and an egoistic self-referentiality work hand in hand with instances of "painless morality" or an empty morality stripped of ethical obligations and an attentiveness to social costs.[51]

We live in a neoliberal age that destroys the most important democratic institutions, values, and relations that connect us. This is evident in the overwrought concentration of power and wealth among the 1 per cent, with its corollary in corporate-induced corruption that leads millionaire politicians such as Trump to have believed that he was above the law and could disregard the Constitution and separation of powers. As, for instance, his use of the Attorney General and the Justice Department to prosecute his enemies and reduce or eliminate jail time for his friends. It is also evident in the institutional, political, and cultural practices that delight in the merging of violence and power to enact cruel policies upon entire populations—women, immigrants, children, Blacks, and Muslims.

This form of malice is evident in recent Supreme Court decisions that reinforced Trump's savage asylum policies. Other examples of the current culture of a profit-crazed barbarism can be found in purposeful creation of a manufactured opioid crisis. This is a crisis produced largely by drug companies that traffic in death, and are responsible for the rising epidemic of suicide rates due to what Anne Case and Angus Deaton labeled "deaths of despair"—caused by social isolation, disenfranchisement, poverty, lack of meaningful jobs, stagnant wages, and cuts in social programs due to tax breaks for the rich and oversized corporations.[52] Cruelty is one of the threads that is closely tied to the workings and legitimation of a fascist politics, as can be seen under modes of governance enacted by demagogues across the globe.

In societies where market values are considered more important than democratic values, hope lives on the margins of society amid the darkness of the moment. Without hope there is no possibility for resistance, dissent, and struggle. Agency is the condition of struggle, and hope is the condition of agency. Hope expands the space of the possible and becomes a way of recognizing and naming the incomplete nature of the present. When hope dies what is also lost is a viable sense of those essential social spheres, public goods, modes of historical consciousness, and collective forms of support necessary for an active and engaged citizenry.

The problem of agency is a precondition for any viable form of individual and collective resistance. It is also crucial to address both changes in consciousness and in rethinking the issue of historical and collective agency as part of the struggle for structural change. Ideological and structural changes can only take place through a formative culture and those institutions and public spheres that make education central to politics itself. The indifference to a discourse regarding who are the historic agents of change in the current moment is not merely deficient politically, it is also complicit with the rise of right-wing authoritarian movements. What emerges in the absence of these institutions, public narratives, and democratic spaces is a neoliberal fascist politics and culture.

This new political formation and punitive monstrosity is defined, in part, by the glitter, spectacles, commodification, technological fanaticism, regressive notions of privatization, and disembodied notions of individualism that dethrone what Hannah Arendt has called "the prime importance of the political."[53] In the face of such reactionary forces, it is crucial to unite various progressive forces of opposition into a powerful anti-capitalist movement that speaks not only to the range of oppressions exacerbated by neoliberalism but also to the need for new narratives that address overturning a system steeped in the machineries of war, violence, aggression, and death. There is certainly a glimmer of hope in the protest movements that emerged after the gruesome murder of George Floyd. These worldwide demonstrations added a new intensity to the struggle for racial and economic justice. They provided a glimmer of hope for building "union between movements stretching across the globe."[54] Hopefully, these massive courageous acts of solidarity will yield a new understanding of collective resistance, politics, and the crucial importance of producing critical and informed agents in the struggle for a socialist democracy.

The plague of a fascist politics and the politics of depoliticization may be on the move, but, as Marx once said, history is open. In the current historical conjuncture, ample possibilities are emerging to recognize that the current crisis of agency is a precondition for addressing not only the crisis of education and politics, but the crisis of democracy itself. Only then, as Frederick Douglass pointed out, can "the conscience of the nation be roused" and the plague of neoliberal fascism challenged and overcome.

The Populist Pandemic and the Plague of Thoughtlessness

There are no dangerous thoughts; thinking itself is dangerous.

Hannah Arendt

We have entered an ominous age of misdirected anger and political danger. A central issue of the ages has been growing support for a right-wing populism that views liberal democracy as both an anachronism and a curse. Meanwhile, many of those who oppose the growth of right-wing movements are turning to more liberal forms of populism, a position that cannot be either equated with right-wing populism or dismissed as equally demagogic. Right-wing populism is defined largely by its authoritarian embrace of bigotry, nativism, racism, and "scapegoating foreigners for social problems, while left 'populism' is generally on the side of democratic values and is anti-racist and egalitarian."[1] Yet progressive forms of populism, in spite of its honored tradition and support of democratic principles and policies, can also be tarnished by the orthodox pitfalls of ideological certainty, a false unity, and a politics of exclusion.

As I mentioned in Chapter 3, the signposts of a growing fascism at home and abroad are clear. Across the globe, politicians spew out inordinate incitements of hatred and bigotry, while legitimating, and often overtly supporting, racism. Liberals cling to notions of freedom and liberty that ignore the power of capital to turn such terms into their opposite. The mainstream media measures the task of pursuing the truth against how their bottom line is affected. One upshot is that the distinction between the truth and state-sanctioned lies is blurred as the bearings by which the truth is determined is driven by the crowd-pleasing pursuit of the spectacle. Under such circumstances, as the philosopher, Richard Bernstein observes, "The possibilities for lying become boundless and frequently met with little resistance."[2] Turning away from the truth in a time when fascist politics is on the rise is not just about the moral dissipation of those who refuse to hold power accountable or engage in moral witnessing; it is also about becoming complicit with a president whose hatred of dissent, justice, law, and democracy darkens and widens every day that he is in office. Fortunately, the architecture of lies and the institutions that support Trump are increasingly being called into question, especially for considering the mass mobilizations that followed the murder of George Floyd. However, it is not clear whether this movement will have any lasting impact on the growing forces of tyranny.

Anti-Semitism and racism became normalized under a president who surrounded himself with policy advisors who either supported Trump's white supremacist and white nationalist views or were too afraid to challenge him on these issues.[3] In the meantime, Trump almost daily tweeted and retweeted racist media messages to his audience of 80 million. Under the leadership of the Trump White House, all elements of the public were under siege by private and corporate interests and right-wing evangelicals, fully sanctioned and emboldened by the Trump regime. Neoliberal policies, which prioritized "protecting the economy before protecting the people," stripped wealth from public goods and turned them into petri dishes for extracting profits and undermining the social contract.[4] Under Trump, the interests of the ultra-rich in an unprecedented and unapologetic manner drove state policy. One effect was the merging of politics and corporate power, which served to undercut every vestige of democracy in the United States.

Tribal identities and right-wing media outlets reveled in Trump's attacks on people of color, immigrants, and his celebration of white identity and defense of citizenship in racial terms. As the leader of the party of white nationalism, Trump helped shape a Republican Party that panicked over the growing population of non-whites in America.[5] He found almost unanimous support among the Republican Party for his defense of voter suppression, his racist attacks on congressional women of color, and his use of racist demagoguery to push the fantasy of white genocide and the threat of migrants and Muslims replacing whites.[6] One brazen expression of his white supremacy ideology took place before the 2020 presidential election when he repeatedly argued that the white suburbs were under siege, ravaged by crime caused by the influx of low-income housing.[7] Stoking racial divisions, Trump's racism was highly visible in his attacks on undocumented workers, Black athletes, politicians, celebrities such as LeBron James, and news anchors such as CNN's Don Lemon.[8]

His campaign against "fake news" drew from the same fascist playbook used by right-wing populist dictators such as Hitler in the 1930s. In its updated version, it engaged in a frontal attack on the truth, dissent, and the oppositional press, evident not only in Trump's attempts to humiliate journalists who asked critical questions but also in his threat of using executive orders to shut down social media platforms such as Twitter. Trump lashed out at Twitter because they added fact-checking labels to two of his tweets after he "falsely claimed that mail-in voting ballots would mean that the November presidential election was 'rigged.'"[9] The United Nations special rapporteur on freedom of opinion and expression, David Kaye, argued that Trump's executive order was "a ploy for him to dominate and eviscerate public oversight of his lies."[10]

Trump's racism has a long legacy, but it erupted on the American stage when he emerged as a "birther," a conspiracy theory narrative that argued that Barack Obama was an illegitimate president because he was born in a foreign country. Trump's presidency brought racism into the center of power as he doubled down on a defense of white supremacy, white nationalism, and racial cleansing. In the few months before the November 2020 election, Trump's racism went into high gear as he downplayed, if not supported, the racism exemplified in Confederate symbols and monuments, and publicly supported voter suppression. In a sense, Trump retooled himself as the president of white supremacists and tied American exceptionalism to white nationalism. Journalist Jamelle Bouie summed up Trump's racist acts and politics of cultural rage and diversion during this period in an illuminating account of Trump's racist pandemic pedagogy. He writes:

> he has re-tweeted a video of a supporter in Florida shouting "white power," threatened to scrap an Obama-era fair housing rule meant to break patterns of segregation (citing its "devastating impact" on suburbs), promised to veto a defense funding bill that would also take the names of Confederate generals off military bases, and called New York City's decision to paint "Black Lives Matter" on Fifth Avenue a "symbol of hate" that was "denigrating" to this "luxury avenue" during this period.[11]

Trump seized upon right-wing populism's image of the strongman who can defy all measures of accountability. Trump's war with Twitter was really part of his intransigent belief that he could say anything he wanted regardless of the degree to which he mangled the truth or, in the worse scenario, used tweets to make racist remarks or incite violence. Trump's belief that he was unaccountable for almost anything he did was on full display in the midst of a series of tweets in which he responded to the massive protests in Minneapolis and other cities over the brutal killing of George Floyd by the police. Trump tweeted that the protesters were hooligans and that those involved in looting in the city could be shot. His exact words were "when the looting starts, the shooting starts." Twitter placed a warning label on the tweet stating that the tweet glorified violence, "based on the historical context of the last line ... and the risk it could inspire similar actions today."[12] Trump later tweeted that if the protesters outside the White House breached the fence, "they would have been greeted with the most vicious dogs, and most ominous weapons, I have ever seen."[13] While many commentators viewed Trump's actions as just another attempt to stifle free speech, his comments regarding "thugs" and violence echo the not-so-hidden codes of racism tinged with the threat of violence. In fact, as *The New York Times* reported, Trump's tweet about shooting Minneapolis protesters appeared to be drawn from a similar comment made in 1967 by the racist Miami police chief Walter E. Headley. Peter Baker, Raymond Zhong, and Russell Goldman write:

Mr. Trump's middle-of-the-night tweet about the Minneapolis protests echoed a comment by Walter E. Headley, the Miami police chief who attracted national attention in the late 1960s for using shotguns, dogs and a heavy-handed "stop-and-frisk" policy to fight crime in the city's black neighborhoods. Mr. Headley announced a "get tough" campaign in a December 1967 news conference that prompted anger among black leaders, The *New York Times* reported at the time. "We haven't had any serious problems with civil uprising and looting," he said, "because I've let the word filter down that when the looting starts, the shooting starts."[14]

Violence, racism, and lawlessness merge in the discourse of right-wing populism. This is especially evident in how looting was taken up by Trump and the conservative media. David Sirota argues that Trump's references to looting came with "all sorts of race and class connotations," suggesting that the only people who loot were protesters, poor people, and elements of the working class who steal televisions, break into liquor stores, or raid convenience stores. Such actions fit well into the familiar script of labeling the working class and poor people of color as perpetrators of crime. This narrow definition of looting allows one to reduce crime to vandalism and a range of street crimes, while ignoring either "rich folk and corporations" who steal billions through "public policy" or "plundering that has become the routine policy of our government on a grand scale that is far larger than a vandalized Target store."[15] As an example, Sirota points to how the pandemic crisis was used to give massive government subsidies used to bail out companies like Boeing, millions of dollars given to oil companies, and billions of dollars given in the form of "temporary tax breaks overwhelmingly to rich individuals and large companies."[16] Juan Cole goes further, arguing that Trump's racist tweet about looting, in which, as I mention above, he quotes the racist Walter Headley, who "would not allow the few African-Americans on his force to be called 'policemen,' only 'patrolmen,' qualifies as a classic example of fascism."[17]

Robin D.G. Kelley argues that the mainstream media's focus on looting functions so as to both dismiss "legitimate organizing work" and fail to understand looting as part of the long history of dispossession and extraction visited upon Black people. According to Kelley:

> The second part of looting is it displaces the looting that is the history of the United States. We know that human bodies, that Black bodies, were looted—that's how we got here—that Indigenous land was looting, seizing that land. We know that for years the housing market has been a kind of form of looting, in which the value of Black-owned homes have been suppressed, Black wages suppressed. The transfer of wealth is a kind of form of looting. But also, if you look at the history of race riots in America, most so-called race riots were basically pogroms, going back to Cincinnati in 1839, 1841, going back to a whole range of so-called race riots in Philadelphia … You know, there's so many examples—Springfield, Illinois, in 1908. And some of that looting is also about taking political power.[18]

As the looter-in-chief, Trump believed that the moral burden imposed on Black people through the systemic violence of the state was not only unjustified but imposed a moral burden on white people because their racial privilege was called into question. Trump hid in the comfort of his lies not only about racial oppression but also with regard to the massive number of deaths that have needlessly taken place under his misdirection in controlling the Covid-19 pandemic. While the death toll in the United States as of July 29, 2020 exceeded 150,000 and thousands of people lost their jobs, Trump tweeted videos to millions of his followers in which a group of discredited doctors dismissed the importance of wearing masks and falsely claimed the antimalarial drug hydroxychloroquine was a cure for Covid-19.[19] Referring to the video, he once again claimed that hydroxychloroquine was a "cure" for the virus, and to prove his point he referenced controversial minister, physician Stella Immanuel, who among other things believes that "demon sex with humans causes health problems" and that face masks are unnecessary.[20] He followed these comments later in the week with the false and dangerous argument that mail-in voting causes massive fraud and that the presidential election could be delayed.

As the pandemic intensified, Trump accelerated and amplified his neofascist discourse and racially divisive speeches as part of his relentless war on democracy, justice, and equality. His virulent attacks against undocumented immigrants, politicians of color, women, and others who didn't fit into his narrow, racially charged view of citizenship and the public sphere echoed a dark past. His vitriol also included his claim that the goal of those fighting for social justice, equality, and the end of institutional racism constituted "a new far-left fascism" designed to "wipe out our history," cause violent mayhem, and implement "their goal [to] end America." Trump was referring to the hundreds of thousands of Americans who, according to *The New York Times*, between May 26 to June 9 engaged in demonstrations in over 2,000 cities, all of whom in Trump's discourse were unpatriotic, if not un-American.[21]

In the ecosystem of right-wing populism, truth is the enemy of politics, and irrationality becomes the bedrock of justifying the unjustifiable, if not unimaginable. Trump's suppression of free speech and mistrust of the press, especially with his use of the term "fake news," has a long history among authoritarian leaders. There is also Trump's use of dehumanizing, bigoted, and conspiracy-laden language—calling undocumented immigrants vermin, animals, and criminals. Add to this list his outrageously false and scurrilous claim that the former congressman Joe Scarborough was responsible for the death of his assistant, Lori Klausutis, some nineteen years ago.[22] For Trump, cruelty as a mode of diversion was a central element in his use of politics as fascist theater—all designed to mobilize his followers. He mocked a reporter for wearing a mask, stating that he was engaging in a form of political correctness, while ignoring the fact that mask-wearing is an act of social responsibility. In one of his tweets he suggested that Nancy Pelosi should be muzzled with a mask and retweeted a post stating that "The only good Democrat is a dead Democrat."[23]

As the global pandemic surged, mass protests erupted in major cities across the United States over the police killings of Black Americans and a crippling economic crisis. Trump responded by accelerating the machinery of state repression and without apology used his media machine to put forth a Nixonian call for "law and order." What was clear here is that Trump weaponized language as a provision of violence, and his rhetoric represented "a bold attempt to use language as a doorway" to resurrect, legitimatize, and replay the horrors of a fascist past.[24] Meanwhile, journalists Matt Zapotosky and Isaac Stanley-Becker[25] observed that Trump is "attacking his political rivals, criticizing a voting practice he himself uses and suggesting that looters could be shot."[26] Trump made it shockingly evident that he would do anything to distract attention from his perilous, failed, and dangerous leadership. For Trump, the first rule of politics was to convince the public that its best moment can be found in escapist entertainment and a dehumanizing theater of hate, bigotry, and cruelty.

Trump's right-wing populism thrived on divisiveness. Under Trump, America became an even more deeply divided country and a failed state, accentuated by the Covid-19 pandemic. Rather than bring the country together, Trump reveled in keeping it "on edge," divided, and united by overwrought anxieties and fears rather than collective responsibilities. Trump proved again and again that he could only exist as the president of a deeply and irreparably divided country. Actually, Trump was the symptom of a divided and sickened country growing ever so more under the rule of a fascist politics, and is the endpoint of years of neoliberal assaults on all vestiges of the common good. As Chauncey DeVega explained at that time:

> Trump is also the leader of a perfidious cabal, which is equally responsible for the human destruction wrought by the coronavirus pandemic. Before Trump was even a credible candidate, the Republican Party had destroyed the country's capacity to govern effectively, hollowed out its infrastructure, and systematically discredited the public's belief that government can be a force for good. The right-wing propaganda machine circulates and helps to legitimate the Republican assault on the truth and reality, the commons and the public good. Republican voters and supporters provide the votes and human energy for the right wing's infernal machine of political and human destruction. Pierce makes an important point, however limited.[27]

Under Trump's presidential reign, a waking nightmare unfolded in the midst of a runaway pandemic. As the economy went into a deep, disastrous decline, one out of four workers were unemployed, and in the midst of mass anxiety and collective fear the language of a far-right-wing populism promoted, without apology, racial hatred once associated with past fascist regimes. Trump's actions spoke to a past that needs to be re-examined so that the echoes of its horrors can be heard in order to salvage memories and insights that offer elements of resistance to what Hannah Arendt once called "the ruins of history."[28] The late Russian writer and journalist Vasily Grossman once issued a warning from another time that seems equally appropriate today. He writes:

> How mighty, how terrible, and how kind is the power of habit! People can get used to anything—the sea, the southern stars, love, a bunk in a prison, the barbed wire of the camps … What creates this abyss is the power of habit. Dull as it seems, it is as powerful as dynamite; it can destroy anything. Passion, hatred, grief, pain—habit can destroy them all.[29]

The Dangers of Right-Wing Populism

Right-wing populism offers a pseudo-democratic notion of politics in which matters of informed judgment, critical agency, and collective action disappear into the symbol of the leader and political bosses "who pretend to be the earthly avatars of 'the people.'"[30] In this discourse, politics becomes personalized in the image of the larger-than-life demagogue, removed from the alleged ignorance of the masses or "herd." The past and present emergence of right-wing populist leaders is exemplified in the rise of Trump, Jair Bolsonaro, and Geert Vilders, among others. Right-wing populism destroys everything that makes a genuine democratic politics possible. But it does more. Trump's claim to populism and his pose as a man of the people was not simply farcical but extremely dangerous, and represented an unprecedented crisis in the annals of American democracy.

It is worth repeating, right-wing populism builds upon and accentuates a long tradition of anti-democratic, militaristic, neoliberal, and racist tendencies that have been smoldering in the United States for decades.[31] It undermines critical thinking, disdains acts of civic courage, dismantles genuine collective action rooted in mass movements, suppresses democratic forms of opposition, and crushes opponents. Its stark Hobbesian division between friends and enemies, unquestioning loyalty and democratic participation contains a propensity for violence rooted in its unforgiving politics of exclusion. The latter is especially troubling at a time in which violence has emerged and is accepted as a defining feature and organizing principle of politics, if not society itself. In this instance, the friend/enemy binary becomes all the more dangerous in a context where history is being erased and ignorance colludes with power to give rise to widening networks of oppression.

Trump made this divisive feature central to his mode of governance. Putting forward coded assertions of white supremacy, Trump acted on a regressive notion of unity that relies on exclusion and a politics of disposability. According to Trump, "The only thing that matters is the unification of the people—because the other people don't mean anything."[32] In Trump's discourse, the call for unity had as its foundation the implication that all opposition is not only illegitimate but constitutes the terrain of the enemy. His notion of "the people" was reduced to a category that mimics the will of the leader whose image of the U.S. was as racist as it was anti-democratic in its deeply authoritarian implications.

The right-wing populist claim to exclusive power, representation, and governance in the hands of the leader is not without its critical moments. For instance, right-wing populist leaders go out of their way to criticize globalization and the elite, but, in doing so, they "claim that only they can represent the people," while putting policies into play that expand the power of the financial elite and their neoliberal imperatives, such as regressive tax cuts and the hollowing out of the welfare state.[33] Populist discourse makes a false claim to a homogeneous notion of "the people" conveniently aimed at erasing the varied identities, interests, and modes of resistance that characterize multiple social groups. Consequently, matters of resistance and social change are packaged into simpleminded calls for unity, which contains the swindle of fulfillment.

The demagogic character of populism can be seen in its use of a language of simplicity, one that avoids complexity, honest dialogue, multifaceted struggles, and the hard work of power-sharing modes of governance. This spirit of populism is at odds with a language that is troubling, calls power into question, disturbs machineries of class, gender, sexual and racial oppression, sharpens the moral imagination, and bears witness to state and corporate violence. Right-wing populism both demonizes and promotes the fear of an internal enemy, distorts information, and suppresses dissent and resistance. In doing so, it attempts to strip democracy of all of its ideals. Populism's language of simplicity and its embrace of an agency-stripping notion of anti-intellectualism is further strengthened by neoliberalism's culture of fear, insecurity, and uncertainty that accentuates a sense of frustration, anger, and political impotence that traps individuals in their own feelings, unable to translate private troubles into broader social and political considerations.

Right-wing populism speaks in the stunted discourse of the perpetrator as victim, refigures the language of war as heroic, and merges the rhetoric of command and racial purity with the discourse of commerce and capitalism. Under right-wing populism, the language of violence parades as the language of war, redemption, walls, barriers, and security. This is a populism without a social conscience, a repackaged neoliberalism that supports authoritarian societies with the empty verbiage of austerity, deregulated capital markets, the dismantling of the welfare state, the denial of climate change, a soaring inequality, and a struggle to whitewash the nation's past.

Populist leaders such as Trump and Bolsonaro rule not for the public interest but for themselves and their ultra-rich allies, furthering the slide toward lawlessness and barbarism. How else to explain Trump's pressuring Israel to ban two Congresswomen of color from visiting Israel after he stated that they should go back to their own countries because they had criticized his policies? How else to explain his relentlessly cruel policies, such as cutting federal support for food stamps for over 3 million people, asserting that immigrants who used government benefits such as housing vouchers or Medicaid should be denied green cards and visas, and his ongoing immigration raids which separated families and traumatized communities? How else to explain Trump's grotesque sense of entitlement and limitless self-regard that translated into a fixation on dominating and humiliating others? How else to understand his sending his version of storm troopers into major cities governed by Democrats in order to create violent clashes as a way to divert attention away from his catastrophic failure to contain the Covid-19 pandemic? These alleged "federal agents" were in effect private contractor forces who operated as Trump's own private army of thugs, not unlike the Brown Shirts Hitler used in his ascendency to power in the 1930s. Awash in lies, Trump has repeatedly downplayed the severity of the coronavirus pandemic, especially in its early stages, and argued for states to reopen their economies. Yet, he had modeling projections in May 2020 that such actions by June 1 would result in a doubling of daily deaths from 1,750 to 3,000 and a "forecast of about 200,000 new cases each day."[34] Borrowing from Stephen Greenblatt's comments made in another context,

> [Trump] is a bully. Easily enraged, he strikes out at anyone who stands in his way. He enjoys seeing others cringe, tremble, or wince with pain. He is gifted at detecting weakness and deft at mockery and insult. These skills attract followers who are drawn to the same cruel delight, even if they cannot have it to his unmatched degree. Though they know that he is dangerous, the followers help him advance to his goal, which is the possession of supreme power.

Right-wing populism thrives on the allure of the spectacle of violence and redirects pent-up anger and aggression into a form of collaborative pleasure and emotional release that becomes complicit with the ugliness of authoritarian modes of governance and morally compromised lives.[35] It shares many elements of a fascist politics, including an ideology of certainty, unhampered by doubt and complexity in its explanation of history and justification for its policies. Its friend/enemy distinction fuels both a politics of disposability that makes some human beings superfluous, and also promotes a culture of fear and terror in which the unthinkable becomes normalized. It disdains the truth, scientific evidence, and empties words of any meaning while elevating lying to the status of a national ideal that legitimates a dystopian mode of governance. A massive corporate-controlled propaganda machine concealed Trump's support for anti-Semitism, his hostility towards science, and his embrace of nativism and racial hatred. Moreover, its authoritarian impulses are hidden under a form of historical amnesia that allows right-wing white nationalists and populists such as Trump to celebrate "authoritarian regimes as models" similar to those that ruled Europe in the 1930s.

Right-wing populism also destroys any notion of the social marked by the principles of compassion, justice, equity, and equality; it also thrives on anti-intellectualism, and the suppression of critical thought, dissent, and social justice. Finally, right-wing populism, like fascism, supports authoritarian governments in which power is concentrated in the hands of the alleged leader.

The Limits of Left-Wing Populism

Populism comes in many forms, and some writers such as Chantal Mouffe and Thomas Frank have argued that the antidote to right-wing populism is left-wing populism.[36] Mouffe insists that left-wing populism works to expose and denounce rising social and economic inequality, criticize the deep cruelties of capitalism, and rightly reveals corrupt middle-of-the road politicians. Mouffe also argues that left-wing populism opposes centrist politics with its investments in neoliberal ideology, finance capital, austerity, deregulation, and corporate power. Frank draws upon a number of historical examples to highlight the radical traditions fought for by left-wing populists, especially economic rights.

Professor Federico Finchelstein has also pointed out that left-wing populism is often marked by its "attention to unequal social and economic conditions ... questioning even the dogmas of neoliberal austerity measures and the supposed neutrality of technocratic business-oriented solutions."[37] Yet, he qualifies the latter by pointing out that left-wing populism undermines its political project "by its claim to exclusively represent the entire people against the elites."[38] Mouffe and Frank ignore this criticism and suggest that the combination of popular sovereignty and equality advocated by left-wing populists offers the greatest challenge to the pervading hold of right-wing populism across the globe, which they argue is the background condition for the erosion of democratic ideals and institutions. Mouffe appropriates Cass Muddle's notion that populism is essentially a clash between the people and the elite and that conflict is a defining feature of contemporary political life.[39] For Mouffe, populism raises the significant question of how democracy is going to be represented and by whom. Rather than viewed as a threat to liberal democracy, Mouffe argues that populism raises valid questions about inequality, the rule of elites, and the question of what kind of democracy people desire.[40]

What is particularly strong about both Mouffe and Frank's arguments is the call for a populist movement rooted in a more comprehensive struggle to recover and expand radical democracy as a political force. For Mouffe, the challenge of left-wing populism is to make clear that the struggle for popular sovereignty has to be part of a broader struggle for democracy. She recognizes that people no longer feel in control of their destinies and her answer to massive forms of alienation is to create a left-wing populist movement that highlights the contradictions between liberal democratic ideals and the anti-democratic politics of the emerging right-wing populism. Democracy in this view becomes a means to fight an ideological war against right-wing adversaries and diverse modes of authoritarianism.

As crucial as some of these arguments are as part of a challenge to confront right-wing populism, they are not unproblematic. Mouffe,

Frank, and many other advocates of left-wing populism overlook the pathologies inherent in all forms of populism. As theorists such as Federico Finchelstein along with John Keane and Jan-Werner Müller point out, these include underestimating how populism is susceptible to being a politically empty category that can be appropriated by almost any political group.[41] Jason Stanley is right in stating that populism as a term ignores more than it reveals, especially regarding the specifics of authoritarian threats. He writes:

> Advocates of the populist thesis emphasize its authoritarian dangers while quietly pushing off stage the more enduring and structural sources of democratic decline such as the dramatic and growing inequalities of wealth and power that have defined the era of global neoliberalism, the marketization of once public goods and steady erosion of procedures of democratic accountability, and the unfettered role of money in political life that further guarantees the ongoing intensification of these processes ... The term populism conveniently facilitates this evasion.[42]

Moreover, populism in all of its forms is too indebted to the personalization of leadership whether such leaders are on the left, such as Bernie Sanders, or on the right, such as Donald Trump. Moreover, as Finchelstein rightly observes, "In all cases, populism speaks in the name of a single people, and does so in the name of democracy. But democracy is defined in narrow terms as the expression of the desires of the populist leaders."[43] Moreover, the notion of an all-encompassing "people" is an abstraction and a crude generalization that ignores the multiple political, ideological, and social differences at work in any society. In addition, left-wing populism runs the risk of being organized around notions of unity that replicate the friend/enemy divide and employ politics as a weapon based on hard and fast notions of exclusion and inclusion. Both forms of populism tend to ignore the hard work of education as a crucial tool for addressing the catastrophe of neoliberalism and its corresponding crisis of subjectivity, identity, and agency.

Critical Education as an Emancipatory Force in Politics

Education has a central role to play in addressing and changing the consciousness of people who occupy either side of the populist divide, as well as people who hold contradictory attitudes towards power, equality, identity, citizenship, asylum, and other central political issues. Crippling binarisms are what Walter Benjamin once called "distractions."[44] They do not produce a collective political consciousness, instead they feed potentially into either the dead end of a rigid orthodoxy or the banality of a culture of immediacy and spectacles. Instead of an empowering change in consciousness, we get a mix of intellectual infantilism and a commodified culture that denounces all thoughts of a critical public consciousness.

Populism on both sides can open the door to conspiracy theories, create what historian Richard Hofstadter called the "paranoid style" of politics, and "morph into a tool of journalistic [if not simplistic] discourse."[45] Though, it must be said this is more a central feature of right rather than left-wing populism. In short, populism can represent a range of perspectives and possibilities while still maintaining its illiberal attributes, including "understanding its own position as the only true form of political legitimacy," while refusing to recognize the validity of its opponents' views, subjecting them to the process of demonization and accusing them of "being tyrannical, conspiratorial, and anti-democratic."[46] In other words, such a perspective becomes sclerotic in its own ideology and political certainty.

Populism, especially in its contemporary forms, functions pedagogically to narrow the scope of power to the role of leaders, whether progressive or reactionary. This weakens a politics of resistance, and potentially undermines the hard work of building a mass anti-capitalist political movement while possibly sabotaging the rise of self-determining and engaged individual and social agents. However, it does more, in its application to any group that challenges power; it loses a sense of political specificity and historical context and tends to overgeneralize the opposition with a homogenizing view of people that conceives of political opponents as enemies. Populism in general runs the risk of pitting groups against each other, and for the left this means often pitting class against race or it cannot move beyond the fracturing of groups into isolated, single-issue movements. In addition, power in all of its complexity is defined to a great extent in simplistic terms as something to resist rather than as a tool of possibility rooted in the struggle over developing democratic institutions.

Beyond Populism

Populism has strong tendencies to criticize elites, but power runs much deeper and is present in economic and political structures as well as ideologies that develop over time, all of which need to be challenged. At the same time, what is needed is a vision and a broad-based movement of informed workers, artists, intellectuals, young people, and others who are challenging not just corporate elites but capitalism itself. Populism runs the risk of becoming synonymous with momentary, if not misdirected, outbursts of anger, discontent, and moral outrage, only to be then appropriated by demagogues. Clearly, the history of left populism does not always follow this script but the danger is still real. Social movements are built not merely on feelings of isolation, anger, and emotional dissatisfaction but also on the hard work of organizing concerted ideological struggles to connect with the problems that everyday people confront, and to create a politics of identification in which people can recognize themselves and join with others not merely to condemn elites but also to radically change the structures of domination.

What is needed is an anti-capitalist movement that can redirect the pain, anger, and rage of the dispossessed toward a radical restructuring of society whose aim is the construction of a democratic socialist social order. The pedagogical task here is to transform anger and emotional investments into forms of critical understanding and the organized desire for collective resistance in multiple sites and platforms—from the streets to all the available media opportunities. The problems people face in the United States and other authoritarian capitalist societies are too deep, extend too far, and command too much power. The structural and ideological sources of oppression must be challenged by building alliances that bring together workers, intellectuals, young people, and diverse anti-capitalist social movements. Such a broad-based social and political formation must learn to speak to and with the dispossessed while addressing how capitalism deprives them of the material conditions of freedom, forcing them to compete over scarce resources, time, and dignity.

Capitalism is the antithesis of democracy and must be overthrown because it cannot provide what Jeff Noonan calls "universal life goods," which translate into "a healthy environment, public healthcare distributed on the basis of need and not ability to pay, and an adequately funded public education system are all universal life-goods without which we cannot live and live fully."[47]

Any challenge to the current rise of right-wing populism must address the need for a politics that contains a language of both critique and hope. This suggests a politics that rouses the passions of people to be more informed while making clear that resistance must be a collective enterprise with struggles unified in their aim to refuse the notion that capitalism and democracy are the same thing. Martin Luther King Jr. was right when he argued that we need a politics that comprehends the totality of the system we are fighting, that there is no struggle without risk, and that struggle is a collective project rooted in a revolution of ethical standards, civic courage, and the dream of a world in which justice and equality merge.

The depoliticizing forces at work under neoliberalism cannot be underestimated in terms of their contribution to the rise of right-wing populism. Widening inequality, widespread alienation, a hardening of culture, the collapse of public goods and civic culture, the dismantling of the social contract, the expanding criminalization of social problems, and a ballooning civic illiteracy, among other forces, all contribute to diverse forms of depoliticization. Under such circumstances, the declining popularity of liberal democracy produces a populace that lacks a sophisticated understanding of how neoliberal fascism infantilizes them politically and undermines their ability to exercise critical judgment, concerted acts of self-determination, and collective resistance. This fighting for a democratic socialist world must make visible the right-wing assault on the basic values and programs that undermine democracy, social justice, and promote widespread misery and suffering. It needs to provide progressive educational programs, use alternative media to educate people in a language they can understand, use demonstrations as pedagogical tools to raise consciousness, and make education central to promoting policies that both undermine capitalism and give meaning to what a socialist society looks like. There will be no change to the power and ideological dynamics of neoliberal capitalism if matters of popular sovereignty, class struggles, and economic equality are not viewed as essential to the collective fights for economic, political, and social justice.

Neither a reactionary nor a progressive populism will provide a strategy capable of challenging the new capitalist formation I term "neoliberal fascism." Populism tends towards extremes and a pseudo-democratic style of politics that embraces an imagined people, oversimplifications, and charismatic and demagogic leaders.[48] Neoliberal fascism must be challenged with a new narrative and vision of what counts as politics at a time in which power has become global and the promises of established liberal elites have become bankrupt politically and ethically. Nancy Fraser rightly argues that we need a political movement in which "a broad spectrum of social actors can find themselves" and address the "challenge of financialization, deindustrialization" and "corporate globalization."[49] She is also right in insisting that the left needs a new political narrative that clearly articulates conjoining "the struggle for emancipation and social equality" while simultaneously informed by a vision that provides a revitalized project for aligning "an egalitarian social movement with an abandoned working class."[50]

Populism neither explains the rise of fascist movements around the globe nor does it provide the answer to challenging them. What is needed is a powerful new vision of politics, one that takes education, agency, and power seriously in its ongoing efforts to develop an alliance among those forces who can imagine and struggle for a world in which neoliberal fascism no longer exists and the promise of a socialist democracy becomes more than a utopian dream. There will be no justice without a struggle and there will be no future worth living without the collective will to struggle.

Section III

The Promise of History

Reading History Against Fascism in the Age of Trump

the great force of history comes from the fact that we carry it within us, are unconsciously controlled by it in many ways, and history is literally present in all that we do. It could scarcely be otherwise, since it is to history that we owe our frames of reference, our identities, and our aspirations.

James Baldwin

Introduction: State of Crisis

American society has turned lethal. This becomes clear given its relentless assaults upon poor children, undocumented immigrants, Black people, and others considered disposable by virtue of their race, ethnicity, religion, and color. Such attacks and the suffering they cause are more characteristics of fascist regimes than of any society making the claim to be a democracy. One measure of democracy in any society is how it treats its children, the poor, and those who are underserved and vulnerable to the registers of dominant power. In this case, the United States has failed miserably.

In an age when historical memory either disappears or is rewritten in the language of erasure and misrepresentation, too many people look away and become complicit with diverse forms of fascism emerging across the globe. Regimes of fear destroy standards of truth, creating easy paths for warmongers, racists, misogynists, and nativists to take advantage of a comatose public. Neoliberal fascism is a new social and political formation, which emerged in full strength in 2016, though its signs were foreshadowed in the early 1980s. It neither replicates in precise forms "historic forms" of fascism, "nor something completely different." Neoliberal fascism combines the savage consequences of economic inequality with the dictates of transnationalism and white supremacy. In addition, it embraces an anti-modernist agenda that is anti-liberal, anti-intellectual, ultra-nationalist, and embraces elements of racial purity in its definition of who is to be included in authentic notions of the community. It functions as a cult and embraces the strongman as the undisputed object of veneration.[1] In addition, it functions as a powerful engine of systemic violence and cruelty, as is obvious in countries such as the United States, India, and Hungary. Neoliberal fascism is the enemy of revisionist forms of history because it disdains any resource that can be used to hold power accountable and translate past events into a form of moral witnessing in the present.

Narratives of Revolt

Any viable resistance to an upgraded form of fascism needs new narratives, a new understanding of politics, power, and resistance in order to counter violence and state terrorism while reviving historical memory as a forum for critically interrogating the unsettling and unspeakable. It also requires a critical understanding and engagement with a culture of real, visceral, and symbolic violence. Politics here takes on an ethical necessity and imaginative ambition. Most importantly, there is a need for a mass movement in which education becomes essential to a politics. Under such circumstances, it is necessary to connect the emergence of right-wing movements to neoliberal capitalism and their core registers of identity, memory, and agency, if not democracy itself.

As capital is liberated from all constraints, historical memory and the institutions that support it wither along with the democratic ideals of equality, popular sovereignty, and the freedom from basic social needs. The upsurge of right-wing movements in the United States is partly fueled by a revolt against political elites, the false promises of liberal democracy, and "blockages" caused by neoliberal modes of governance. In this political and ethical void, right-wing movements emerge as a form of politics in which any gesture toward giving a real voice and power to people is substituted for the power of demagogues who claim to speak on their behalf.

Right-wing populism began as a revolt against a neoliberal winner-take-all-society and was quickly appropriated by demagogues such as Donald Trump to address a mix of economic anxiety, existential uncertainty, and the fear of undocumented immigrants, refugees, and asylum seekers. Instead of learning from a past filled with genocidal wars waged in the name of difference, the emerging fascist tyrants enshrined a form of unlearning that privileged moral comas while recounting endless narratives of hate that vilified immigrants, Black and brown people, refugees, peaceful demonstrators, and undocumented children as chosen enemies of the paragons of racial cleansing.

Something sinister and horrifying is happening to alleged liberal democracies all over the globe. Democratic institutions such as the independent media, schools, the legal system, the welfare state, and public and higher education are under siege. Public media are underfunded, schools are privatized or modeled after prisons, the funds for social provisions disappear as military budgets balloon, and the legal system is positioned more and more as an engine of racial discrimination and the default institution for criminalizing a range of behaviors.

The echoes of a fascist past are with us once again resurrecting the discourses of bigotry, exclusion, and ultra-nationalism. Right-wing extremist parties have infused a fascist ideology with new energy through an apocalyptic populism that constructs the nation through a series of racist and nativist exclusions, all the while feeding off the chaos produced by the dynamics of neoliberalism.

Under such circumstances, the promises of a liberal democracy are receding as present-day reactionaries work to subvert language, values, civic courage, history, and a critical consciousness. Brazilian President

Jair Bolsonaro, for instance, has pledged to rid his country's educational system of all references to the work of radical educator, Paulo Freire. In the United States, Trump accelerated his attacks on public and higher education by cutting budgets and appointing Betsy DeVos, a billionaire and sworn enemy of public education and advocate of school choice and charter schools, as the U.S. Secretary of Education.[2] In addition, education in many parts of the globe has increasingly become a tool of domination as market fundamentalists and reactionary politicians imprison intellectuals, close down schools, undercut progressive curriculum, attack teacher unions, and impose pedagogies of repression, often killing the imaginative and creative capacities of students while turning public schools into a conveyer belt that propels students marginalized by class and color into a life of poverty or worse—the criminal justice system and prison.[3] In the age of Covid-19, public and higher education are even more vulnerable as faculty positions are cut and pedagogy is reduced to endless methodological considerations around which social media platforms are best for online teaching.

In the current historical moment two worlds are colliding. First, there is the world of neoliberal globalization which is in crisis mode because it can no longer deliver on its promises or contain its own ruthlessness. Hence, there is a worldwide revolt against global capitalism that operates mostly to fuel forms of right-wing populism and a systemic war on democracy itself.[4] Power is now enamored with amassing profits and capital and is to an increasing extent addicted to a politics of social sorting and racial cleansing.[5] Second, there is a genuine series of fluctuating democratic revolts and struggles in which millions across the globe are protesting police violence and systemic racial injustice. This mass rebellion is rewriting and revising an updated script for democratic socialism, a script that can both challenge the neoliberal world of finance capital while rethinking the meaning of politics, if not democracy itself.

At the same time, what is not in doubt is that, all across the world, the global thrust toward democratization that emerged after the Second World War has given way, once again, to tyrannies. As alarming as the signs may be, the public cannot ignore how a fascist politics took root in the United States. Such a threat was exacerbated in the public consciousness and at a time when academic discipline and intellectual rigor have lost favor with the American public. One outcome has been the replacement of the value of historical consciousness with a form of social and historical amnesia.

One measure of this trend is obvious in the fact that history is no longer a required course in most institutions of higher education, and has as a selected course of study declined into near oblivion. For example, "fewer than 2 percent of male undergraduates and fewer than 1 percent of females major in history, compared with more than 6 percent and nearly 5 percent, respectively in the late 1960s."[6] Some colleges have threatened to abolish their history departments. Ironically, this is happening at a time when forms of public knowledge and civic literacy have declined exponentially. One consequence is that an increasing number of Americans are ignorant of the past, making them vulnerable to the simplistic appeals of demagogues. Ignorance has lost its innocence and is no longer synonymous with the absence of knowledge. It has become malicious in its refusal to know, to disdain criticism, to undermine the value of historical consciousness, and to render invisible important issues that lie on the side of social and economic justice. Ignorance has become the organizing principle of a pandemic pedagogy that collapses fact and fantasy, truth and lies, evidence and opinion.

Making Education Central to Politics

James Baldwin was right in issuing his stern warning in *No Name in the Street* that "Ignorance, allied with power, is the most ferocious enemy justice can have." As is well known, Trump's real and pretended ignorance lit up the Twitter landscape almost every day. He denied climate change along with the dangers that it posed to humanity; he shut down the government because he could not get the funds for his border wall—a grotesque symbol of nativism—and he mangled history with his ignorance of the past. For instance, he once implied in a speech that Frederick Douglass was still alive and was only now getting the recognition he deserved. Trump's ignorance is legendary, if not shameful, but he models a dangerous form of presidential historical ignorance that suggests the problems suffering people face are part of the natural order and that they face such problems alone. His endless lies covered up the need to place facts, events, and ideas in a historical context. Privatizing almost everything, he constantly suggested in his manner and discourse that it was useless to translate private troubles into broader systemic considerations. His politics and discourse reproduced the notion that in their isolation people should be made unaware that history's great liberating force is that "having a sense of history is knowing that whatever happens to us or to our world we are not alone. It has happened in some form before."[7]

This lethal form of ignorance fused with a reckless use of state power that held both human life and the planet hostage. The historian David Bright claims that Trump's "essential ignorance of history, of political processes, [and] the Constitution," rather than his authoritarianism, was "his greatest threat to our democracy."[8] According to Bright, Trump's grasp of history operated at a level of understanding one would expect from a fifth grader, or worse.[9] However, beyond the production of a depoliticizing and dangerous form of ignorance and shrinking historical horizons, there is also the rewriting of historical memory. Trump not only distorted history but also made it and in doing so suggested a contempt for knowledge, which he manipulated for political purposes. Ignorance in high places was a boon to history deniers and conspiracy theorists, and legitimated the authoritarian assumption that history is only made by strongmen. It gets worse.

Without an informed historical consciousness, it is easier for authoritarians to engage in the corruption of politics coupled with explicit expressions of cruelty and a "widely sanctioned ruthlessness."[10] How else to explain the separation of children from their parents at the southern border in the United States, and the creation of internment centers that were exposed as an assault on civil rights and human dignity? John Steppling rightly notes that "the forced separation of children form their mothers or fathers was a conscious policy of cruelty and racist hatred, but also an unconscious expression of primordial scapegoating impulses."[11] There is a reiteration of history here that is too horrifying to ignore, and yet it is largely unheeded.

Once again, it is hard to imagine a more urgent moment for making education central to politics. If we are going to develop a politics capable of awakening our critical, imaginative, and historical sensibilities, it is crucial for educators and others to develop a collective language that rewrites the traditional notion of politics. Such a language is necessary to enable the conditions to forge collective international resistance against Trump's legacy of forging what Noam Chomsky called "a global reactionary alliance under the U.S. aegis, including the "illiberal democracies" of Eastern Europe (Hungary's Orbán, etc.) and Brazil's grotesque Bolsonaro."[12] Such a movement is important to resist and necessary in the ongoing fight to overcome the tyrannical fascist nightmares that threaten the United States, India, Turkey, and a number of other countries in Europe plagued by the rise of neo-Nazi parties and right-wing movements. In an age when civic culture is collapsing and a culture of compassion gives way to a culture of cruelty, it is all the more crucial to take seriously the notion that a democracy cannot exist or be defended without informed and critically engaged citizens.

Education both in its emancipatory symbolic and institutional forms has a central role to play in fighting the resurgence of fascist cultures, mythic historical narratives, and the emerging ideologies of white supremacy and white nationalism.[13] Moreover, as fascists across the globe are disseminating racist and ultra-nationalist images of the past, it is essential to reclaim critical pedagogy as a form of popular education, historical consciousness, and moral witnessing. This is especially true at a time when historical and social amnesia have become a national pastime matched only by the masculinization of the public sphere and the increasing normalization of a fascist politics that thrives on ignorance, fear, hatred, and the suppression of dissent.

Oppression is no longer defined simply through economic structures. A neoliberal culture of precarity and uncertainty has resulted in job insecurity, declining wages, the slashing of retirement funds, and the weakening of the welfare state, all of which are largely addressed through right-wing cultural apparatuses that frame such conditions through a pandemic pedagogy that functions as part of a broader politics of fear, hatred, and bigotry. Education, particularly in the social media, operates with great influence as a sounding board for right-wing nihilism, poisonous conspiracy theories, and the pus-filled discourse of white supremacy groups. Such platforms have become a powerful pedagogical portal for circulating fascist ideas, legitimating hate-fueled violence, and promoting ugly racist rhetoric that undermines democratic ideals. At the same time, education is not simply about domination, nor is it only about schooling. Popular education reaches far beyond the classroom, and, while often imperceptible, or viewed as apolitical entertainment, is crucial in using the new media to challenge and resist the rise of fascist pedagogical formations and their rehabilitation of fascist principles and ideas.[14]

Against a numbing indifference, despair, and withdrawal into the private orbits of the isolated self, there is a need to create those formative cultures that are humanizing, foster the capacity to hear others, sustain complex thoughts, and engage in solving social problems. There is a need for narratives and pedagogical practices that are inspiring, energizing, and suggest that working men and women and others have the power to make a difference in shaping the future. We have no other choice if we are to resist the increasing destabilization of democratic institutions, the assault on reason, the collapse of the distinction between fact and fiction, and the taste for brutality that now spreads across a number of countries, including the U.S., like a plague. The pedagogical lesson here is that fascism begins with hateful words, the demonization of others is considered disposable, and then moves to an attack on ideas, the burning of books, the disappearance of intellectuals, and the emergence of the carceral state and the horrors of detention jails and camps. As educator Jon Nixon suggests, pedagogy "provides us with a protected space within which to think against the grain of received opinion: a space to question and challenge, to imagine the world from different standpoints and perspectives, to reflect upon ourselves in relation to others and, in so doing, to understand what it means to 'assume responsibility.'"[15]

This is even more reason for educators and others to address important social issues and to defend public and higher education as democratic public spheres. It is all the more reason to support the teaching of history as a protected space within which to teach students to think against the grain, hold power accountable, embrace a sense of citizenship and civic courage, and to "learn about the world beyond the confines of their home towns, and to try to understand where they might fit in."[16] We live in a world in which everything is now market-driven, transformed into what authors Michael Silk and David Andrews call "spectacular spaces of consumption" and subject to the vicissitudes of the military-security state, all the while accompanied by the rise of a fascist politics rooted in the rallying passions of ultra-nationalism, racism, and an apocalyptic populism.[17] One effect is the emergence of what the late historian Tony Judt called an "eviscerated society"—"one that is stripped of the thick mesh of mutual obligations and social responsibilities to be found in" any viable democracy.[18] This grim reality has been called a "failed sociality"—a failure in the power of the civic imagination, political will, and the promises of a radical democracy.[19] It is also part of a politics that strips the social of any democratic ideals.

The Language of Fascist Politics

Trump's presidency was symptomatic of the long decline of liberal democracy in the United States into a corrupt political and economic oligarchy, but its presence signified one of the gravest challenges, if not dangers, the country faced in over a century. A spectacularized culture of lies, ignorance, corruption, and violence was fueled by a range of orthodoxies shaping U.S. life, including social conservatism, market fundamentalism, apocalyptic nationalism, religious extremism, and unchecked racism—all of which occupied the centers of power at upper reaches of power. Historical memory and moral witnessing gave way to a bankrupt white supremacist notion of nostalgia that celebrated the most regressive moments in U.S. history.

Fantasies of absolute control, racial cleansing, unchecked militarism, and class warfare were fundamental to a US social order that turned lethal—evident in the militarizing of schools and public spaces, and the centrality of a war culture as an organized mode of governance. This was a dystopian social order marked by hollow words, an imagination pillaged of any substantive meaning, cleansed of compassion, and used to legitimate the notion that alternative worlds are impossible to entertain. What we witnessed was an abandonment of democratic institutions, however flawed, coupled with a full-scale attack on dissent, thoughtful reasoning, and the social imagination. Trump degraded the office of the presidency by normalizing the unthinkable, legitimating the inexcusable, and defending the indefensible. Under such circumstances, the United States moved into the dark shadows of a present burdened by a horrifying resemblance to an earlier period of fascism with its language of racial purification, hatred of dissent, systemic violence, intolerance, and the Trump administration's "glorification of aggressive and violent solutions to complex social problems."[20]

The history of fascism offers an early warning system and teaches us that language, which operates as a modality of violence, desperation, and the troubled landscapes of hatred, carries the potential for resurrecting the darkest moments of history. It erodes our humanity, and makes many people numb and silent under the glare of ideologies and practices that mimic and legitimate hideous and atrocious acts. This is a language that eliminates the space of plurality, glorifies walls and borders, hates differences that do not mimic a white public sphere, and makes vulnerable populations—even poor young children— superfluous as human beings. Trump's language, like that which characterized older fascist regimes, mutilated contemporary politics, disdained empathy and serious moral and political criticism, and made it more difficult to criticize dominant relations of power. His brutalizing and petulant language of command and unchecked vanity also fueled the rhetoric of a war culture, a supercharged masculinity, the rise of public anti-intellectuals, and a resurgent white supremacy.

The corruption of language is often followed by the debasement of memory, morality, and the eventual disappearance of books, ideas, and human beings. Trump's language of disappearance, dehumanization, and censorship echoed and downplayed the barbarism of another time. His regressive use of language and denial of history is still with us and must be challenged so that the emancipatory energies and compelling narratives of resistance can be recalled in order to find new ways of challenging the ideologies and power relations that put them into play. Trump's predatory use of language and public memory were part of a larger authoritarian politics of ethnic and racial sorting that evokes the legacy of state violence that historically has been waged against those populations considered unknowable, unspeakable, and disposable.

The shift toward a fascist politics cannot be laid exclusively at Trump's feet. The language of nativist and white nationalist values of a nascent fascism have been brewing in the United States for some time. It is a language that is comfortable viewing the world as a combat zone, a world that exists to be plundered, and one that views those deemed different because of their class, race, ethnicity, religion, or sexual orientation as a threat to be feared, if not eliminated. When Trump used debasing rhetoric that portrayed undocumented immigrants as criminals, rapists, and drug dealers he was doing more than using ugly epithets, he was also materializing such discourse into policies that rip children from their mothers' arms, put the lives of immigrants at risk, and impose cruel and inhumane practices that assault the body, mind, and basic human rights. When he called peaceful protesters "thugs" and critics "unpatriotic" he used code for legitimating the unleashing of his personal militia who wore uniforms to make themselves look like soldiers, who then attacked, abducted, and unconstitutionally arrested demonstrators in a number of America's cities.

A Resurgent Fascist Politics

While it is fruitless to believe that there is perfect mirror for measuring a resurgent fascism, it is crucial to recognize how the "crystalized elements" of an updated fascism have emerged in new forms in the shape of a U.S.-style authoritarianism. Yet, too many intellectuals, historians, and media pundits have denied the legacy and presence of fascist politics in the United States. In part, this may be because history is written by the winners, but also because serious historical analyses is ignored in a culture of immediacy and instant gratification. In an age of selfies and tweet storms, time is reduced to short bursts of attention as the slowing down of time necessary for focused analytical thought and imaginative contemplation withers. Author Leon Wieseltier argues that we live in an era in which "words cannot wait for thoughts [and] patience is a ... liability."[21] In the current age of instant gratification, history has become a burden, treated like a discarded relic that no longer deserves respect. The past is now either too dangerous to contemplate, is relegated to the abyss of willful ignorance, or is rewritten and appropriated in the interests of the anti-democratic forces of ultra-nationalism, nativism, and social Darwinism, as is taking place in countries such as Poland and Hungary.[22] However frightening and seemingly impossible in a liberal democracy, neither history nor the obvious signs of a fascist politics can be easily dismissed, especially with the simplistic rejoinder that demagogues such as Trump did not create concentration camps or engineer plans for genocidal acts. Echoes of a fascist past were strikingly evident in degrading and inhumane conditions in many of the migrant detention sites, many of which "hold children as young as 5 months old."[23]

On the caging of children in prisonlike detention centers, the *New York Times* reported that many of the children were suffering from hunger, were housed in cramped cinder block cells with only one toilet, were sleeping on cement floors, and were subject to a number of illnesses including scabies, shingles, and chicken pox. According to the *Times*, lawyers who visited the Clint, Texas detention center described seeing:

children in filthy clothes, often lacking diapers and with no access to
toothbrushes, toothpaste, or soap ... Warren Binford, director of the
clinical law program in Willamette University in Oregon said that in
all her years of visiting detention and shelter facilities, she had never
encountered conditions so bad—351 children crammed into what she
described as prisonlike environment.[24]

Fascist politics, in its more recent updated capitalist formation, has
a long history of covering up its crimes against humanity, especially
the most egregious acts of genocide. Trump and his top immigration
officials may not have perpetuated overt acts of genocide with his nativist
policies and acts of unimaginable cruelty in incarcerating immigrants,
especially children. Nevertheless, he followed a fascist script in denying
"reports that migrant children were being held in horrific conditions in
federal detention facilities," even as the accounts of disease, hunger, and
overcrowding multiplied over time.[25] Moreover, like his counterparts in
NATO and the EU there was a silence about who creates these refugee
populations across the globe. Lying as an asset to egregious forms of
evil has a long history among demagogues.

What is distinctive about Trump is that he lied even in the face of
irrefutable evidence to the contrary.[26] Accordingly, Trump's lies and
attempted cover-ups functioned as a form of depoliticization. Lying
was performed as a tool of power, promoting forms of manufactured
ignorance in which it became difficult for the public to separate fact
from fiction in order to recognize the violence and injustices imposed
by the Trump administration on those populations it considered
disposable. Given Trump's embrace of an upgraded version of Hannah
Arendt's notions of thoughtlessness, cruelty, and the banality of evil as
central elements of totalitarianism, it is difficult to argue that fascism
was at the time a relic of the past.

Simply because the Trump administration did not replicate in an
exact fashion the sordid practices of violence and genocide reminiscent
of fascist states in the 1930s does not mean that it had no resemblance
to such a history. In fact, the legacy of fascism becomes even more
important at a time when the language, policies, and authoritarian
ideology of the Trump administration echoed a dangerous "warning

from history" that could not be ignored.[27] Fascism does not disappear because it does not surface as a mirror image of the past. Fascism is not static and the protean elements of fascism always run the risk of crystallizing into new forms. Fascism in its contemporary forms is a particular response to a range of capitalist crises that include the rise of massive inequality, a culture of fear, precarious employment, ruthless austerity policies that destroy the social contract, the rise of the carceral state, and the erosion of white privilege, among other issues.

Fascism is also obvious by its hatred of the public good, by what author Toni Morrison calls its "desire to purge democracy of all of its ideals," and its willingness to privilege power over human needs and render racial difference as an organizing principle of society.[28] What must be remembered in a time of tyranny is that historical consciousness is a crucial tool for unraveling the layers of meaning, suffering, the search for community, the overcoming of despair, and the momentum of dramatic change, however unpleasant this may be at times. No act of the past can be deemed too horrible or hideous to contemplate if we are going to enlarge the scope of our imaginations and the reach of social justice, both of which might prevent us from looking away, indifferent to the suffering around us. This suggests the need for rethinking the importance of historical memory, civic literacy, and critical pedagogy as central to an informed and critical mode of agency. Rather than dismiss the notion that the organizing principles and fluctuating elements of fascism are still with us, a more appropriate response to Trump's rise to power is to raise questions about what elements of his government signaled the emergence of a fascism suited to a contemporary and distinctively updated political, economic, and cultural landscape.

Reading History and the World Critically

In an age when memory is under attack, civic literacy and a critical reading of history become both a source of hope and a tool of resistance.

If reading history and critical forms of education are central to creating informed citizens, it is fundamental for educators to connect the past to the present and to view the present as a window into those horrors of the past that must never be repeated. A critical reading and teaching of history provides educators with a vital resource that helps inform the ethical ground for resistance—an antidote to demagogic pandemic pedagogy and politics of disinformation, division, diversion, and fragmentation. Moreover, memory as a form of critical consciousness is crucial in developing a form of historical consciousness that can work to offset a willful ignorance that provides the conditions that both enable and reinforce a fascist politics.[29] In the face of this nightmare, thinking and judging must be connected to our actions.[30] At the very least, as scholar Angela Davis points out, learning to think critically about power, politics, and economics while developing a robust historical consciousness provides the opportunity and space for people to say no and refuse "to settle for fast solutions, easy answers [and] formulaic resolutions."[31] In this instance, "historical learning is not about constructing a linear narrative but about blasting history open, rupturing its silences, highlighting its detours, acknowledging the events of its transmission, and organizing its limits within a rigorous and compassionate engagement with human suffering, values, and the legacy of the often unrepresentable or misrepresented."[32]

In the current era, the corruption of discourse has become a defining feature of politics, reinforced largely by an administration and a right-wing media apparatus that does not simply lie but also works hard to eliminate the distinction between fantasy and fact. Underlying this collapse of reason and informed judgment is the creation of models of agency more susceptible to becoming complicit with fascist modes of governance and the lure of the strongman.

Under the reign of a manic neoliberalism, time and attention have become a burden, subject to what philosopher Byung-Chul Han calls an "excess of stimuli, information, and impulses [that] radically changes the structure and economy of attention. Perception becomes fragmented and scattered."[33] The contemplative attention central to reading critically and listening attentively have given way to a hyperactive flow of information in which thinking is overcome by speed, compulsion, sound bites, fragments of information, and a relentless stream of disruptions. As Han notes, this is a type of violence in which the fragmented mind undercuts the capacity to think dialectically, undermining the ability to make connections, imagine capaciously, and develop comprehensive maps of meaning and politics.[34] At work here is a form of pandemic pedagogy that depoliticizes and leaves individuals isolated, exhausted, unaware of the forces that bear down on their lives, and susceptible to a highly charged culture of stimulation.

The terror of the unforeseen becomes ominous when history is used to hide rather than illuminate the past, when it becomes difficult to translate private issues into larger systemic considerations, and people willingly allow themselves to be both seduced and trapped into spectacles of violence, cruelty, and authoritarian impulses. Reading the world critically and developing a historical consciousness are two important preconditions for intervening in the world. That is why critical reading and reading critically were so dangerous to Trump, his acolytes, and those who hate democracy. Democracy as both an ideal and site of struggle can only survive with a public attentiveness to the power of history, politics, and the rigor of informed judgments and thoughtful actions. It can only survive when we are willing to engage the power to think otherwise in order to act otherwise.

The never-ending crisis produced by neoliberalism, with its financial ruin for millions, its elimination of the welfare state, its deregulation of corporate power, its unchecked racism, and its militarization of society, has to be matched by a rupture in the realm of common sense. Such a rupture should be one that embraces historical memory, rejects the normalization of fascist principles, and opens a space for imagining alternative worlds that can be brought into being. While the long-term corrosion of politics and the threat of fascism in the U.S. will not end by simply learning how to read critically, the spaces opened by learning how to think critically create a bulwark against cynicism and foster a notion of hope that can be translated into forms of collective resistance. In the fascist script, historical memory becomes a liability, even dangerous, when it functions pedagogically to inform our political and social imagination.

This is especially true when memory acts to identify forms of social injustice and enables critical reflection on the histories of repressed others. For instance, the haunting images of hungry, sick, and frightened children in migrant detention centers do more than rupture the myth-making rhetoric of the American dream, they also invoke the revival of historical memories that tie the present to a fascist past. Moreover, critics who ignore such warnings by refusing to learn from the past reinforce Walter Lippmann's cautionary insights a century ago when he argued that "when a nation creates the conditions in which its citizens have little or no knowledge of past," it is opening the door for them to "become victims of agitation and propaganda, subject to the appeals of quacks and charlatans."[35] The merging of a manufactured ignorance and an obstinate refusal to learn from history sets the stage for a right-wing populism eager to vent real existential anger in a hatred of others and a politics wedded to the rhetoric of disposability and elimination.

Unsurprisingly, historical memory as a form of enlightenment and demystification is surely at odds with the way Trump used history as a form of social amnesia and political camouflage. For instance, Trump's 1930s slogan, "America First," marked a regressive return to a time when nativism, racism, misogyny, and xenophobia defined the American experience. This inchoate nostalgia rewrote history in the warm glow and "belief in an essential American innocence, in the utter exceptionality, the ethical singularity and manifest destiny of the United States."[36] Philip Roth aptly characterizes this gratuitous form of nostalgia in his *American Pastoral* as the "undetonated past." Innocence in this script is the stuff of mythologies that distort history and expunge the political significance of moral witnessing and historical memory as a way of reading, translating, and interrogating the past as it impacts, and sometimes explodes, the present.

Under Trump, both language and memory were disabled, emptied of substantive content, and the space of a shared reality crucial to any democracy is eviscerated. In this context, strict categories of identity canceled out notions of shared responsibilities and what might be termed a "more radical practice of citizenship."[37] History and language in this contemporary political script were paralyzed in the immediacy of tweeted bombast, the thrill of the moment, and the comfort of a cathartic emotional discharge. The danger, as history has taught us, occurs when words are systemically used to cover up lies, and the capacity to think critically.

Indifferent to the historical footprints that mark expressions of state violence, the Trump administration used historical amnesia as a weapon of (mis)education, power, and politics, allowing public memory to wither and the architecture of fascism audaciously to manifest itself at the highest levels of government. This accounts for Trump's attack on the New York Times 1619 project which highlighted the legacy of slavery in the U.S.—a blatant attempt to censor repressed narratives and historical consciousness. The fight against a demagogic erasure of history must begin with an acute understanding that memory always makes a demand upon the present, refusing to accept ignorance as innocence.

As reality collapsed into fake news, moral witnessing disappeared into the hollow spectacles of right-wing media machines, and into state-sanctioned weaponry used to distort the truth, suppress dissent, and attack the critical media. Trump used Twitter as a public relations blitzkrieg to attack everyone from his political enemies to celebrities who criticized him.[38] For Trump, language operated through the medium of slogans, bigotry, and violence. Words were turned into an undifferentiated mass of ashes, critical discourse reduced to rubble, and informed judgments exiled to a distant radioactive hate-filled horizon. Culture carried the imprint of a madness that seems everywhere, reflecting a kind of collective psychosis lodged in a White House surrounded by bunkers, cement walls, and guard dogs.

Shouting replaced the pedagogical imperative to listen and reinforced the stories neoliberal fascism told us about ourselves, our relations to others, and the larger world. Under such circumstances, monstrous deeds were committed under the increasing normalization of civic and historical modes of illiteracy, if not ignorance. One result was that comparisons to the Nazi past withered in the false belief that historical events are fixed in time and place and can only be repeated in history books. In an age marked by a war on terror, a culture of fear, and the normalization of uncertainty, social amnesia became a powerful tool for dismantling democracy. Indeed, in this age of forgetfulness, American society appeared to revel in what it should have been ashamed of and alarmed over.

Even with the insight of history, comparisons between the older orders of fascism and Trump's regime of brutality, aggression, and cruelty were considered by many liberal commentators to be too extreme. There are costs to such caution: failing to learn the lessons of the past, or, even worse, ignoring the past as a source of moral witnessing and resource for speaking for those no longer able to speak.[39] Knowing how others in the past, such as those involved in the anti-war movement of the 1960s, successfully fought against elected demagogues such as Trump is crucial to a political strategy that challenges and works to reverse an impending global catastrophe.

The story of a fascist past needs to be retold not to simply make comparisons to the present, though that is not an unworthy project, but to be able to imagine a new politics in which new knowledge will be built, as Arendt states: "new insights ... new knowledge ... new memories, [and] new deeds, [will] take their point of departure."[40] This is not to suggest that history is a citadel of truth that can be easily mined. History offers no guarantees and it can be used in the interest of violence as well as for emancipation.

Trump's selective appropriation of history waged war on the past, honoring rather than questioning fascist politics. Even more reason why, with the rise of fascist politics, there is a need for modes of historical inquiry and stories that challenge the distortions of the past, transcend private interests, and enable the American public to connect private issues to broader historical and political contexts. Comparing Trump's ideology, policies, and language to a fascist past offers the possibility to learn what is old and new in the dark times that have descended upon the United States. The pressing relevance of the 1930s is crucial to address how fascist ideas and practices originate, and adapt to new conditions, and how people capitulate and resist them as well.

Education and the Radical Imagination

The emerging authoritarianism in many countries today raises questions about the role of education, teachers, and students in a time of tyranny. How might we imagine education and the teaching of history as central to a politics whose task is, in part, to create a new language for students, one that is crucial to reviving a radical imagination, a notion of social hope, and the courage to struggle collectively? How might public and higher education and other cultural institutions address the deep, unchecked nihilism and despair that grew alongside the Trump presidency? How might educators be persuaded not to abandon democracy, and take seriously the need to create informed citizens capable of fighting the resurgence of a fascist politics? Fascism thrives on surveillance, arrest, crushing dissent, spreading lies, scapegoating those considered disposable, and attacking any vestige of the truth. Fascism is the modern-day form of a pandemic depoliticizing machine that renders individual and collective agency powerless to exercise the conduct, sensibilities, and practices endemic to a robust form of citizenship. When fascism is strong, democracy is not simply weak or under siege, the very institutions that inform and educate a public begin to disappear. As educational reformer John Dewey once argued, "democratic conditions do not automatically sustain themselves," they can only survive in the midst of a critical and formative culture that "produces the habits and dispositions-in short-a culture to sustain it."[41]

Political science professor Melvin Rogers, reiterating Dewey's warning, rightly argues that most critics of Trump ignored Dewey's crucial insights and how they might have been applied to the refusal to normalize Trump's fascist politics or relied too heavily on the false assumption that the country's checks and balances and fundamental institutions by default would protect us from an impeding fascism. He is worth quoting at length:

> Dewey's worry is as urgent today as it was in 1939. Those who believe the strength of our institutions will win the day miss the slow but steady effort to undermine the social fabric that makes them possible—by habituating us to cruelty, by treating facts as fictions, and by suspending the idea that we each, regardless of our national affiliation, are worthy of respect. Underneath the policies of the Trump administration is a test of the moral culture of Americans—to see what they can stand and what they will endure. When he refuses to disclose his taxes, he tests our desire for transparency. When he dismisses the media, he tests our commitment to truth. When he abets the gutting of institutions like the EPA, he tests our reliance on research and facts. Taken together his bet is a direct challenge to Dewey. How closely are the American people paying attention to the actual processes threatening our institutions rather than all the bread and circuses? How can we be so sure Trump's transgressions will amount to a momentary blip along the arc of America's future? Checks and balances do not have an agency of their own. In relying on the inertia of institutions, we forget that a democracy is only as strong as the men and women who inhabit it.[42]

Democracy cannot exist without a critically informed and engaged public. Educators, artists, journalists, and other cultural workers have a crucial obligation to defend public and higher education as a public good rather than defining such institutions through market-driven values and modes of accountability defined by the financial and corporate elite. Nevertheless, raising public consciousness, especially among students, is not enough. Students need to be inspired and energized to address important social issues, learn to narrate their private troubles as public issues, and to engage in forms of resistance that are both local and collective, while connecting such struggles to more global issues.

Democracy begins to fail and political life becomes impoverished in the absence of those vital public spheres of public and higher education in which civic values, public scholarship, and social engagement allow for a more imaginative grasp of a future that takes seriously the demands of justice, equity, and civic courage. Democracy should be a way of thinking about education, one that thrives on connecting equity to merit, learning to ethics, and agency to an investment in and strengthening of the public good. Education is crucial as an analytical tool in making the elements of a fascist politics visible while situating the latter historically in order to gain some perspective on its real danger in the present.

Given the current crisis of politics, agency, history, and memory educators need a new political and pedagogical language for addressing the changing contexts and issues facing a world in which capital draws upon an unprecedented convergence of resources—financial, cultural, political, economic, scientific, military, and technological—to exercise powerful and diverse forms of control. If, as educators, we are to take seriously the role of nurturing in our students a robust civic imagination and social imagination, we need to develop not only a pedagogical discourse of critique and transformation but also a more comprehensive narrative that draws from history while embracing a newfound democratic sense of social, economic, and political justice. Against the rootlessness and atomization produced by neoliberal fascism, we need a language that finds its meaning not through the market-driven dictates of privatization, the propriety of a sterile individualism, and an ethos of war and eviscerating competiveness, but in relation to others, a larger sense of community, and a radical revival of the social contract. Another challenge faced by such a language is the need to create political formations capable of understanding the current plague of apocalyptic populism and fascist politics as a single integrated system whose shared roots extend from class and racial injustices under financial capitalism to ecological problems and the increasing expansion of the carceral state and the military-industrial-academic complex.[43]

Fascism in its American appearance offered a narrative of nativism and bigotry as an answer to the systemic misery and suffering produced by capitalism's machinery of death and its savage embrace of racial and social cleansing. The phantoms of a dark past were once again set free like a plague on American society. The ghosts of fascism should terrify us, but most importantly they should educate us and imbue us with a spirit of civic justice and collective action in the fight for a substantive democratic social order. We live in dangerous times and there is an urgent need for more individuals, institutions, and social movements to come together to resist the current regimes of tyranny, see that alternative futures are possible, and understand that, by acting on these beliefs through collective resistance, radical change will happen.

Such a struggle will not be easy and will not come through momentary demonstrations, or through the elections. What is needed is a massive unified movement that takes as its major weapon the general strike, using it to shut down the fascist state in all of its registers. Only then can power be used to rethink and restructure American society through forms of collective power in which democracy and its radical ideals of liberty, freedom, and equality can come to fruition.

Law and Disorder in the Age of Organized Forgetting

Injustice anywhere is a threat to justice everywhere.

Martin Luther King, Jr.

The Age of Crisis and Apocalyptic Prophecies

We can no longer talk about fascist politics without speaking about the plague of lawlessness. At the core of fascist politics is a persistent attack not only on the rule of law, and crucial political and economic institutions but also on the formative cultures, values, and modes of critical agency that make a democracy possible. We live in an age of relentless crisis—an age marked by the collapse of civic culture, ethical values, and democratic institutions that serve the public good. Language now operates in the service of violence and ignorance has become a national ideal.[1] Religious fundamentalism, white supremacy, and economic tyranny now inform each other, giving rise to an updated recurrence of fascist politics.[2] Nazi Germany proved with frightening clarity that the rule of law and its institutions can be easily transformed and implemented into agents of state violence, if not domestic terrorism.[3] What Trump has proven with utmost audacity and little regret is that no institution is immune from the reach and power of a fascist politics.

Apocalyptic prophecies now replace thoughtfulness and sustained acts of social responsibility. In this age of nightmarish prophecies, right-wing populist regimes fuel conspiracy theories and normalize lying as a way to degrade public discourse. In addition, demagogues promote emotion over reason as a way to legitimate a culture of conformity, and elevate society's pleasure quotient through the registers of vengeance, brutality, and bigotry. Trump's ongoing criminal behavior and pernicious policies, pointed to a crisis of civic literacy and the inability of the public to understand how society broke apart, became more cruel, and receded from the language of justice, critique, and the promise of a substantive democracy. A culture of withdrawal, privatization, and immediacy reinforced an indifference to public life, the suffering of others, and what Hannah Arendt once called "the ruin of our categories of thought and standards of judgment."[4] The space of traditional politics continues to be occupied by a culture driven by an ongoing politics of corruption, diversion, and disappearance. This is a political space that weakens civic culture and fails to offer a comprehensive and critical analysis of a series of crises extending from the impeachment process "to the use of the criminal-justice system to reward friends and punish enemies."[5] In the absence of a comprehensive politics capable of defining the related parts and threads that point to a society in crisis, violence, especially as mediated through a predatory neoliberalism and a politics of white supremacy, has become the regulative principle of everyday life.

Evidence of the distinctive nature of today's crisis on both a national and global level can be glimpsed in the political and cultural forces that shaped President Trump's impeachment, the Brexit fiasco, and the rise of authoritarian demagogues in Brazil, Turkey, and Hungary, among other countries.[6] This is a general crisis whose roots historically and in the current era lie in the resurgence of global neoliberalism with its embrace of finance capital, massive inequities in wealth and power, the expansion of the racial punishing state, and the creation of an age of precarity and uncertainty. This is a crisis that was produced, in part, through a full-scale attack on the welfare state, labor, and public goods. Under such circumstances, democracy has become thinner: the social sphere and social contract did not occupy an important place in Trump's America.

As Nancy Fraser points out, "these forces have been grinding away at our social order for quite some time" and constitute not only a crisis of politics and economics, which is highly visible, but also an ideological crisis which is not so visible.[7] Put differently, the crisis of politics and the attention it has drawn have not been matched by public recognition of a crisis of understanding and critical insight. Instead, as the global economy has unraveled, the backlash against the so-called political elites and established forms of liberal governance has, until the mass mobilizations over the murder of George Floyd, an unarmed Black man, by Derek Chauvin, a Minneapolis police officer, produced movements for popular sovereignty that under-emphasized the crucial call for equal rights and social justice. This historical crisis not only refigured the social sphere as a site of commercialism, conformity, and commodified infantilism, it also redefined matters of individual and social agency through the mediation of images in which self-alienation was reinforced within a culture of immediacy, disappearance, and spectacle. The hyper-capitalism that has framed politics for the last forty years is at odds with any viable notion of a socialist democracy. Undermining both economic and social rights, it further intensified and expanded systemic racism by repudiating and disdaining any notion of reform that addressed the relationship between economic justice and racial justice.

In the wake of mass mobilizations across the globe, the terror of neoliberal fascism can no longer escape visibility. In the face of unchecked police violence, the establishment of white supremacy as a governing principle at the highest levels of government, and the rise of a series of pandemic crises, a virus that turned racist came into full view at the same time that racist violence became viral. Moreover, the concern for survival which dominated so many lives was transformed in a collective burst of outrage and anger into a demand for racial and economic justice. The Italian philosopher Giorgio Agamben's notion of bare life, in which those who are excluded can be killed with impunity, had reached its limits with the accumulating murders of Black men and women by the police, fueling what appeared to a turning point in a politics sharpened by an ability to see, think, and demonstrate with clarity the force of massive collective resistance.

Trump's ministry of fake news was collapsing in the wake of a delegitimation process fueled by a series of events that included his impeachment hearings, which revealed the inner workings of corruption, and a pandemic crisis that made clear that capitalism and the market cannot address serious social problems, especially in this case a public health crisis. The misuse of the past in the service of Trump's authoritarianism revealed its inner ideological workings in the White House. Trump responded to the growing outrage against systemic racism and state violence by defending the appearance of the Confederate flag at NASCAR events and exhibiting his support for leaving in place Confederate statues and memorials. The emotions produced through Trump's language of bigotry, cruelty, and dehumanization and a hatred of those considered other were increasingly seen by young people and others marching in the streets as the building blocks for the nativist wall under construction on the southern border and the wall that went up around the White House, revealing it as a wartime bunker under siege by those fighting for a radical democracy.

Under Trump, lawlessness was the soul of an updated neoliberal fascism which near the end of his presidency was no longer in the shadows as its connection to the horrors of the past became increasingly evident. Lawlessness binds the connection among barbarism, corruption, and the politics of disposability and in the United States has its roots in a long, shameful legacy of racism, exploitation, and human suffering. To understand how it was unmasked is to begin not with the ideological, political, and medical crisis that emerged with the Covid-19 pandemic but with Trump's impeachment trial which served to open up a new discourse about established power relations regarding how to think dangerously, challenge the language of command, and hold power accountable, however timid the overall attempt might have been.

The impeachment hearing, regardless of the fact that it did not go far enough, put Trump's authoritarian regime into question, pulling back the curtains to reveal a pandemic of chaos, disorder, corruption, and utter disregard for the law, and assaults on American democracy. The drama that took place in the House of Representatives revealed a politics of the unthinkable, and yet it only scratched the surface of

Trump's substituting of personal gain and financial interest for the national interest and making a politics of lawlessness a governing ideal. Brian Klaas offers a short list worth repeating:

> Trump has encouraged and aided ethnic cleansing, and possible genocide, against the Kurds in Syria. He has engaged in multiple abuses of power, including obstruction of justice. He has tried to bribe and extort the Ukrainian president. He has violated the emoluments clause of the United States Constitution in any number of ways. He has ordered administration officials not to comply with subpoenas issued by Congress. He has spread racist or anti-Semitic conspiracy theories. He has threatened violence against leading Democrats, the news media and others who dare to criticize him.[8]

It is impossible to separate this maelstrom of corruption and disorder from the backdrop of neoliberal capitalism. In the age of multiple pandemics, the promises of neoliberalism were revealed as a swindle, and one result was that the pandemic pedagogy that created the knowledge, ideologies, values, and cultural workstations that legitimated it began to crumble. Central to this significant historical event was that the issue of political education and a politics of social responsibility became more visible, reinforcing the need for people to think critically and be informed in order to hold power accountable and learn how to govern rather than be governed. Education as a force for both domination and emancipation was being rethought, once again within a historical moment that gave rise to both new crises and new possibilities for rethinking politics itself.

The Politics and Performance of Impeachment and the Rot of a Fascist Politics

The impeachment hearings of Donald Trump appeared as a crisis without a history, at least a history that could illuminate, not just comparisons with other presidential impeachments but also a relationship to a previous age of tyranny that ushered in horrors associated with a fascist politics in the 1930s. In the age of Trump, history did not teach us lessons from the past; it was used to divert and elude the most serious questions raised about a politics of corruption and lawlessness. The legacy of earlier presidential impeachments, which include Andrew Johnson and Bill Clinton, provided a comparative historical context for analysis and criticism. While Trump's impeachment attempt was often defined as a more serious constitutional crisis, given his attempt to use the power of the presidency to advance his personal political agenda, it is a crisis that willfully ignored the conditions that gave rise to Trump's presidency along with its recurring pattern of authoritarian behavior, policies, and practices.

The impeachment process with its abundance of political theater and insipid media coverage mostly treated Trump's crimes not as symptoms of a history of conditions that have led to the United States' slide into the abyss of authoritarianism, but as the failings of individual character and a personal breach of constitutional law. It is only in the aftermath of the impeachment process, the acceleration of the Covid-19 pandemic, and the outpouring of protests against police violence that the concealed truths that reveal Trump as the endpoint of a long-simmering authoritarianism have been starkly revealed and increasingly challenged.

The authoritarian storm clouds that emerged with the Covid-19 pandemic and the mass street protests highlighted that Trump's impeachment battle were part of the wider historical and global struggle taking place over democracy. This was apparent in Trump's attack on "the independence of the courts, the business community, the media, civil society, universities and sensitive state institutions like the civil service, the intelligence agencies and the police."[9] It was also evident in the expansion under the Trump regime of what Peter Maass calls the "accessories and devices of dictatorship." He writes:

> the accessories and devices of dictatorship have expanded with infectious ruthlessness in American cities. The police swinging batons wildly, the paramilitary forces refusing to identify themselves, the hysterical president trying to incite war, the vigilantes in league with the

police, military helicopters clattering overhead, the general marching in the streets in combat fatigues, the state TV network loosing its tales of sabotage and mayhem—it's all there, loud and clear.[10]

Trump's militarism was particularly evident when he mobilized military units and other repressive forces to disperse demonstrators peacefully protesting police violence and institutional racism. His weaponization of language was on full display when he labeled racial justice protesters "a bunch of maniacs," and "terrorists." Trump's bellicose discourse was also circulated in the right-wing media and increasingly implemented by forces of repression in the streets. His son, Eric Trump, went even further, using a racist slur when at a Tulsa rally he referred to Black Lives Matter activists as "animals."[11]

Central to such attacks is a form of reactionary educational politics—what I have referred to throughout this book as pandemic pedagogy-that became pivotal to Trump rationalizing his accelerating defensive and highly irrational actions in response to the Covid-19 crisis and ongoing street rebellions protesting police brutality, institutional racism, and the systemic negation of human rights and life. Pandemic pedagogy is both a form of public pedagogy responsible for the conditions created by the Covid-19 pandemic and a term that refers to the virus-like spread of racist discourse. In part, it refers to a "political conjuncture in which the anti-Black cultures of white supremacy are spreading and multiplying through online platforms, print media, city streets and town squares within, across, and beyond, the Western world."[12] A snapshot of Trump's virulent pandemic pedagogy—a pedagogical account infused with lies, racial slurs, misrepresentations—was on full display in his campaign rally in Tulsa, Oklahoma in June 2020. According to Joe Sommerlad and Danielle Zoellner writing in the British *Independent*, Trump made the following comments.

> On stage at the BOK Center, the president mocked the dangerous respiratory disease that has killed some 121,000 Americans as the "kung flu", likened it to the "sniffles" and admitted he had ordered his team to "slow the testing" for Covid-19 because the infection statistics were so unfavourable to him in an election year.[13]

The racism, incompetence, and disdain for science and public health merge together, further suggesting that Trump's crimes far exceeded what was stated in the impeachment documents to include lies, threats, and his flirtation with extra-legal violence.[14] This would also include his attack on the truth, especially his attack on the oppositional press and media, which he labels as the "enemy of the people." In addition, there was his use of Twitter to spew out verbal grenades that exploded in bursts of nativism and vitriol aimed at his critics and people of color who do not fit into his white nationalist view of citizenship and the public sphere.[15] As the bully-in chief, Trump has a long history of producing inflammatory, racially charged rhetoric.[16] Moreover, in doing so, he weaponized language into a tool of hatred and transformed politics into a spectacularized theater of bigotry, humiliations, and violence.

Ralph Nader argues that Trump's most distinguishing impeachable offenses resided in his "abuses of the public trust" which ranged from his "obsessive pathological lying and falsifications" and "endless racism and bigotry in words and deeds" to his support for voter suppression and his "incitement of violence on more than one occasion."[17] The *Washington Times* Fact Checker certainly backs up Nader's assertion about Trump's lying with the claim that "three years after his inauguration, Trump ... made more than 16,200 false or misleading claims. That boils down to six such claims a day in 2017, nearly 16 a day in 2018, and more than 22 in 2019."[18]

Needless to say, there was more at work here than Trump blurring the line between truth and fiction as a way of preventing individuals from distinguishing between good and evil, democracy and authoritarianism. There is also, as the historian Timothy Snyder observes, a politics of lying that represents a page out of the fascist playbook and evokes a history whose political legacy speaks to the present in compellingly related and horrifying ways.

> Fascists despised the small truths of daily existence, loved slogans that resonated like a new religion, and preferred creative myths to history or journalism. They used new media, which at the time was radio, to create a drumbeat of propaganda that aroused feelings before people

had time to ascertain facts. And now, as then, many people confused faith in a hugely flawed leader with the truth about the world we all share ... Fascists ruled for a decade or two, leaving behind an intact intellectual legacy that grows more relevant by the day.[19]

According to Nader, not only is Trump a pathological liar, he has also shredded and violated the Constitution, undermined its critical separation of power, and "illegally ordered his staff or ex-staff to ignore Congressional subpoenas to testify and provide documents"; he has also ignored Congress's right to declare war by inciting an unlawful crisis with Iran.[20] Literary figures such as Bertolt Brecht and Sinclair Lewis, along with politicians such as Henry A. Wallace, have long argued that if fascism came to America it would be wrapped in the symbol of the flag, the language of patriotism, and the cover of democracy. In his *Anatomy of Fascism*, the historian Robert O. Paxton argued that the texture of North American fascism would not mimic traditional European forms but would be rooted in the language, symbols, and culture of everyday life in America. According to Paxton:

> No swastikas in an American fascism, but Stars and Stripes (or Stars and Bars) and Christian crosses. No fascist salute, but mass recitations of the Pledge of Allegiance. These symbols contain no whiff of fascism in themselves, of course, but an American fascism would transform them into obligatory litmus tests for detecting the internal enemy.[21]

There is a lesson to be learned here regarding how history is reproduced in the present. First, there was Trump's killing of a high-ranking Iranian general "based on thin evidence with an eye towards domestic politics."[22] Second, there was Trump's threat to use "dominating force" and unleash the National Guard and police upon demonstrators peacefully protesting police violence against people of color. Third, there was Trump's relentless language of violence designed to embolden second-amendment gun-rights activists towards committing violence and to dehumanize certain populations while attempting "to harness the emotion of nostalgia to the central themes of fascist ideology—authoritarianism, hierarchy, purity and struggle."[23] Fourth, Trump's authoritarian impulses and fascist politics took a dangerous turn when he authorized the use of military-clad federal law enforcement officers to round up and detain protesters in Portland, Oregon.

Wearing camouflage khakis, striking a menacing hyper-militarized warrior pose, the troops offered no proof of identification, drove around in unmarked cars, pulled people off the streets with no probable cause, and provided no sense of whose directives they were acting under, or who was to be held accountable for their actions. Ted Wheeler, the Mayor of Portland, called such actions "an attack on our democracy."[24] Nancy Pelosi, the Speaker of the House, tweeted in reference to Portland that "Trump and his storm troopers must be stopped."[25] Oregon Gov. Kate Brown (D) said in a statement, "This is a democracy, not a dictatorship," "We cannot have secret police abducting people in unmarked vehicles. I can't believe I have to say that to the President of the United States."[26]

We have seen this before under Hitler in Germany, Augusto Pinochet in Chile, and in other dictatorships. When such actions appeared in the past, dissidents, demonstrators, and intellectuals disappeared, were beaten, tortured, and interrogated in undisclosed sites, and in the worse scenarios were murdered. What happened in Portland suggests that the war on terror had shifted from abroad to the homeland. Such actions may have been Trump's attempt at trial run for an authoritarian state. It is not implausible to assume that Trump's was attempting to produce civil unrest in order to enhance his purported role as the law and order president in order to enhance himself as a strong candidate for re-election. Barr appeared to support this position by indicating at the time that he was willing to send 200 federal agents to Kansas City, Missouri, and Chicago, with a lesser number going to Albuquerque.

These events mimic, if not recall, an older period in history when Hitler, following the crisis produced by the Reichstag fire, seized upon the ensuing fear, terror, and war fever to further consolidate his power. For Trump, the actions of pushing the United States to the edge of war through a military strike on Iran, killing Iranian Gen. Qassem Soleimani, and using the military to stifle domestic protests reinforced the seriousness of the charges of lawlessness brought against him during his impeachment hearings. It also made visible his ongoing crimes and misdeeds, while suggesting, as Elizabeth Warren pointed out, that he will do "whatever he can to advance the interests of Donald Trump."[27] Trump's haphazard decision to threaten a war with Iran also puts Americans at risk of terrorist attacks and undermines previous efforts to roll back Iran's nuclear program.[28] He strained relations with China and a host of friendly European countries. At the same time, former national security advisor John Bolton says that Kim Jong Un found Trump laughable and stated that "Russian President Vladimir Putin thinks he 'can play' President Trump like a 'fiddle.'"[29]

Moreover, Trump's political incompetence and ignorance was matched by a war fever that expresses itself as a self-serving fascistic affirmation of his steroid-charged hyper-masculinity and his admiration for military power and authoritarian pageants generally associated with demagogues who use such displays as a tool to produce respect among their followers. Trump's authoritarian response to the various protest movements that broke out across the United States revealed his "blunt-force view of the military" to promote his own political interests, even at the expense of the civil rights of peaceful dissenters.[30] Sending active-duty troops to gas and fire rubber bullets at American citizens made clear the degree to which the U.S. government had ushered in a politics that mimics the grim lessons of a menacing and authoritarian past.

The Politics of Invisibility and the Language of Violence

Prior to Trump's impeachment hearings, there were serious political debates regarding Trump's lawlessness, but they never went far enough. The debates focused mostly on issues such as the inadequacy of the Democrats' efforts to impeach, arguments regarding whether the impeachment charges went enough, and the more favorable view that the impeachment process, however limited, was necessary to stop Trump from using the resources of the government to influence other governments to interfere in American elections for his own personal and political gains.[31]

There were also more extreme views, largely coming from Trump and his supporters. Some argued that the impeachment process was pure theater—a staged theatrical hoax; others such as Senator Lindsay Graham and Mitch McConnell claimed that the process was rigged, and was an attempt on the part of the Democrats to win favor in the 2020 elections. Trump himself angrily dismissed the impeachment process as corrupt, claiming, among other things, that he was the victim of a socialist plot. In the aftermath of the failed impeachment trial, Trump continued to produce a well-worn pattern of threats and vengeful acts against his critics. For instance, he stated that House Intelligence Chairman Adam Schiff "should be arrested for treason."[32] In addition, Trump suggested that Schiff should be "be violently punished" in a manner of justice displayed by dictatorships such as Guatemala. Jean Spanbauer, a Trump supporter, mused online that "Shifty Shiff [*sic*] needs to be hung."[33] At work here is more than the indiscriminate insult or infantile mocking.

Language in this instance is an enabler of violence, functioning to divert and punish. According to Victor Klemperer, an expert on Nazi Germany, this type of language has a precedent in the Third Reich in which it operated "as part of a linguistic malignant disease designed to spread the poison of mass seduction [and] destroy the intellect which defies it."[34] As Ishaan Tharoor observes, "the use of such volatile and dehumanizing language in the current moment is not innocent and often leads to violence."[35] According to Tharoor, "There are immediate consequences to such demagoguery, not least in the form of far-right terrorist attacks and violence carried out by people inflamed by this sort of rhetoric."[36]

Political Theater in the Age of Relentless Lies

Within the current crop of competing discourses that analyzed the impeachment proceedings, the Democrats presented themselves as the "last line of defense between constitutional democracy and tyranny,"[37] while Republicans repeated conspiracy theories and accused the Democrats of producing a show trial whose purpose was the ultimate reversal of Trump's 2016 election to the presidency. The Republicans were particularly egregious and used the hearings to badger witnesses, and showcase their "emotive hand-wringing, faux exasperation and yelling, all the while making outlandish claims that turned the hearings into a 'propaganda circus.'"[38] In some cases, more insightful commentary was produced.

One particular instance came from legendary journalist Bill Moyers who viewed the impeachment hearings as a potential site for a lesson in civic education. For Moyers, the value of the impeachment proceedings meant making visible "things you would never know otherwise."[39] Bringing the concept of civic education to understanding the impeachment process is crucial, but what people learn from such events is limited by what is actually revealed both within and outside of the hearings. In this case, Trump's impeachment process in the House was reduced to a political spectacle and served to undermine reason and informed judgment while promoting a steady stream of the performative diversions produced through a regimen of ignorance, self-serving lies, and the triumph of illusion.

Unfortunately, the mainstream 24/7 news cycle, with its relentless torrent of dramatic sound bites, did its best to turn the House impeachment hearings into a political theater by largely focusing on the political risks Democrats faced by conducting the hearings.[40] In addition, the media mostly adhered to the empty tactic of providing balance while avoiding any attempt to tell the truth about a present that had collapsed into a disdain for human rights, enacted cruelty as an act of patriotism, justified oppression in the name of national security, viewed undocumented immigrants as disposable, allowed elections to be bought by the highest bidder, demonized and threatened critics, and regarded the truth as a liability.[41] Trump's closest allies, such as Jair Bolsonaro in Brazil, mimicked his cruelty and wore it like a badge of honor.

For Bolsonaro, this was on full display when in the midst of the pandemic ravaging his country with over a half million cases and over 30,000 dead, he stated in a heartless display of cruelty: "We are sorry for all the dead, but that's everyone's destiny."[42] The consequences of Bolsonaro's indifference to addressing the pandemic crisis in Brazil has been catastrophic. It became more personal when, not surprisingly, given his refusal to take safety precautions, he eventually was infected with the virus, as was later his denier in arms, Donald Trump. As of July 27, 2020, over 2,400,000 were infected in Brazil and the death toll had reached close to 87,000. Bolsonaro's moral indifference morphed into what could be appropriately labeled as a war crime. Such a charge is bolstered by the fact that he has modeled himself after Mussolini, openly supporting his brutalizing masculinity on Facebook with the quote: "It is better to live one day as a lion than a hundred years as a sheep."[43]

Vichy Republicans without Apology

While the Republican and Democratic Parties shared a fundamental commitment to the ideology and institutional structures of neoliberal capitalism, the Republican Party was far more extreme in its critique of the American press, judiciary, dissent, labor unions, workers' rights, and its support for reversing environmental protection laws. Ken Burns, the acclaimed filmmaker, columnist George Will, and *New York Times* opinion writer Paul Krugman, among others, have labeled Trump's loyal party followers Vichy Republicans, referring to the war-era collaborationist Vichy government of France—run by cowardly French sympathizers and appeasers who gave their faithful loyalty to their Nazi German occupiers.[44] Not unlike the Vichy government that collaborated with the Nazis in the 1940s, Trump's Republican "party of sycophants" bought into the script of ultra-nationalism, and closed their eyes to Trump's racism, remained silent in the face of his unchecked fantasies of power, and supported his sanctioning of state violence at home and abroad.[45]

Trump's merging of enemies at home with enemies at the border is particularly disturbing. Capitalizing upon the media to circulate this theater of fear, Trump shaped television viewing to suggest that the general public (white) was under threat not only from "outsiders" on the southern border but also those deemed as internal dissidents, rioters, people of color, and enemies of the American state. Patriotism was now exhibited in the symbol of paramilitary security forces protecting individual rights, jobs, and threats from the undocumented brown "hordes" and the Black "anarchists" and "terrorists" who interchangeably posed an existential threat to the American way of life. As Andrew Gawthorpe observed, "sending camouflage-clad forces to battle both America's external enemies and its internal dissenters is supposed to send the message that ultimately, the latter are just as dangerous to the nation as the former."[46]

This is a party that has chosen to look away in the face of Trump's lies, crimes, violence, and repeated acts of corruption. The corruption in Trump's presidency has been repeated so often that it became normalized. This short list alone speaks volumes to Trump's corruption. For instance, his campaign chairman and deputy campaign chairman were sent to prison; the president's university was shut down as a scam; Trump was tried and then retaliated against those who testified against him; he put his son's wedding planner in charge of federal housing in the northeast United States and pressured the post office to punish Jeff Bezos, the owner of the *Washington Post*, because he didn't like the *Post*'s critical reporting on his policies. These episodes barely scratch the surface of the numerous corrupt acts in which this president engaged.

The Republican Senate ignored all of these issues, refusing to take an impartial look at these infractions during the impeachment inquiry. Instead, they invoked what has become a mantra for them, pledging to support Trump at all costs, and did everything possible to muddle the public discourse by floating conspiracy theories, calling the proceedings a hoax, and attacking the character of witnesses.[47] Under the Trump regime, the Republican Party was more than willing to engage in a Faustian bargain with incipient authoritarianism. If the Republican Party once stood for basic principles such as small government, family values, fiscal soundness, and national security, that was no longer true. Instead, its most paranoid and racist elements controlled the party. The

Republican Party's move to the right intensified in the 1990s under the influence of Newt Gingrich and Karl Rove, and later with the rise of Sarah Palin and the defeat of the centrist Mitt Romney in 2012.

Today, the Republican Party has almost unilaterally become a party of white supremacists, blood-and-soil nationalists, and political swindlers who activate white panic, voter suppression, and define citizenship in racial terms.[48] They supported, through either fear or blind loyalty, Trump's ideological policies, race baiting, and dangerous foreign policy strategies, regardless of the excesses and ongoing assault on the country's democratic institutions.[49] This included a racist campaign strategy, ongoing attempts at voter suppression, caging immigrant children, savage attacks on undocumented immigrants, devaluing critics by calling them treasonous, slashing of social provisions such as food stamps, and serial lying by Trump.[50] This was a president who refused to wear a mask when he appeared in public and at his indoor rallies (until the death count was out of control), all the while titillating his supporters by using a racist term in naming the virus. In addition to the ignorance, stupidity, and political opportunism displayed by Trump and his administration, there was also a descent into lawlessness and the abyss of fascist politics.

The Politics of Lawlessness and the Plague of William Barr

Theodor W. Adorno argued in "The Meaning of Working through the Past" that "the past that one would like to evade is still very much alive."[51] This was particularly evident in the debilitating pronouncements of William Barr, Trump's Attorney General, regarding his defense of unchecked executive authority, which he believed should be unburdened by any sense of political and moral accountability. Tamsin Shaw is right in suggesting that Barr bears a close resemblance to Carl Schmitt, "the notorious ... 'crown jurist' of the Third Reich."[52] Barr placed the president above the law, defined as a kind of unitary sovereign. In addition, he appeared to relish in his role as a craven defender of Trump, all the while justifying a notion of unchecked executive authority in the face of Trump's endless lies, racist policies, and lawlessness that echo the dark era of the 1920s and 1930s.

His attacks on the FBI and the Justice Department's Inspector General, and his threat to remove police protection from Black communities who are not loyal to Trump, were at odds with any viable notion of defending the truth and "the most basic tenets of equality and justice."[53] James Risen claims that Barr "turned the Justice Department into a law firm with one client: Donald Trump [and that] under Barr, the Department of Justice had two objectives: to suppress any investigation of President Trump and his associates, and to aggressively pursue investigations of his political rivals."[54]

It gets worse. Shamelessly, Barr issued a directive to National Guard soldiers and police to attack individuals peacefully protesting racist police violence outside of the White House in order to clear a path for Trump's walk to St. John's Episcopal Church for a photo op. In the photo op, Trump stood before the church awkwardly holding a Bible in his hand, echoing a history one associates with the Ku Klux Klan and iconographic images that might have been used in D.W. Griffith's 1915 racist film, *The Birth of a Nation*. Prior to the photo op, Barr ordered the "National Guard soldiers and police to break up a crowd of peaceful demonstrators, which they did by clubbing them with batons, firing tear gas canisters into crowds, and shoving people to the ground." One pastor, Michael Wilker, one of the leaders of the Washington Interfaith Network, called Trump's actions an "abomination," placing Trump's actions in the context of an earlier fascist history. According to Wilker,

> During Nazi Germany, Adolf Hitler used the symbols of the Lutheran church—our own church—as a way to divide Christians from one another, and especially to deny the humanity of Jews in Germany. It's the same thing Trump is doing here: he is using the symbols of the church as a way to divide the church from one another and to divert our attention from the actual suffering and killing that's going on. [It was] a demonic act.[55]

Just before the assault, Trump delivered a speech on the nationwide uprising sparked by the killing of George Floyd.[56] He used the speech as a pretext to appoint himself as the "president of law and order" and came close to declaring war on the American people. As Kristen Clarke stated on *Democracy Now*:

> Here, Trump single-handedly seeks to deploy the military to states all across our country over the objections of state officials and with the sole and singular purpose of silencing Americans. In many ways, this is the death of democracy, because people who are out right now have one singular goal: to ensure that at this moment we not turn our backs on the long-overdue work that's necessary to rid our nation of the scourge of police violence that has resulted in innumerous deaths of unarmed African Americans.[57]

In spite of the overwhelming evidence of a violent, racist police culture in the U.S., Barr has stated publicly that "he did not believe racism was a systemic problem in policing, echoing other top administration officials' defense of an important part of President Trump's base as protests against police killings of unarmed black people continued across the nation."[58] Barr along with Trump's acolytes were not simply the victims their own bad judgment; they lacked a moral compass, embraced the banner of white supremacy, willingly supported what appeared to be racial anxieties about the decline of "white civilization," and emerged as a menace to the American people and to democracy itself. A strong believer in an imperial presidency, Barr relinquished the role of the Justice Department as an independent agency and repeatedly attempted to subvert the law he should be upholding.

In light of such actions and the refusal of the Republican members of Congress to speak out against such activities, it is not surprising that conservative journalist George Will declared that Barr and Trump's congressional enablers "gambol around [Trump's] ankles with a canine hunger for petting."[59] This criticism is not unfounded given Barr's legal illegalities and ideological cover for Trump's dangerous lackeys, such as Senate Majority Leader Mitch McConnell and Senator

Lindsay Graham, both of whom shamed themselves during the impeachment hearings. For example, McConnell's Vichyite propensity for collaboration with the White House was on full display when he publicly denounced the impeachment process while it was in progress, claiming he had already made up his mind. Moreover, as an unabashed defender of Trump, he shamelessly stated that he would work hand in hand with the Trump administration during the impeachment process to make sure Trump would not be removed from office.

McConnell was not alone. Senator Lindsay Graham stated that he had already made up his mind about Trump committing a criminal conspiracy, which he dismissed, and that he would do everything he could to make impeachment "die quickly" in the Senate.[60] Such blind and dangerous support for Trump the vulgarian warrants Will's claim that Trump is a "malignant buffoon" and that those who support him should be removed from office.[61]

There appeared to be no limits to Barr's defense of the indefensible, particularly as a way of placating Trump's vindictive and vengeful actions towards those he believed have wronged him or his close associates. In June of 2020, Barr convinced Trump to fire Geoffrey S. Berman, the United States attorney in Manhattan. Berman had pursued a number of cases on members of Trump's inner circle that irked Trump. The cases included the arrest and prosecution in 2018 of Michael D. Cohen, Trump's longtime lawyer and fixer; an investigation into the wrongdoings of a Turkish state-owned bank (an investigation Trump had promised Turkish president, Recep Tayyip Erdogan, he would end), and later an inquiry started by Berman's office into Rudolph W. Giuliani, Trump's close supporter and personal lawyer. Speaking on CNN, Rep. Adam Schiff (D-CA), Chairman of the House Permanent Select Committee on Intelligence, stated that Barr "is the second most dangerous man in the country."[62]

Barr's use of the Department of Justice as a tool to implement the president's personal and political demands and pardons was on full display when a Justice Department official recounted to Congress that

Barr had intervened in a sentencing recommendation "because of politics." Aaron S.J. Zelinsky, a prosecutor, stated that Barr overrode the decisions of career prosecutors to "seek a more lenient prison sentence for Mr. Trump's longtime friend Roger J. Stone Jr."[63]

What followed, unsurprisingly, was a blatantly corrupt use of presidential clemency power and interference in the Justice Department when Trump commuted the prison sentence of Roger Stone, who was convicted of seven felony crimes. Speaker Nancy Pelosi called the move an act of "staggering corruption."[64] Senator Mitt Romney (R-Utah) echoed Pelosi, calling it an act of "unprecedented, historic corruption: an American president commutes the sentence of a person convicted by a jury of lying to shield that very president."[65] Adam Schiff, the Democratic representative of California and lead prosecutor in the impeachment trial stated: "With Trump, there are now two systems of justice in America: one for Trump's criminal friends and one for everyone else ... Under Trump and Barr, the rule of law has been corrupted."[66]

Abigail Tracy in *Vanity Fair* added to the charge of corruption and pointed to the growing rot in the Justice Department, and in doing so quoted David Laufman, a former Justice Department official who stated, "We're now seeing continuous, unbridled, and apparently shameless efforts to corrupt the Department of Justice and undermine its governing principles by manipulating cases and installing pliable officials for political purposes."[67] This is not merely about corruption and incompetence, but lawlessness, which is the essence of fascist politics. As Hannah Arendt noted in her work on totalitarianism: "If lawfulness is the essence of non-tyrannical government [then] lawlessness is the essence of tyranny."[68]

In spite of Trump's celebration of demagogues such as Kim Jong Un, whom he called a "real leader," and overtly fascists leaders such as Jair Bolsonaro in Brazil and President Rodrigo Duterte of the Philippines, the Republican Party has stood unified behind Trump's blatant move towards authoritarianism.[69] Paul Krugman goes so far as to claim that modern conservatives live inside a cult and are "turning into government by the worst and dumbest."[70] At the same time, he makes it clear that there is more than massive degree of stupidity at work in the Trump administration; there are also the dark clouds of authoritarianism which extend far beyond the political career of Donald Trump. Krugman writes: "For whatever may happen to Donald Trump, his party has turned its back on democracy. And that should terrify you. The fact is that the G.O.P., as currently constituted, is willing to do whatever it takes to seize and hold power."[71]

The importance of Trump's and Barr's repeated acts of lawlessness go far beyond the historical moment in which they occurred. They reinforce an image of a party that, in the face of egregious crimes by the president and increasingly by his Attorney General, either remained mute or overtly supported him in a show of ideological certainty—what Robert Jay Lifton calls an act of "absolute purification" and a cult-like totalizing vision that reproduced a politics of "malignant normality."[72]

Barr has been rebuked by a federal judge for misrepresenting the Mueller Report to the Congress; over 1,000 former Department of Justice officials called for him to resign, and 80 percent of active faculty professors and deans at George Washington University Law School, from which Barr graduated in 1977, signed an open letter calling for his resignation. The letter is a searing indictment of Barr's transgressions and acts of lawlessness and contained the following summary of his illegalities.

William Barr's actions as Attorney General since 2019 have undermined the rule of law, breached constitutional norms, and damaged the integrity and traditional independence of his office and of the Department of Justice. He obfuscated and misled the American public about the results of the Mueller investigation. He wrongfully interfered in the day-to-day activities of career prosecutors, and continues to do so, bending the criminal justice system to benefit the President's friends and target those perceived to be his enemies. He participated in the forcible removal from public space of peaceful protesters, exercising their First Amendment rights to speech and assembly in order to protest racial injustice. His actions have posed, and continue to create, a clear and present danger to the even-handed administration of justice, to civil liberties, and to the constitutional order.[73]

Barr, along with Trump and his Republican allies, ignored these criticisms. Barr and other members of Trump's cabinet believed that crime is the result of moral factors, which is both *false* as the sole condition for alleged criminal behavior and *ironic*. Ironic because, given their complicity with Trump's criminogenic behavior, the Vichy Republicans exhibited nothing more than a massive flight from any semblance of morality. In a brilliant analysis of Republican Party leaders as Trump's enablers, who readily echo past Vichy collaborators, Anne Applebaum argues that Trump "built a Cabinet and an administration that serve[d] neither the public nor his voters but rather his own psychological needs and the interests of his own friends on Wall Street and in business and, of course, his own family … All the while he fanned and encouraged xenophobia and racism, both because he found them politically useful and because they are part of his personal worldview."[74] Beyond the seductive lure of power, there is also at work here the transition from a nascent fascism to full-fledged embrace of fascist politics.

The contemporary elements of tyranny at work in the United States and across the globe pointed not only to a crisis of leadership and the rise of demagogues such as Trump on the domestic and global stages but also the conditions and crisis that produced "the discontent of millions of people, facing economic instability, climate insecurity, mass migrations, technological change, cultural shifts around gender and race—people who in turn seem all too willing to embrace the politics of fear and blame."[75] The pandemics of our time are shot through with the scourge of entrenched inequalities and its effects on class, race, social privilege, gender, occupation, and age, all of which determines who is most vulnerable not only to the virus but also to "work conditions and environments, as well as access to good-quality healthcare, diet, and facilities to prevent disease—e.g., regular water supply, sanitation, housing that allows physical distancing/quarantine, personal protective equipment (PPE), etc."[76]

Pandemic Disimagination Machines

The crisis of truth and politics is now matched by a mainstream and corporate-controlled digital media and screen culture, and other cultural apparatuses, that revel in political theater, and embrace a numbing ignorance, produce fractured narratives, and trade in racial hysteria.[77] In addition, as a powerful regulatory workstations, they authorize and produce a culture of sensationalism designed to increase ratings and profits at the expense of truth. As a form of pandemic pedagogy, they undermine a complex rendering of social problems and suppress a culture of dissent and informed judgments. Their depoliticizing logic is rampant in the entertainment fields, celebrity culture, and the advertising industries, with their perpetual motion fantasy machines at work 24/7. This pandemic pedagogy functions to shape human agency, desire, and modes of identification in the logic of consumerism while privileging a hyper form of masculinity and legitimating a friend/enemy distinction.

We live in an age in which theater and the spectacle of performance empty politics of any moral substance and contribute to the revival of an updated version of fascist politics. Thoughtlessness has become a national ideal as the corporate-controlled media mirrors the Trump administration's demand that reality be echoed rather than be analyzed, interrogated, and critically comprehended. Politics is now leaden with bombast, words strung together to shock and numb the mind, and images overwrought with a self-serving sense of righteousness and anger. Trump shamelessly reinforces such a cultural politics by showing propaganda videos at presidential news conferences.

What is distinct about this historical period, especially under the Trump regime, is what Susan Sontag has called a form of aesthetic fascism with its contempt of "all that is reflective, critical, and pluralistic."[78] One distinctive element of the current moment is the rise of pandemic disimagination machines such as Fox News, conservative talk radio, and Breitbart Media, which function as overt and unapologetic propaganda machines that trade in nativism, misrepresentations, and racist hysteria, all wrapped in the cloak of a regressive view of patriotism. This is particularly true for Fox News, which Margaret Sullivan calls a "a shameless propaganda outlet which makes billions of dollars a year as it chips away at the core democratic values we ought to hold dear: truth, accountability and the rule of law."[79]

Joel Bleifuss furthers this argument, stating that Fox News "the most-watched cable news network, function[ed] in its fealty to Trump like a real-world Ministry of Truth from George Orwell's *1984*, where bureaucrats 'rectify' the historical record to conform to Big Brother's decrees."[80] Trump's fascist politics and fantasies of racial purity could not have succeeded without the disimagination machines, pedagogical apparatuses, and the practitioners needed to make his "vision not just real but grotesquely normal."[81] What Trump made clear is that the weaponization of language into a discourse of racism and hate was deeply indebted to a politics of forgetting and was a crucial pedagogical tool in the battle to undermine historical consciousness and memory itself.

Corporate-controlled disimagination machines mostly functioned within a market-driven culture to cater to Trump's Twitter universe, unchecked bombast, and culture of humiliation (often aimed at them), all the while prone to isolating social issues, individualizing social problems, and making the workings of power superficially visible. This was obvious in the mainstream's continuous coverage of his initial daily press briefings, which my friend Oscar Zambrano describes as "like watching a disease in progress that is infecting us all: a parallel to coronavirus."[82] Unfortunately, high ratings were more important than refusing to participate in Trump's disinformation spectacles.[83]

Politics as a spectacle saturates the senses with noise, cheap melodrama, lies, and buffoonery. This is not to suggest that the spectacle that shapes politics as pure theater is meant merely to entertain and distract. Trump turned the channels of entertainment into a new kind of politics. He invented a new form of pandemic pedagogy, one that grew out of and used the power of digital media. He used it to bypass traditional channels of communication and dialogue, speaking directly to his followers and producing an echo sphere of hate unparalleled in that it flowed from the highest levels of power.

While elements of the liberal press were highly critical of Trump, they were eclipsed by a digital media spectacle, and more mainstream coverage. In this case, the corporate-controlled media rarely challenged Trump's language of war in terms of how it fed into his broader exercise of an authoritarian mode of governance. Under such circumstances, war as a permanent social relation was normalized, and became the primary organizing principle of society and politics. War is still the operative and defining feature of language and the matrix for all relations of power. Its more dangerous threat came from Trump's hesitation about stepping down if he lost the election, and his repeated attempts to call his critics communists, socialists, "anarchists" and "left-wing fascists," all the while using the military to incite civil conflict.

The militarization of the media, and culture itself, operates as a form of social and historical amnesia. That is, in both form and content it separates the past from a politics that in its current incarnation turned deadly in its attack on the values and institutions crucial to a functioning democracy. In this instance, resemblances to a fascist past remained hidden, invisible beneath the histrionic shouting and disinformation campaigns that railed against alleged "enemies of the state" and "fake news," which were euphemisms for dissent, holding power accountable, and an oppositional media. A flair for the overly dramatic represented an additional element of pandemic pedagogy that attempted to eliminate the distinction between fact and fiction, lies and the truth. As allegiance to the truth disappeared at the highest levels of government, it was replaced by the celebration of the strong over the weak, an emphasis on unlimited authority, and relations of domination and repression, which became the unifying symbols of Trump's brand of fascist politics. In Trump's world view, the leader was the all-powerful symbol of the present and future and this mimicked what Susan Sontag once called fascist art which "glorifies surrender," "exalts mindlessness," "the righteousness of power" and the "right to have total power."[84]

In the current historical moment, the spectacle of militarization functions as part of a culture of distraction, division, and fragmentation, all the while refusing to pose the question of how the United States shares elements of a fascist politics that connect it to a number of other authoritarian countries such as Brazil, China, Turkey, Hungary, the Philippines, and Poland. On the pretext of protecting the public in the midst of the pandemic, many countries employed forms of digital surveillance, used emergency powers to repress dissent, engaged police violence against those occupying unsafe spaces, shut down conventional and social media, and waged war against alleged political enemies. In the midst of the pandemic, all of these countries embraced a form of fascist politics that combined an unraveling of constitutional law with the discourses of hate, nativism, and state repression. In this dark period, the militarization of everyday life exhibited elements of a fascist past and in doing so created a form of depoliticization in which the public largely refused to "pose the question why Hitler and Nazi Germany continue to exert such a grip on modern life."[85]

Forgetting History and the Legitimation of White Supremacy

A crucial lesson to be learned from the absence of history is not only how ignorance becomes normalized but also how the absence of critical thought allows us to forget that we are moral subjects capable of changing the world around us. The reign of Donald Trump constituted a crisis in need of being fully confronted both historically and in terms of a comprehensive politics that allows us to learn from the alarming signs that came from the Trump administration. Such a crisis contained elements of a past that suggested we could not look away or give in to the assault on the past as a matter of intellectual responsibility.

History offers a model to learn something from earlier turns towards authoritarianism and makes it more difficult to assume that fascism is merely a relic of the past.[86] Memories of fascist terror are not only present in the rise of white supremacist demonstrations of hate and bigotry that took place in a number of cities defending Confederate monuments and protesting against Covid-19 health restrictions, but also in the Trump White House which was home to white supremacists such as Stephen Miller, who was a high-level advisor to Trump and was viewed by many as the architect of his draconian immigration policies. Miller's white supremacist views were on public display when over 900 of Miller's emails were leaked by former Breitbart editor Katie McHugh. Among the trove of emails, Miller commented on and provided reference to white nationalist websites such as VDARE and celebrated the racist novel, *The Camp of the Saints*. According to Jared Holt, an investigative reporter at *Right Wing Watch*, Miller "also reportedly espoused conspiracy theories about immigration, backed racist immigration policies introduced by President Calvin Coolidge that were praised by Adolf Hitler, and deployed slang popular in white nationalist circles to reference immigration."[87] Judd Legum argues that Miller also "obsessed over the loss of Confederate symbols after Dylann Roof's murderous rampage,"[88] a view that may have later shaped Trump's doubling down on protecting Confederate monuments. In July 2020, the Southern Poverty Law Center, which documents hate groups across the U.S., added Miller's name to its database of extremists because of his white supremacist views and influence in shaping many of Trump's most egregious racist policies.[89]

In spite of a barrage of calls from a number of politicians calling for Miller's removal from the White House, Trump held firm, reinforcing the widely accepted notion that Trump is a white nationalist entirely comfortable with white supremacist ideology.[90] Since Trump waged a presidential campaign using the language of white nationalism, it is not surprising that he brought such extremist views into the White House.[91] Of course, removing Miller would not have changed much. Miller was not the only white supremacist in the Trump administration. Nor could his presence hide the fact that white supremacy has been a staple of the Republican Party for decades, evident in the history and contemporary presence of high-profile Republican politicians such as

Strom Thurman, Jeff Session, former Representative Steve King, Tom Tancredo, and Dana Rohrabacher.

Moreover, the long legacy of white supremacy in the United States should not undercut the distinctiveness of Donald Trump's white supremacist views which he boldly embraced while escalating and normalizing white nationalist sensibilities, practices, and policies unlike any president in modern times. His scapegoating of minorities and demonization of politicians, athletes, and other critics of color reflected more than a divide-and-rule strategy; it was an updated strategy for mainstreaming the death-haunted elements of fascism.

Fascism has deep roots in American history, and its nativist legacy and anti-intellectualism has always incorporated notions of racial cleansing, the dehumanization of other groups, and an embrace of white nationalism and supremacy. This legacy lives on in different forms in Trump's view of America. How else to explain Trump's embrace of birtherism, his racist anti-immigration policies, his public support for right-wing groups marching on state capitals protesting Covid-19 restrictions,[92] and his appropriation of the early twentieth-century nativist and pro-fascist slogan "America First"?

Unsurprisingly, Trump used the vast reach of his social media platforms to retweet a video to his millions of followers in which a man at a retirement community riding in a golf cart bearing "Trump 2020" and "America First" signs yells the racist phrase "white power!" at a group of counter-protesters.[93] While Trump later deleted the video, "he did not condemn the 'white power' statement or specifically disavow the sentiment expressed by his supporters."[94] A few days later, as if he wanted to reinforce for his base his obsession with violence, white supremacist brutality, and deep disdain for the widespread protests over racial violence and police violence, he "retweeted a video of a white man and woman brandishing a semiautomatic rifle and a handgun at peaceful black demonstrators in St. Louis."[95] What Trump relentlessly affirmed whenever he addressed matters of race reinforces James Baldwin's argument that "White is a metaphor for power."[96] How else to explain Trump's comment that "people love" the Confederate battle flag, and that it has a place in American society because it's about freedom of speech, as if its legacy as a symbol of slavery and the fact that it is a racist, painful, and hurtful symbol to Black Americans did not matter.[97] In his debate with Joe Biden, he refused to denounce white supremacy making clear that he embraced it as a national ideal.

Trump's lawlessness and fascist policies cannot be explained away by his overcharged narcissism, ignorance of history, or the fact that his authoritarian tendencies do not perfectly match those of Hitler or Mussolini. Trump's fascist politics were historically and culturally specific, wrapped in a discourse of ultra-nationalism, militarism, and racial cleansing that is as American as apple pie. As Sarah Churchill observes, American fascism has its own symbols, slogans, and appropriation of national customs. She writes:

> American fascist energies today are different from 1930s European fascism, but that doesn't mean they're not fascist, it means they're not European and it's not the 1930s. They remain organized around classic fascist tropes of nostalgic regeneration, fantasies of racial purity, celebration of an authentic folk and nullification of others, scapegoating groups for economic instability or inequality, rejecting the legitimacy of political opponents, the demonization of critics, attacks on a free press, and claims that the will of the people justifies violent imposition of military force. Vestiges of interwar fascism have been dredged up, dressed up, and repurposed for modern times. Colored shirts might not sell anymore, but colored hats are doing great.[98]

The Americanization of fascism was also evident in Trump's war on the free press and free speech. Trump consistently waged war on the "lying media" and elevated the spurious notion of fake news to the level of a common-sense assumption. The derogatory term has a strong resemblance to Hitler's demonization of "lugenpresse" —the lying press. Rick Noack states that "The defamatory word was most frequently used in Nazi Germany. Today, it is a common slogan among those branded as representing the 'ugly Germany': members of xenophobic, right-wing groups. This Nazi slur was also used by some of Trump's followers."[99] Trump legitimated a culture of lying and cruelty, and furthered a collapse of civic justice. He intensified and furthered the process of making people superfluous and disposable while producing a fog of ignorance. The latter gives contemporary credence to Hannah Arendt's claim in *The Origins of Totalitarianism* that "The ideal subject of totalitarian rule is not the convinced Nazi or the convinced Communist, but people for whom the distinction between fact and fiction (i.e., the reality of experience) and the distinction between true and false (i.e., the standards of thought) no longer exists."[100]

Toward Insurrection among an Educated Citizenry

The historian David Blight has written that Trump's "greatest threat to our society and to our democracy [was] not necessarily his authoritarianism, but his essential ignorance—of history, of policy, of political process, of the Constitution."[101] Former national security advisor John Bolton, in his book *The Room Where It Happened*, reinforces Blight's perception of Trump. Bolton states that Trump was "stunningly uninformed," lacked basic political and geographical knowledge—thought Finland was a part of Russia—and was unaware that the UK had nuclear weapons.[102]

Blight is only partly right in that the greatest threat to our society is a collective ignorance that legitimates forms of organized forgetting, modes of social amnesia, and the death of civic literacy. This is a threat that empties politics of any substantive democratic meaning and value. The notion that the past is a burden that must be forgotten is a centerpiece of authoritarian regimes, one that allows public memory to wither and the threads of fascism to become normalized. While some critics eschew the comparison of Trump with the Nazi era, it is crucial to recognize the alarming signs in his administration that echoed a fascist politics of the past. As Jonathan Freedland points out, "the signs are there, if only we can bear to look."[103] No democracy can survive without an informed and educated citizenry, one attuned to the importance of historical memory as a bedrock of moral witnessing and political action.

The impeachment hearings offered more than their stated limited aims in that they had real value as a form of civic education. That is, they laid bare a politics of evasions and structured silences that both ignored the most serious of Trump's crimes and failed to examine a number of political threads that together constitute elements common to a global crisis in democracy. In this context, the impeachment hearings exhibited a form of lawlessness that cannot be disconnected from those neoliberal institutions that reproduce a colonial past, "propagate imperialist violence and extraction [and] continue to function as a fortress that excludes and a prison that incarcerates its disenfranchised and oppressed."[104] The impeachment process revealed how power works through a politics of denial and as such creates the conditions for neoliberal power relations to be useful in "the transfer of wealth to the privileged by justifying capitalism's hegemony."[105] This is a politics that is built into all of America's infrastructures, ranging from the educational and voting systems to its banking and housing industries. What the mass rebellions brought to public attention by confronting power and domination, particularly the police violence against Blacks, is that systemic racism and capitalism's system of dispossession, exclusion, and "harrowing intersecting inequalities" must be defeated.[106]

It will not be an easy task to make change both purposeful and radical. Any call for radical change has to be systemic and must include, as Martin Luther King, Jr. once argued, a revolution of values as well a recognition that "the problems of racial injustice and economic injustice cannot be solved without a radical redistribution of political and economic power."[107] King recognized that changing values was akin to changing consciousness and that education was central to creating a mass movement of collective resistance rooted in revolutionary change rather than in a call for liberal reforms. King's politics were comprehensive and intersectional because he recognized that the "giant triplets of racism, extreme materialism, and militarism" mutually informed each other as part of a wider edifice of violence in the United States.[108] His call to "transform the jangling discords" bodes well today because it makes clear that there will be no fundamental change if the fractured and often siloed forms of oppression and the structures that support them are not brought down together.

What the mass rebellions against racial violence illustrated is that solidarity among individuals cannot be assumed and must be fought for as part of a wider struggle to break down the walls of ideological and material repression that isolate, depoliticize, and pit individuals and groups against each other. Community and a robust public sphere cannot be built on the bonds of common fears, isolation, and oppression. Authoritarian governments will work to contain both any semblance of democratic politics and any attempts at large-scale transformations of society. Power lies in more than understanding and the ability to disrupt, it also lies in a vision of a future that does not imitate the present and the courage to collectively struggle to bring a radical democratic socialist vision into fruition. The time has come not for patience, but for struggle and mass resistance—a revolutionary insurrection—against both the horrors of racism, militarism, searing inequality, police brutality, and the malignancy of a society that elevates profit over human needs.

Section IV

Thinking Beyond Plagues

The Plague of Inequality in the Age of Pandemics

I am convinced there is only one way to eliminate these grave evils [of capitalism], namely through the establishment of a socialist economy, accompanied by an educational system which would be oriented toward social goals.

Albert Einstein

Inequality under neoliberal capitalism is a cancer that functions as a form of slow violence that attacks the social fabric, the welfare state, and the body politic.[1] All the more visible, and with intensifying violence and speed as a result of the pandemic crisis, it relentlessly subjects workers, the disabled, the homeless, the poor, children, people of color, and frontline hospital and emergency workers and others considered at risk to lives of anxiety, misery, and in some cases death.[2] Many people are just one hospital bill or failed harvest away from slipping into extreme poverty. Austerity policies have become mechanisms of suffering and displacement, robbing workers of their jobs, a decent income, and nutritious food and forcing them to live from paycheck to paycheck. In some cases, people who cannot afford health care are being put in jail because of unpaid medical bills.[3] The statistics on inequality globally are scandalous. Oxfam International 2019 reports:

> [T]he world's richest 1% have more than twice as much wealth as 6.9 billion people who make up 60 percent of the planet's population. Meanwhile, around 735 million people are still living in extreme poverty … the super-rich are paying the lowest levels of taxes in decades while 10,000 people die each day because they lack access to affordable health care. In addition, over 100 million people are pushed into extreme poverty due to healthcare costs.[4]

Economic and racial inequality is not marginal to American society; it is the underlying governing structure that nourishes the medical, economic, and racial pandemics currently at work in the United States. Yet, inequality historically under neoliberal capitalism has been either largely ignored or underemphasized by the mainstream press or treated as part of the natural order.[5] Prior to the pandemic, the gap between the rich and the poor widened to dangerous levels without being seen as a major societal and political problem. For instance, in 2018, the world's 26 richest men had as much wealth as the poorest half of the world's population, some 3.8 billion people. Nearly 3 billion people, half of the world's population, live on less than $2.50 a day and "more than 1.3 billion live in extreme poverty—less than $1.25 a day."[6] In the United States, the wealthiest three billionaires – Jeff Bezos, Bill Gates, and Warren Buffett —have as much wealth as the bottom half of the U.S. population combined.[7]

In an age of increasing inequality, punishing class divisions, extreme poverty, the collapse of democratic institutions and rising death tolls, neoliberal capitalism is a specter that needs to be more fully understood and challenged. In the current historical moment, rapidly escalating levels of inequality cannot be separated from the political formations in which they are legitimated and reproduced. At the very least, neoliberalism and inequality with their historical and contemporary roots and anti-democratic and authoritarian tendencies need to be denaturalized, removed from the calculus of common sense, and challenged as a political, economic, and ideological regime of dispossession, control, and exclusion.

As the Covid-19 crisis raged out of control in the United States, it became clear that iniquitous relations of power and wealth correlate with the loss of public goods, disinvestment in essential institutions to protect public health, and the concentration of wealth in the hands of a financial elite. Under neoliberalism, economic justice and the common good are both detached from economic prosperity, and viewed with disdain. At the same time, the state is transformed into a racialized corporate regime that refuses to invest in social goods such   as public and higher education, public health systems, and hospitals, and rejects any economic model that moves more toward equality and sustainability.[8] One unfortunate result of concentrating wealth and power in the hands of the rich has been a devaluation of those scientific institutions, research programs, and medical experts that were necessary in addressing and containing the pandemic in the first place.

Referring to the Trump administration, Tim Dickinson remarked in *Rolling Stone*, "The White House's inability to track the disease as it spread across the nation crippled the government's response and led to the worst disaster this country has faced in nearly a century."[9] Moreover, as the Covid-19 plague accelerated, it made visible profound racial divides, mediated by a mix of disgust for the most vulnerable and shameless opportunism exhibited by the ruling elite. In this context, the death rate among Black Americans was triple that of whites, and essential workers bore the risk of not only death but also low wages, and inadequate, if any, health care. In the meantime, the government threw billions of dollars into "slush funds for the largest corporations."[10]

As thousands poured into the streets protesting police violence, the scourge of economic and racial inequality were highlighted as a life-threatening plague that has a long history in the United States. What initially began as a medical crisis emerged as a political and economic crisis, laying bare a menacing political disaster steeped in police violence and a punishing degree of racism. It also laid bare a health-care system that was underfunded and iniquitous, especially with respect to those populations marginalized by race and class. The pandemic may have been indiscriminate in terms of those it infected, but its effects bore down disproportionately on poor people of color proving Martin Luther King, Jr.'s' claim that "Of all the forms of inequality, injustice in health care is the most shocking and inhumane."[11] Of course, Blacks and others pushed to the fringes of society had been denied quality health care, health insurance, and adequate medical treatment. As Ed Yong observes,

Of the 3.1 million Americans who still cannot afford health insurance in states where Medicaid has not been expanded, more than half are people of color, and 30 percent are Black. This is no accident. In the decades after the Civil War, the white leaders of former slave states deliberately withheld health care from Black Americans, apportioning medicine more according to the logic of Jim Crow than Hippocrates. They built hospitals away from Black communities, segregated Black patients into separate wings, and blocked Black students from medical school. In the 20th century, they helped construct America's system of private, employer-based insurance, which has kept many Black people from receiving adequate medical treatment. They fought every attempt to improve Black people's access to health care, from the creation of Medicare and Medicaid in the 60s to the passage of the Affordable Care Act in 2010.[12]

The pandemic plague brought home with startling visibility and consequences the failure of neoliberal capitalism to provide universal health care, meaningful jobs, paid sick leave, and other economic rights that "should be considered part of our social contract, not special benefits for those who are lucky enough to be employed by companies that grant discretionary benefits."[13] It also highlighted the long legacy of racial injustice, dispossession, exclusion, and immiseration at the roots of a capitalist system marked by what David Harvey calls "the huge amount of rot beneath the surface glitter of conspicuous consumerism, indulgent individualism, and flamboyant architectural interventions … separating enclaves of wealth and privilege from the gap-toothed blocks of aging buildings and vacant lots where jobs are scarce and where life is hard and all too often short."[14] How else to explain the daily existence of millions of Americans who had to endure decaying and disabled infrastructures, underfunded and decaying schools, failing public transportation systems, water systems filled with lead, dilapidated housing, rising rates of suicide, and other deaths rooted in despair, hopelessness, and dejection? All of which amounted to zones of social abandonment fueled by a slow violence endemic to the workings of machineries of social death.[15]

Pandemic Nightmares

The pandemic has destabilized economic institutions and laid bare the ideological swindle of neoliberalism with its plague of massive inequality in wealth, power, and access. Global capitalism was severely weakened, at least temporarily. The neoliberal state failed in the face of the pandemic, exposing its fault lines, revealing its inability to protect the poor, essential workers, and the most vulnerable from disproportionate levels of risk and death. The pandemic made evident the wreckage of structural, social, and economic inequality, revealing it in all of its cruelty and effects—effects understood less as timeless conditions than as a predictable expression of a society in which wealth and the allocation of power are concentrated in relatively few hands. In what can be seen as a cruel form of political irony, the poor, homeless, incarcerated, and unemployed were viewed as a general threat to society—as possible carriers of the virus—making their status and deprivations more visible. However, this transpired less through the language of human rights than through a discourse of fear and preventive health measures.

In some cases, the pandemic brought to the surface underlying currents of immiseration and a collapse of moral values pervasive in the ideology of extreme individualism and the retreat back into the privatized space of the self. This was obvious in the growing demand on the part of many pro-Trump anti-mask, gun toting protesters to reopen the economy, against the advice of medical experts. The narratives informing these demands often took an ugly turn at many protests across the country. For instance, one Tennessee activists' sign asserted: "Sacrifice the Weak/Re-open TN."[16]

In a Chicago protest, a woman displayed a sign with a Nazi slogan. Armed far-right demonstrators rallying against social distancing in Michigan displayed swastikas and other Nazi insignia. President Trump referred to them as "very good people." This is similar to the same language he used to defend neo-Nazis and white nationalists in

Charlottesville where violence was enacted in the name of "blood and soil." He referred to the latter as "very fine people."[17] Nazi references and symbols are not alien to the Trump administration. At one point the Trump campaign used a large red triangle to criticize Antifa, a decentralized, if not loose, collection of anti-fascist activists. The symbol was used by the Nazis during the Second World War to classify political prisoners such as communists and anarchists in the concentration camps. Facebook removed the ads, stating that they violated their policy "against organized hate."[18]

What the Covid-19 plague exposed is a neoliberal narrative pushed for decades by both political parties, which argued "that illness, homelessness, poverty, and inequality are minor aberrations in an otherwise healthy society."[19] Today this narrative appears transparently false. In addition, the pandemic drew unprecedented attention to how interdependent we are on each other. In doing so, it resurrected a notion of the social that leaves little room for tolerating a society where "over 31 million are without health insurance … more than 38 million people live below the poverty line [and] 140 million are poor."[20]

The pandemic made visible the borders and walls that blocked out large parts of the working class, especially poor Blacks and Latinos who support the fundamental structures necessary for sustaining the daily life of the entire population. It revealed the shocking cruelty and apparatuses of inequality that decides which lives are worth living and which lives are designated as precarious and thus dispensable.[21] In this instance, structural inequality and corporate power were uncovered not only as an injustice, but as a real threat to human life, the planet, and democracy.

In spite of the bankruptcy of neoliberalism with its attack on public goods and social safety nets, the issue of economic inequality is still pushed to the back burner in media coverage among the mainstream press. This takes place regardless of the fact that the Trump administration in the midst of a raging pandemic could no longer cover up the failures of an economic and racial state that devastated society. These failures include the government's inability to provide adequate testing, ventilators, and protective equipment for frontline and emergency workers, largely due to its unwillingness to support a federal plan that would have provided robust investments in an equitable health-care system, a strong welfare system, and crucial social provisions. Instead, the Trump administration expanded and deepened those structural forces and policies that privilege the rich, essentially supporting the amassing of huge profits in the hands of the few over social needs.

Pandemic Pedagogy and the Politics of the Spectacle

The Covid-19 pandemic revealed the social costs of accelerating inequality over the last forty years, all the while stripping government of its civic functions and subjecting more and more people to housing shortages, discrimination, voter suppression, low-wage jobs, and the turning of cities into combat zones. The scourge of inequality is especially visible regarding the underfunding and discriminatory practices of health care, which is treated as a commodity that imposes a crippling financial burden on millions of Americans who don't have health insurance or whose insurance policies are threadbare and vastly inadequate.[22] One outcome of the pandemic uprising was the unmasking of a neoliberal ethos rooted in massive inequalities, which can no longer be explained away and were on full display in mass unemployment, record number of job losses, and a health crisis that were unprecedented in American history.

Not only has inequality become comparable to gasoline being thrown on a burning fire in the midst of the current pandemic, its unethical tactics have been used in the midst of the Covid-19 crisis to lavish privileges on the rich by transferring monumental amounts of "wealth from the bottom of the economic ladder to the top," furthering the gap between the financial elite and the poor.[23] Neoliberalism never runs away from a crisis because it relentlessly attempts to appropriate it for its own use, giving new energy to what has been called by Joseph

Schumpeter "creative destruction."[24] David Harvey captures the violent dynamic integral to creative destruction in the following comments:

> The effect of continuous innovation ... is to devalue, if not destroy, past investments and labour skills. Creative destruction is embedded within the circulation of capital itself. Innovation exacerbates instability, insecurity, and in the end, becomes the prime force pushing capitalism into periodic paroxysms of crisis ... The struggle to maintain profitability sends capitalists racing off to explore all kinds of other possibilities.[25]

In this scenario, capitalism does not use such crises to address reasons for their underlying causes and destructive effects. On the contrary, they become fodder for thinking how capitalism can invent new ways of using a crisis to its own advantage—all the time remaining "indifferent to the moral consequences of unbridled capitalism," whether it be the polluting of the atmosphere, defunding of public goods, or furthering income inequality.[26] For example, in the age of the Covid-19 pandemic, the financial and political elite used the radioactive fog of mass anxiety and fear-mongering in order to legislate reforms that in actuality served to reward themselves and further deepen the gap between the rich and the poor. This unethical and corrupt shift in policy was done not only through legislation such as the 2020 U.S. financial stimulus package but also through a pandemic pedagogy that convinced the general public of its legitimacy through a barrage of corporate and mainstream propaganda disseminated through numerous media platforms.

Parading as common sense, pandemic pedagogy attempts to persuade the general public that it is in their best interest rather than in the interest of the ruling financial elite, big corporations, investment houses, and the mammoth banks to reorganize society around gaping class and racial divisions. This double-dealing policy reveals the brutality and avarice at the heart of neoliberal capitalism. Given its greed for profits and profiteering from people suffering or dying because they are poor or considered economically unproductive, neoliberalism is an utterly destructive socio-economic system and bears the marks of a monstrous social order. Inequality sharpens the social divide and in doing so worsens class, racial, and gendered divisions.[27]

As Max Fisher writing in the *New York Times* observes, inequality and poverty in the midst of the Covid-19 pandemic exacerbates the possibility of transmission and death for everyone, but especially for those populations that traditionally have been considered disposable by virtue of their class and racial marginalization. He writes:

> As the coronavirus spreads across the globe, it appears to be setting off a devastating feedback loop with another of the gravest forces of our time: economic inequality. In societies where the virus hits, it is deepening the consequences of inequality, pushing many of the burdens onto the losers of today's polarized economies and labor markets. Research suggests that those in lower economic strata are likelier to catch the disease. They are also likelier to die from it. And, even for those who remain healthy, they are likelier to suffer loss of income or health care as a result of quarantines and other measures, potentially on a sweeping scale.[28]

It gets worse. Even as Trump's Twitter storms and incessant lying fell flat in attempting to divert the underlying failure of his administration to address the pandemic crisis, the mainstream press focused very little on the issue of deepening inequality and more on surging unemployment metrics. Trump's Tweets were ugly distortions in the pandemic wars that were both flatly untrue and dangerous. So much so that Twitter censored the most egregious tweets.[29] Surprisingly, inequality and societal class divisions were downplayed in the press in spite of the fact that inequality is crucial in analyzing both "the weakness in our health care infrastructure and social safety nets— institutions that Trump ... willfully undermined."[30] It is only recently that the mainstream media began to focus on how diverse individuals and groups both experienced the pandemic and suffered the risks and consequences differently. Anthony DiMaggio at the time provided an insightful commentary on this issue:

> We face a rapid rise in jobless claims, with various estimates suggesting unemployment reached between 16 to 20 percent by late April. But it

is not clear why it unemployment should be seen as a more important economic metric than inequality, at a time when COVID-19 is disproportionately ravaging neighborhoods populated by poor people of color, and low-pay service workers on the frontlines of the crisis … Inequality is also highly significant when considering that lower income Americans are more likely to work in jobs that require extensive contacts between individuals, whereas higher-income white-collar workers have been able to escape regular contacts with others by retreating into remote work tele-jobs that radically reduce their potential contacts with Covid-19-positive individuals.[31]

Under such circumstances, what emerged in the midst of the current pandemic crisis was not only an economic collapse but also a crisis of ideas, language, morality, and the inability of capitalist societies to solve practical, if not essential, social and economic problems. Human rights had no place in this discourse. What must be made visible is that inequality is not normal, ignorance is not innocent, power is not benign, and violence is not an abstraction. Racial and economic inequality have become visceral, stark in their damage to human bodies, minds, and sense of agency. In the age of pandemics, it is crucial to create a language that undermines neoliberalism's disimagination machines; that is, it is crucial to match our discourse around health and economic crises with discourse focused on the crisis of ideas laid bare by Covid-19.

The affliction of multiple crises is all the more reason to embrace the philosopher Jürgen Habermas's concept of the legitimation crisis, with its emphasis on exposing blockages, dysfunctions, economic downturns, and the production of a language of normalization. This is one example of a discourse of critique that offers new possibilities for analyzing inequality and injustice not merely as an economic issue but also as a pedagogical and ideological concern. I do not want to suggest that critical education is central to politics only through its ability to merely provide a rational argument or to speak truth to power. Or to suggest that the strength of argument can change the political balance of power exclusively through an appeal to interpretation, rationality, and the force of dialogue. These are important pedagogical considerations, but they do not go far enough.

Ideas are produced, legitimated, and circulated through powerful cultural apparatuses that have enormous weight in determining not only their version of the truth but the forcefulness and rationality of an argument itself. Ideas gain their merit, in part, through the institutions that produce them, and as such merit the importance of recognizing that the knowledge/power/agency connection is both a battle over ideas as well as over cultural apparatuses and institutions, and the power relations that create them.[32] In this instance, critical thinking is transformed into critical consciousness, which deals with not only the force of ideas but also the power relations that legitimate them and the task of understanding "how knowledge is related to the power of self-definition."[33] Matters of critique now merge with the imperative of actions bringing together not merely critical ideas and balanced judgment, but theory and informed action.

The Swindle of Individual Responsibility and the Politics of Disposability

In the midst of the Covid-19 pandemic, the face of inequality became more visible as the American public was bombarded by shocking images of long food lines, the stacking of dead bodies, long lines of refrigerated trucks symbolizing the plague of death, desperate individuals and families applying for unemployment benefits, hospital workers putting their lives on the line (and in some cases dying), and warnings to stay away from others for fear of catching the virus. What this pandemic revealed in all its ugliness are the lethal mechanisms of systemic inequality, deregulation, the dismantling of the welfare state and the growing dangerous assault on the environment. Beneath the massive failure of leadership from the Trump administration was the sordid history of concentrated power in the hands of the 1 percent, brazen corporate welfare, political corruption, and the merging of big money and politics. This apparatus of repression functions to deny those most vulnerable access to health care, a living wage, worker protection, and the development of a strong labor movements capable of challenging corporate power, as well as the cruelty of austerity and right-wing policies that maim and kill hundreds of thousands, as was evident in the effects of the pandemic.

The brutality of neoliberal capitalism and its reproduction of iniquitous relations of wealth and power were openly defended in the call to reopen the economy by restricting or eliminating protective measures that would slow the pace of the virus. Once again, most at risk were those populations who were considered disposable, such as people of color, undocumented immigrants, the poor, the elderly, and the working class. Inequality made a mockery of social distancing, especially for health-care workers who lacked adequate protective gear, and even more so for migrants, the elderly, the poor, and those mostly people of color incarcerated in prisons, jails, and detention centers, who lacked any form of protection or adequate medical services.

Vulnerable populations were held hostage to policies that failed to protect them while simultaneously being told to sacrifice their lives in the interest of filling the financial coffers and ideological waste bins of the corporate elite and the political zombies that rule the United States. How else to explain that Senate Republicans wanted to cut an extension of emergency unemployment supplement benefits under the CARES Act from $600 to $200 a week on the grounds that the absurdly low $600 a week was a disincentive to work. It was not as if there were plenty of jobs available in a deep economic recession; and if there were such jobs, many of them were dangerous to perform. These would include jobs such as driving a bus, working in a meatpacking plant, or teaching in a public school. This was a form of zombie politics, with the morally dead punishing America's unemployed.

Each day, the grim numbers indexing infections and deaths are accompanied by the call to wash hands, wear masks, and practice social distancing. These are crucial medical practices, but they collapse matters of power, politics, and class differences into an individualized and personalized script, one that mimics a neoliberal ethos. For instance, while the call for lockdowns seemed reasonable in the midst of the Covid-19 crisis, there was often little understanding of how such practices affected the stark realities of inequality. Shalmali Guttal is quite perceptive on this issue and writes:

> Inequalities also determine whose interests shape the responses to the pandemic. The most common response by many governments has been to impose lockdowns that severely restrict the movement of people and goods, curtail service provision, and practically halt economic activity, including food production, storage, and distribution, but without the required testing, tracing, and treatment, and little or no support for those who do not have homes where they can distance (or even shelter from weather and pollution) and for whom the loss of daily income leads to hunger. Across Asia, millions of informal sector, agricultural, and construction workers are stranded without incomes, shelter, food, water, and healthcare. Restrictions on movement, closure of local markets, absence of credit, etc., have hit small-scale food producers hard, setting the stage for food shortages and food price hikes.[34]

What was also forgotten in this medical narrative was how the pandemic of inequality demanded a much more comprehensive view of global politics and its relationship to the then raging Covid-19 crisis. Crucial here is the need to prioritize both public health and social justice for everyone and not just those in the developed world caught in the eye of the viral storm. For instance, UNICEF noted that "one in three people in the world do not have access to clean water and that more than 300 million Africans do not have running water. The pandemic is devastating the world's poor, even before the coronavirus has fully affected them."[35] Little was said either by politicians or the mainstream media on how the pandemic might affect children already suffering from mass starvation. Four United Nations agencies in 2020 warned that with the impact of Covid-19 on food production the 140,000 children on the brink of starvation could rise to 270,000 million.

The global plague amplified the misery produced by inequality, a politics driven by the rule of big money, and the production of modes of agency fit for a dystopian science-fiction film. The plague is a form of zombie politics, which is an avatar for death and cruelty and the production of the walking dead among the financial elite who suck the life out of the common good, public values, and democracy itself. Moreover, the Covid-19 pandemic amplified matters of uncertainty, existential anxiety, and the ever-present fear of death. Such sentiments not only invoked a new understanding of how we are all connected but also what it means to embrace public health as a public good, and the terrible cost its absence inflicts on individuals reduced to the sheer task of survival.

The mutually dependent notions of social justice and equality need to be rethought through a broader understanding of the commons and what we should share as essential services and resources in a robust socialist democracy. In addition, this has to be done in a political framework that refuses to bail out neoliberal institutional, political, and economic structures controlled by the financial elite and big corporations. The language of neoliberalism is exhausted and should be considered the enemy of democracy and economic justice, particularly as it plays out as form of "racial capitalism" and fascist politics.[36] David Harvey is right, "capital is the problem, not the solution."[37]

Tales of a Failed State

In Trump's America, no spaces were left untouched by neoliberal capitalism with its financialization and commercialization of everything from social services and education to public transportation. The pandemic revealed the toxic underside of neoliberal capitalism with its assault on the welfare state, its undermining of public health, its attack on workers' rights, and its affirmation of the economy and the accumulation of capital over human needs and life itself. The coronavirus pandemic and the pandemic of inequality called into question the false and dangerous neoliberal notion that all problems are a matter of character and personal choices.

The global pandemic shattered once and for all the notion that private troubles cannot be translated into larger systemic considerations.

Curtis Bradford of San Francisco, testifying at a virtual social justice assembly sponsored by the Poor People's Campaign, spoke movingly, with his own personal statement, on the notion that poverty was a systemic rather than an individual problem: "The war on the poor in this country seeks to blame the poor people for their circumstances. It wanted me to believe that I was the problem. I'm still here despite the odds, and I no longer buy into the narrative that poverty is my fault."[38]

There are many lessons to be learned from a crisis that has revealed the barbarism of neoliberal capitalism and a governing regime insensitive to human rights and human needs. First and foremost the intersecting inequalities that propagate capitalism as an economic and ideological system must be made visible and challenged. Second, we must learn from the history that created the conditions that made the pandemic and Trump's presidency even imaginable. Thirdly, we must rethink both politics and the future we want.

Neoliberal capitalism has created a society in which markets act without ethical restraints, enshrine an "unembarrassed opportunism" as part of the laws of nature, and subordinate everything to a cost-benefit analysis.[39] Workers' real wages have declined for decades and have done so in proportion to the growing sense of outrage and anger that have fueled right-wing populist movements and the rise of authoritarians such as Trump. Neoliberalism has unleashed a wave of fear and insecurity that runs the risk of further depoliticizing individuals caught in the paralyzing grip of trying to survive.

The neoliberal pandemic of economic and racial inequality was and is a form of organized looting conducted by the corporate and ruling elite and is the fundamental problem in denying millions of people the most basic human needs and political and social rights. In this merging of capitalism and inequality, justice and compassion disappear. As does the legitimacy of a predatory capitalism system, one that fails to provide quality education, universal health care, decent jobs, a living wage, and a viable social contract. Social and economic inequality has become a form of organized state violence that nourishes the seeds of racial cleansing, white supremacy, militarism, and culture of cruelty. It is all the more dangerous since it is part of a social order that combines a brutalizing economic system, a machinery of racial purity and cleansing, and an updated form of fascist politics. Under Trump, neoliberal savagery was vastly intensified as the drive for profits existed in equal measure to the denigration of human life. Thom Hartmann captures the cruelty of Trump's administration, referring to it as a death cult and pointing to a number of death-dealing policies endorsed by him and his acolytes which caused enormous suffering and pain. He writes:

> They revel in their efforts to end Obamacare and cut millions of Americans off healthcare. They celebrate last night's resumption of federal executions. They enthusiastically authorize the use of formerly banned pesticides that cause cancer and neurological damage to children. Trump's first official action was to allow coal and oil companies to dump more waste in our rivers, poisoning people downstream. As children were being slaughtered in classrooms across America, Trump doubled down on supporting the NRA. Numerous children have died in U.S. detention facilities, yet they continue to give millions of dollars to Trump's contributor corporations to continue holding these children in deplorable, disgusting conditions. The Republicans in Congress are fighting all efforts to extend more unemployment relief to American families, further stressing out people in ways that inevitably, history tells us, lead to domestic violence and suicide.[40]

The neoliberal engine of grotesque inequality attempts to turn everyone into a form of human capital, produces punishing class divisions, commercializes all human relations, and obliterates the conditions for democracy. Moreover, it functions as a form of domestic terrorism, raining potential death on the 18.2 million who lack adequate health insurance or income to seek treatment when sick, having made them more susceptible to the worst effects of Covid-19.[41] Inequality has become synonymous with the politics of disposability, terminal exclusion, racism, and police violence. It is the thread that links class divisions, racism, and disproportionate deaths suffered by people of color from Covid-19. Inequality runs through and shapes every institution in American life and cannot be separated from an updated form of capitalism that is more and more organized on fascist principles and a lethal anti-democratic politics.[42]

The Abyss of Fascist Politics

Soaring inequality in the United States has brought to the surface of politics the raw realities of an updated form of fascism. This was particularly true under the Trump administration where shocking levels of economic inequality and draconian austerity policies conjoined with fascist ideals.[43] This unprecedented convergence included: a disdain for human rights, a rampant anti-intellectualism, a populist celebration of white nationalism,[44] the cult of leadership, the protection of corporate power, the elevation of emotion over reason, rampant cronyism, a disdain for dissent and intellectuals, and the "more or less explicit endorsement of violence against political enemies."[45] Massive inequality allowed the ruling elite to colonize the media, marshaling their power to trade in the incendiary rhetoric of fear, divisiveness, and demonization, while using language to inflame violence and weaponize the primary tools of communication.

Under the Trump administration, fantasies of authoritarian control coupled with a ruthless appropriation of power were fed by an iniquitous political system interlaced with white nationalism, racism, and class divisions. How else to explain a president who refused to criticize violent acts produced by white supremacists, called peaceful demonstrators protesting systemic racism domestic terrorists, and refused to change the names of ten U.S. Army bases, all in Southern states, "named after Confederate generals who fought for slave-holding states in the Civil War?"[46] Moreover, Trump defended Confederate monuments, memorials, and statues by condemning their removal and setting up a task force in the Department of Homeland Security to protect what he termed without irony "our historic landmarks." Kristen Holmes and Geneva Sands reported in *CNN Politics* that "Trump personally instructed Interior Secretary David Bernhardt to restore the only Confederate statue in Washington, DC, after it was torn down last week."[47] Surely, such a move provided another example of Trump's white supremacist values.

As has been well documented, the major terrorist threat to the U.S. does not come from protesters turning their attention to symbols and monuments glorifying slavery, but from white supremacists and right-wing extremists. Trump's embrace of right-wing extremism was further exemplified when he instructed the Department of Homeland Security to disband its unit focusing "on domestic terrorism and white supremacist groups."[48] As the United States fell deeper into the abyss of a fascist politics, Trump presented himself as the defender of the losers, those slavery advocates who lost the Civil War. On the other hand, he returned the brutal logic represented in the film *Wall Street* in which triumphant greed is celebrated as a national virtue and power is reduced to a corporate value. The latter was evident in Trump's massive tax cuts for the wealthy and big corporations, the roll back of environmental regulations, the defunding of public goods, and the dismantling of social provisions, together amounting to full-fledged attack on what remained of the welfare state.

The endpoint of the scourge of racial and economic inequality can be seen not only in an administration that embraced white supremacy and ultra-nationalism but also in the massive deprivations and misery endured by those at the bottom of the economic ladder. It was also present in the form of a president and Republican Party that viewed without apology the organization of the American state on fascist principles.[49] What other interpretation can explain Trump's warning that he would use U.S. military force to crush protesters calling for the end of police violence and systemic racism, while threatening them with "vicious dogs" and "Ominous Weapons"?[50]

As massive numbers of people were in the streets speaking out, Trump declared that he would deploy the National Guard "in sufficient numbers that we dominate the streets."[51] In a phone call with governors, he told them, "You have to dominate [and if you don't] you're going to look like a bunch of jerks." His consigliere and enforcer Bill Barr parroted Trump's false claim that Antifa represented a well-organized group leading the movement protesting police violence and tearing down statues celebrating Confederate criminals. Trump appeared to be surrounded by what Adam Weinstein in the *New Republic* called "violence addicts" who wanted to put the U.S. on a war footing in order to squash demonstrators. He argued that politicians such as Donald Trump, Bill Barr, Tom Cotton, the war-crazed senator from Arkansas, and the border patrol all appeared to speak to the Republican base with the well-received message: "Join the fascist party. We're winning."[52]

Trump's fascist principles were quite evident in displays of political opportunism in which he flaunted the dangers of Covid-19 in order to speak to large crowds that, in the midst of a pandemic, ran the risk of large numbers of people being infected and possibly dying. He defied health guidelines and endangered others even after he contracted the virus. He tried to force the governors of the states to open public schools in spite of the warnings by health officials that such a move could endanger the lives of children. Health experts agreed that opening schools in poor districts or in communities that have high rates of community transmission represents a moral and medical catastrophe waiting to happen. Not only are Trump's Vichy Republicans willing to sacrifice the lives of children to bolster his re-election campaign, they have refused to provide the necessary funds needed to implement base-line safety requirements and equipment. This would include, at the very least, updated air ventilation systems, proper disinfectants, testing options, money to hold double sessions, more support staff, and school construction to ensure proper classroom spacing. White House Press Secretary Kayleigh McEnany, speaking to reporters, stated that even if studies indicated that it was unsafe to open schools, "science should not stand in the way" of opening schools, in spite of the fact that Covid-19 infection rates were reaching record levels in a number of U.S. states.[53]

Deploying troops against demonstrators who are exercising their first amendment rights represents another example of Trump's disregard for the law and constitutional rights, particularly when such actions polled favorably for his re-election. As I noted earlier, Trump first endangered the lives of protesters in Lafayette Square outside of the White House so he could have a clear path to hold up a Bible for a photo op aimed at his base. Later he would issue threats and use federal troops again in Portland to make it clear that he would militarize American cities to crush the ongoing protests against police violence.[54] In the end, this was a losing strategy.

This is more than fascist agitprop. What this militarized action suggests is that fascism and its brutalizing logics are never entirely interred in the past, and that the conditions that produce its central elements are with us once again, ushering in a period of modern barbarity that appears to be reaching towards homicidal extremes.[55] Trump's infatuation with dictators, his attack on civil rights, his concentration of executive power, expansion of the military budget, and ultra-nationalism have little to do with a democracy and a great deal to do with providing a snapshot of a society that has tumbled into the abyss of fascism. As I have stressed in *The Terror of the Unforeseen* and *American Nightmare: Facing the Challenge of Fascism*, there may be no perfect fit between Trump and the fascist societies of Mussolini, Hitler, and Pinochet, but the basic tenets of hyper-nationalism, pervasive racism, misogyny, and disgust with the rule of law suggest that "the essential message is the same."[56] Fascism is often an incoherent set of assumptions combined with anti-intellectualism, ultra-nationalism, and a demonizing rhetoric aimed at a group singled out as different and underserving of human rights. It is worth repeating. Fascism does not operate according to an inflexible script. On the contrary, it is adaptive, and its mobilizing furors are mediated through local symbols, as it normalizes itself through a country's customs and daily rituals. Sarah Churchill in reference to the United States makes a strong case about how American fascism would "deploy American symbols and American slogans" so it would not seem alien to the American public.[57] What we saw with Donald Trump were these symbols emerging from the highest offices of government and emblazoned, however haphazardly, across the American landscape.

Fascism is often the endpoint for democracy in a state of terminal crisis; and inequality is its breeding ground. The workings of finance capital with its relentless attack on the welfare state, people of color, the social contract, poor youth, and the public good have made visible the presence of an undisguised fascism at the center of political power. Consistent with this fascist ethos is a soaring inequality that feeds the political premise that some people are disposable, their lives not valued, and their existence a liability, particularly for a racist elite motivated by the search for profits and accumulated capital. Under such circumstances, the elderly, disabled, undocumented immigrants, and people of color, among others, are objects of a near sociopathic disdain by those who drive the machineries of class divisions, racial inequality, mass incarceration, and terminal exclusion in a society saturated with violence and death.

Until the Covid-19 pandemic and ensuing rebellion over George Floyd's murder, these populations were viewed by most of the American public as unspeakable, unknowable, not worthy of narration, agency, and dignity. What has come to light as a result of the pandemics is both the value of essential workers and a newfound awareness of the often hidden-zones of social abandonment they inhabit. The Covid-19 pandemic and the pandemic of police violence are now undeniably viewed through the machineries of social and economic inequality that produce brutalizing structures of racial violence. The lethal nature of such inequality is often legitimated in the false discourses and liberal appeals to meritocracy and the meritocratic myth of picking oneself up by the bootstraps.

Below this erasure of systemic inequality lies a malignant culture of cruelty, unchecked privilege, a dystopian model of disposability and the dark echo of a fascist past. The Trump administration reinforced a serious history lesson by proving that fascism never goes away, but is always just beneath the surface of society and can erupt at any time.

Donald Trump is a symptom of America's long descent into racial and economic injustice, and as such manifested the deep, lingering rot of a society rooted in white supremacy and class privilege, which his administration wore like a badge of honor. The plague will be with us for some time and its presence proves once again that resistance is not an option but a necessity.

Conclusion: Thinking Beyond
a Covid-19 World

Ordinary people with extraordinary vision can redeem the soul of
America by getting in what I call good trouble, necessary trouble.

John Lewis

The Covid-19 pandemic, which spread rapidly across the globe on March 2020, unleashed both a dystopian nightmare and the opportunity to rethink matters of politics ethics, power, and social change. In the first instance, the struggle to contain the virus ushered in a profound re-examination of globalization, racism, inequality, militarism, and ultra-nationalism. Matters of life and death were examined within a broader economic, social, and political context. The bodies of individuals dying in escalating numbers were connected to a political and ecological body that was gasping to breathe. The debates over public health were expanded to include a broader dialogue over the welfare state and the merging of political, personal, and economic rights. Body counts were connected increasingly not only to a virulent virus but also to various forms of state violence. Matters of life and death, and issues concerning whose lives were valued and whose were not were examined through the interrelated registers of class, race, gender, and other political categories. Previous zones of disposability and spaces of terminal exclusions could no longer be ignored because they not only carried within them the fear of spreading the virus but also served as symbols of a failing state and a brutalizing capitalist system.

The social sphere once again proved crucial to maintaining not just public health but democracy itself. Reducing politics to the realm of the personal now seemed as absurd as privatizing health care. Inequality, often cloaked in the scandalous narratives of free choice, deregulation, and privatization, proved to be a paralyzing force in providing the most essential tools to fight Covid-19—from testing and ventilators to hospital beds and personal protective equipment. The need for science, evidence, and transparency in both the medical and the political spheres became more obvious in order to challenge the fact-denying populism of authoritarians such as President Trump, Brazilian President Jair Bolsonaro, and other hard-right nationalists. Refusing to acknowledge scientific evidence, the right-wing authoritarians waged a war against their own scientists, domestic rivals, and chief medical officers. They also waged a culture war against foreign powers such as China, employing racial slurs, in their dastardly attempts at diversion and political opportunism. And in doing so they sacrificed thousands of lives.

Solidarity, compassion, international cooperation, and the recognition that we are all connected, though in vastly different ways, gained a new resurgence within the public imagination and among diverse groups fighting for economic justice and popular sovereignty. The correlation between failed democracies and the rise of right-wing extremism, populism, and updated forms of fascism became more obvious. The pathogens carried by a deadly virus could no longer be separated from the political and economic pathogens that fuel an updated version of neoliberal fascism. What became increasingly clear, especially among young people and people of color, is that hope for humanity does not lie in a future that mimics the present, especially a present that reproduces massive inequality, exploitation, ecological destruction, war, colonization, and commodification of everyday life.[1] The stark realities of diverse forms of oppression and domination have become more visible and were and still are being challenged in streets all over the globe. Education has once again become a crucial element of politics rooted in a vision that is infused and energized with a new sense of hope and collective struggle.

Any movement for change will need a new vision and political framework to contest the rise of neoliberal fascism in the United States and across the globe. Central to such a task is the recognition that democracy and capitalism are not synonymous. Moreover, any call for institutional and structural transformation must "plot the creation of more democratic and socially just [institutions], animated by a different political economy and a different structure of social relations."[2] Crucial to such a project is the recognition that capitalist market relations based on profit maximization are tragically unequal to the challenge of addressing major social problems that include soaring poverty, spiraling inequality, ecological devastation, injurious forms of deregulation, mounting homelessness, food insecurity, and public safety.[3]

Also central to such a recognition is the need to challenge "the dominant notion of who the agents of change should be," emphasizing that they should be "those most impacted by injustice."[4] Under neoliberal capitalism and the rise of a fascist politics, the agents of change must include working people, immigrants, poor people of color, marginalized young people suffering under debt and in the paralyzing grip of austerity measures, as well as those populations considered disposable, marginalized by class, race, ethnicity, and religion. There are no automatic agents of radical change, nor can such agents emerge exclusively from within single-issue movements. No individual or group automatically offers political guarantees. Agency is an educational and political issue and has to be developed through the hard work of the merging of consciousness raising and meaningful activism.

The urgency of building solidarity among different groups cannot be overestimated. Moreover, this call for unity must be developed as part of a mass international force that can address the interrelated issues of economic inequality, racism, war, peace, and militarization, among other issues.[5] Fundamental change does not privilege one specific group, though it should exclude those in dominant positions of power from taking the lead in any radical movement against injustice, inequality, and the brutalizing machinery of neoliberal capitalism. The agents of change should be all those individuals and groups willing to fight for a more just world, and in doing so be willing to exercise the civic courage and willpower to join with others in a massive show of collective resistance that unites people with different skills, actions, and capacities. Agency in the assistance of justice and emancipation does not come easily to the oppressed or anyone else and must take the issue of education, popular consciousness, and critical pedagogy seriously.

The fight over education must include the important pedagogical work of producing a shift in consciousness that is capable of providing the knowledge, skills, and capacities that enable people to speak, write, and act from a position of empowerment. This means that educators, activists, and public intellectuals must produce narratives in which people can recognize their problems, learn how to translate private issues into larger systemic contexts, and identify with issues that will enhance their capacities to think critically and act meaningfully. This means disrupting the normalizing plague of common sense and unsettling strategies of domination and depoliticization. This suggests changing established rules of understanding and recognition in order to make visible a corrupt social order so that its multiple and interrelated forms of injustice can be resisted and changed. Making power relations visible entails both a language of critique and hope. Without hope there is no viable sense of agency and without agency there is no sense of vision for a better future. Moreover, it is crucial to recognize the threads that run through diverse injustices so that alliances can be formed that give power to the development of a mass movement in the fight for a democratic socialist society.

Within this moment of uncertainty and change, the time has come for new political formations and mass displays of civic courage to resist and change a script that legitimates police violence, military surveillance operations, and the militarization of everyday life. Young people who have and continue to march in the streets and challenge the long history of deeply rooted inequality, racism, and state violence are both criticizing established relations of power and acting on their belief that change is possible. In doing so, they have raised new hope in the struggle to establish a democratic socialist world. The generation driving this global rebellion refuses to have their future cancelled out and to be written out of the script of democracy. They are not only refusing to look away from multiple forces of oppression, they have embraced Martin Luther King Jr.'s warning that "He who accepts evil without protesting against it is really cooperating with it."[6] In that sense, they are part of a new awakening, one that embodies a spirit of revolt and struggle that is motivated by the call for radical change. Such change must address the false equation between democracy and capitalism, and in doing so reclaim and rethink the interconnection between racism and class injustice, on the one hand, and politics and inequality on the other.

Neoliberal capitalism has morphed into pandemic of ugliness and mass suffering, and has spawned a regime of disgraced fake leaders. The entire United States is now shaped by the malignant rot of racism, class discrimination, and unchecked bigotry. Only by recognizing these interrelated elements of oppression as part of a broader politics of neoliberal fascism can mass protest be transformed into movements for real ideological and structural change. The call for radical change in the streets is matched by the spread of anti-Black white supremacy in the realms of governing and diverse online platforms, and print media across the globe. To fight this plague of neoliberal fascism and economic domination, a radical understanding of politics has to think in terms that are interrelated, comprehensive, systemic, and intersectional. Only then will a mass movement for radical change be able to reveal "the propagation of capitalism as a system of harrowing, intersecting inequalities, manifest globally and locally, for the benefit of the privileged."[7]

The major challenge for the success of a mass international movement is the task of bringing together emancipatory social movements and change agents from members of the working class and young people to the numerous groups fighting diverse forms of oppression. What is needed is a thread to hold such groups together in new forms of alignment that translate into an international movement for building a socialist democracy. Such a movement will only be successful if it dismantles a class and racist system that is organized around the twin pillars of iniquitous wealth, income, and power, on the one hand, and the virulent ideology of racial cleansing and a politics of disposability on the other. Capitalism in its updated neoliberal fascist forms is the most dangerous plague the world now faces. Any collective movement for equality and justice needs a new vision, language, and politics. This is a time to rethink the meaning of agency, popular sovereignty, and what a socialist democracy would look like. As Shalmali Guttal eloquently puts it, it is crucial to rethink what politics means for rebuilding a post-Covid-19 world.

> This is a time when we, as the public, can and must develop and socialize our proposals for rebuilding strong public infrastructure and systems for public health, goods, services, social protection, human rights, and democracy, with special provisions for the most vulnerable: the precariat, migrant workers, small-scale food producers, indigenous peoples, and, among all these, women, who are usually the primary care providers. This is a time when we can start to transform our societies and countries toward equality, justice, and universal realization of human rights by building solidarity, economic and political systems from the ground up.[8]

As theorists such as Angela Davis, Robin D.G. Kelley, and Cedric Robinson have argued, capitalism has been racialized and cannot be abstracted from an emancipatory notion of political struggle. In other words, capitalism is racial capitalism. What is crucial at this important historical conjuncture is the willingness on the part of social movements to develop a notion of popular education and critical pedagogy "which will allow people to understand the interconnections of racism, heteropatriarchy, capitalism."[9]

The ugly connection between racism and capitalism and its updated versions of white supremacy in America cannot be abstracted from system of neoliberal fascism that is criminogenic in its production of human misery, exploitation, exclusion, and death. Any viable notion of social transformation needs also to connect with international struggles as a way of making visible other forms of resistance while recognizing that the nation state is not the only site of power and reform, especially given the need to develop a revolutionary global agenda.[10] There is also the need to reimagine the connection between freedom, agency, and justice. Freedom has to be understood as the freedom to participate in and shape society rather than being removed from it. This notion of freedom to become operative cannot be privatized or reduced to a simple championing of the individual over the social sphere. Nor can it be removed from the dual notions of ethical and social responsibility. Freedom must be grounded in not only political and personal rights but also economic rights. The fight for economic and racial justice cannot take place without extending the notion of freedom to economic rights. Personal and political rights are crucial but mean little when one's sense of agency is limited to the fight for daily survival. Economic or social rights are central to any viable notion of agency and citizenship rights.

As the Poor Peoples Campaign in the United States argues, such rights can take the form of strengthening unions, "protecting and expanding the right to vote, ending mass incarceration, honoring Indigenous rights, canceling student and medical debt, protecting and expanding Social Security, enacting a federal jobs program, protecting the right to unionize, and establishing universal healthcare."[11] There is also a need to create the public goods and social spaces that generate new forms of solidarity and institutions that expand the possibility for valuable knowledge, critical thinking, and new social relations. Michelle Alexander is right in claiming that "Our only hope for our collective liberation is a politics of deep solidarity."[12]

Inclusion is not just a matter of upholding civil and human rights; it is also central to a movement for radical change. This issue has not been lost on young people fighting to create a democratic socialist society. The protesters are multiracial, conscious of the hypocrisy and deceit at the heart of neoliberal society with its gaping inequities in wealth, power, and access, and they appear fully conscious of the need for radical change. They are not simply protesting the killing of George Floyd, nor are they exclusively denouncing police violence, however brutal and symbolic. They are revolting against the entire infrastructure of injustice that runs through American society and the often-erased memories and outcomes of the long legacy of racial violence at the core of American history. At the heart of this movement is the belief that American society is both corrupt and unjust and that it can be changed. A number of principles seem to have guided the intensity of this movement, principles that are crucial for it to develop further into a revolutionary and emancipatory force. The value of historical memory as a tool of knowledge and resistance is a central feature of the new rebellion.

Questions regarding historical memory and moral witnessing suggest that the current violence in American society has a long history of resistance that needs to be resuscitated, critically engaged, and gleaned. This unpacking of history is crucial for its ability to contribute to a class and racialized politics that is comprehensive in its understanding of politics and power and redemptive in its ability to incorporate and move beyond acts of moral witnessing. Historical context matters because it offers important traces, fragments from the past that inform the present, illuminate what is new, and provide insights into imagining alternative forms of social life, solidarity, and the possibility of new political formations.

We still have the opportunity to reimagine a world in which the future does not mimic the predatory neoliberal present. What is crucial to remember is that no democracy can survive without an enlightened citizenry. Moreover, solidarity among individuals cannot be assumed and must be fought for as part of a wider struggle to break down the ideologies and modes of pedagogical repression that isolate, depoliticize, and pit individuals and groups against each other. Community and a robust public sphere cannot be built on the bonds of shared fears and the discourse of bigotry and hatred. At the same time, what cannot be forgotten is that power lies in more than understanding and the ability to disrupt the status quo—-it also lies in a radical vision of the future coupled with the courage to struggle collectively to bring into being a new society.

Such a world would erase the massive gap between rich and poor, the deserving and undeserving. At stake here, at the very least, is the need to produce new forms of global solidarity, especially with reference to the creation of a democratic global health structure and network. This should be a world that brings together the struggles for justice, emancipation, and social equality. More urgent than ever is the need to struggle for a world that imagines and acts on the utopian promises of a just and democratic socialist society.

We live in an era in which elements of a fascist politics have reemerged in new and deadly forms. The crisis we face today far exceeds any one issue such as police violence, poverty, or racism. We face a form of capitalism that is as barbaric as it is lethal. The expression "I can't breathe" refers to numerous Blacks who have been the subject of police violence throughout history, though it might refer to all the victims of a surging neoliberal fascism that marks out the "death zones of humanity" on a global scale.[13] If Pablo Picasso's painting *Guernica* was appropriated as an early twentieth-century symbol of fascist terror, the words "I can't breathe" have become the twenty-first-century symbol of mass terror, just as the emergence in the United States of refrigerated trucks serving as mass graves speaks to the amplification of capitalism's ruthless logic of disposability in a time of crisis.

Though it remains to be seen, the spirit of revolt that grew in the U.S. and a host of other countries in 2020 suggests that we witnessed more than mass protests and a series of short-lived demonstrations. A new political horizon opened up that points to a growing rebellion against the lethal merging of racism, class divisions, and the punishing registers of inequality. The failed state has lost its oxygen and is on life support. Hopefully, the growing rebellion will breathe new life into a transformed social order, forged within the crucible of a radical demand that democracy finally fulfills its promises and ideals.

Democracy needs a vision. The election of Joe Biden as President of the United States ends the reign of Trump's fascist politics. Yet, a central question remains regarding what were the forces that purged America of its democratic ideals and norms, however weak, allowing Donald Trump to become the president. The ghosts of fascism may have been pushed back in the shadows but they have not disappeared.

Notes

Preface

1   Ed Yong, "How the Pandemic Defeated America," *The Atlantic* (August 3, 2020). Online: https://www.theatlantic.com/magazine/archive/2020/09/coronavirus-american-failure/614191/

2   Kamalakar Duvvuru, "Is India Displaying Signs of Neo-Fascism?," *Countercurrents.org* (July 29, 2019). Online: https://countercurrents.org/2019/07/is-india-displaying-signs-of-neo-fascism/#_ednref29

3   Angela Y. Davis, *Abolition Democracy* (New York: Seven Stories Press, 2005), pp. 90–91.

4   Cynthia Haven, "'Historical Consciousness' Can Be Double-Edged Sword, Historian Says," *Stanford News* (February 25, 2009). Online: https://news.stanford.edu/news/2009/february25/james-campbell-history-022509.html

5   Amy Goodman, "Angela Davis on Abolition, Calls to Defund Police, Toppled Racist Statues & Voting in 2020 Election," *Democracy Now* (July 3, 2020). Online: https://www.democracynow.org/2020/7/3/angela_davis_on_abolition_calls_to

6   Andrew Gawthorpe, "Trump is Unleashing Authoritarianism on US Cities— Just in Time for the Election," *Guardian* (July 23, 2020). Online: https://www.theguardian.com/commentisfree/2020/jul/23/trump-authoritarianism-portland-cbp-election

7   Frank Bruni, "So This Is Your Idea of Freedom," *The New York Times* (July 22, 2020). Online: https://static.nytimes.com/email-content/FB_sample.html?action=click&module=nl-index-see-the-latest

8   John Keane, "Democracy and the Great Pestilence," *Institute for Human Science* (April 10, 2020). Online: https://www.iwm.at/closedbutacitve/corona-focus/john-keanedemocracy-and-the-great-pestilence/

Chapter 1

1   See, for instance, Julia Lynch, *Regimes of Inequality: The Political Economy of Health and Wealth* (London: Cambridge University Press,

2020); Thomas Piketty, *The Economics of Inequality* (New York: Belknap Press, 2015); Paul Farmer, *Infections and Inequalities: The Modern Plagues*, updated edition with a new preface (Berkeley: University of California Press, 2001).

2　Henry A. Giroux, *The Terror of the Unforeseen* (Los Angeles: LARB Books, 2019).

3　Bram Ieven and Jan Overwijk, "We Created This Beast," *Eurozine* (March 23, 2020). Online: https://www.eurozine.com/we-created-this-beast/

4　Henry A. Giroux, *Against the Terror of Neoliberalism* (New York: Routledge, 2008); Nancy Fraser, *The Old is Dying and the New Cannot Be Born: From Progressive Neoliberalism to Trump and Beyond* (New York: Verso, 2019).

5　Ieven and Overwijk, "We Created This Beast."

6　Jill Lepore, "A Golden Age for Dystopian Fiction," *New Yorker* (May 29, 2017). Online: https://www.newyorker.com/magazine/2017/06/05/a-golden-age-for-dystopian-fiction

7　Pankaj Mishra, "Get Ready, a Bigger Disruption is Coming," *Bloomberg Opinion* (March 16, 2020). Online: https://www.bloomberg.com/opinion/articles/2020-03-16/coronavirus-foreshadow-s-bigger-disruptions-in-future

8　Mark Fisher, *Capitalist Realism: Is There No Alternative?* (Winchester, UK: Zero Books, 2009), p. 12.

9　Lefen and Overwijk, "We Created This Beast."

10　Henry A. Giroux, *Neoliberalism's War on Higher Education*, 2nd edition (Chicago: Haymarket Books, 2019).

11　Glenn Kessler, Salvador Rizzo, and Meg Kelly, "President Trump Has Made 15,413 False or Misleading Claims Over 1,055 Days," *Washington Post* (December 16, 2019). Online: https://www.washingtonpost.com/politics/2019/12/16/president-trump-has-made-false-or-misleading-claims-over-days/; Harry Stevens and Shelly Tan, "From 'It's going to disappear' to 'WE WILL WIN THIS WAR' How the President's Response to the Coronavirus Has Changed Since January," *Washington Post* (March 31, 2020). Online: https://www.washingtonpost.com/graphics/2020/politics/trump-coronavirus-statements/?utm_campaign=wp_to_your_health&utm_medium=email&utm_source=newsletter&wpisrc=nl_tyh&wpmk=1

12   Christian Stöcker, "Conspiracy Theories in the Age of COVID-19," *Der Spiegel International* (March 17, 2020). Online: https://www.spiegel.de/international/germany/conspiracy-theories-in-the-age-of-Covid-19-a-86ed07e7-7009-405c-a1c7-58e83f6ab790

13   Bill Quigley, "Six Quick Points about Coronavirus and Poverty in the US," *CounterPunch* (March 12, 2020). Online: https://www.counterpunch.org/2020/03/12/six-quick-points-about-coronavirus-and-poverty-in-the-us/

14   Amy Kapczynski and Gregg Gonsalves, "Alone against the Virus," *Boston Review* (March 12, 2020). Online: http://bostonreview.net/class-inequality-science-nature/amy-kapczynski-gregg-gonsalves-alone-against-virus?utm_source=Boston+Review+Email+Subscribers&utm_campaign=53eec847f3-MC_Newsletter_3_11_20_COPY_01&utm_medium=email&utm_term=0_2cb428c5ad-53eec847f3-41081485&mc_cid=53eec847f3&mc_eid=15b082ac54

15   Min Li Chan, "Public Matters," *The Point Magazine* (April 20, 2020). Online: https://thepointmag.com/quarantine-journal/#public-matters

16   Wendy Sawyer and Peter Wagner, "Mass Incarceration: The Whole Pie 2020," *Prison Policy Initiative* (March 24, 2020). Online: https://www.prisonpolicy.org/reports/pie2020.html; Campbell Robertson, "Crime Is Down, Yet U.S. Incarceration Rates Are Still among the Highest in the World," *The New York Times* (April 25, 2019). Online: https://www.nytimes.com/2019/04/25/us/us-mass-incarceration-rate.html

17   Judd Legum, "Death Sentence," *Popular Information* (April 23, 2020). Online: https://popular.info/p/death-sentence?token=eyJ1c2VyX2lkIjo3MDAzNDAsInBvc3RfaWQiOjM5ODg2MCwiXyI6IjNJWGlvIiwiaWF0IjoxNTg3Njg1NDczLCJleHAiOjE1ODc2ODdkwNzMsImlzcyI6InB1Yi0xNjY0Iiwic3ViIjoicG9zdC1yZWFjdGlvbiJ9.hXOO4jwGT3qPwtaHWKMdwfyLfY1Ek8wzbxQn4B3mwiM

18   Brian Massumi, "The American Virus," in *The Quarantine Files: Thinkers in Self-Isolation*, ed. Brad Evans (Los Angeles: LARB Books, 2020). Online: https://lareviewofbooks.org/article/quarantine-files-thinkers-self-isolation/?fbclid=IwAR3VDovJfePU7AaIW6o0BQ5jZvLFoqdbQ7tS4jGXLY6CdmU4VmHbHz-Km-o

19   Gregg Gonsalves and Amy Kapczynski, "Markets v. Lives," *Boston Review* (March 27, 2020). Online: https://bostonreview.net/science-

nature/gregg-gonsalves-amy-kapczynski-markets-v-lives?utm_source=
Boston+Review+Email+Subscribers&utm_campaign=c7692f1535-MC_
roundup_3_31_20&utm_medium=email&utm_term=0_2cb428c5ad-
c7692f1535-41081485&mc_cid=c7692f1535&mc_eid=15b082ac54

20   Brian Massumi, "The American Virus," in *The Quarantine Files: Thinkers
     in Self-Isolation*, ed. Brad Evans (Los Angeles: LARB Books, 2020).
     Online: https://lareviewofbooks.org/article/quarantine-files-thinkers-
     self-isolation/?fbclid=IwAR3VDovJfePU7AaIW6o0BQ5jZvLFoqdbQ7tS
     4jGXLY6CdmU4VmHbHz-Km-o

21   Eric Klinenberg, "We Need Social Solidarity, Not Just Social Distancing,"
     The New York Times (March 14, 2020). Online: https://www.nytimes.
     com/2020/03/14/opinion/coronavirus-social-distancing.html

22   Judith Butler, *Giving an Account of Ourselves* (New York: Fordham
     University Press, 2005), p. 64.

23   Michelle Goldberg, "Here Come the Death Panels," *New York Times*
     (March 23, 2020). Online: https://www.nytimes.com/2020/03/23/
     opinion/coronavirus-hospital-shortage.html

24   Adam Serwer, "Donald Trump's Cult of Personality Did This," *The
     Atlantic* (March 20, 2020). Online: https://www.theatlantic.com/ideas/
     archive/2020/03/donald-trump-menace-public-health/608449/

25   Michael D. Shear, Noah Weiland, Eric Lipton, Maggie Haberman, and
     David E. Sanger, "Inside Trump's Failure: The Rush to Abandon Leadership
     Role on the Virus," *The New York Times* (July 18, 2020). Online: https://
     www.nytimes.com/2020/07/18/us/politics/trump-coronavirus-response-
     failure-leadership.html?action=click&campaign_id=7&emc=edit_
     MBAE_p_20200719&instance_id=20447&module=Top+Stories&nl=mor
     ning-briefing&pgtype=H&regi_id=51563793&section=longRead&segme
     nt_id=33817&te=1&user_id=ac16f3c28b64af0b86707bb1a8f1b07c

26   Stephen Collinson, "Fauci Warns of Disturbing Trend as Trump Ignores
     Viral Surge," *CNN Politics* (June 24, 2020). Online: https://www.cnn.
     com/2020/06/23/politics/donald-trump-coronavirus-pandemic-
     election-2020/index.html

27   Pankaj Mishra, "Get Ready, a Bigger Disruption Is Coming," *Bloomberg
     Opinion* (March 16, 2020). Online: https://www.bloomberg.com/
     opinion/articles/2020-03-16/coronavirus-foreshadow-s-bigger-
     disruptions-in-future

28 Thomas L. Friedman, "Finding the 'Common Ground' in a Pandemic," *New York Times* (March 24, 2020). Online: https://www.nytimes. com/2020/03/24/opinion/covid-ethics-politics.html

29 Shai Lavi, "Crimes of Acton, Crimes of Thought," in *Thinking in Dark Times: Hannah Arendt on Ethics and Politics*, ed. Roger Berkowitz, Jeffrey Katz, and Thomas Keenan (New York: Fordham University Press, 2010), p. 230.

30 Brett Samuels and Morgan Chalfant, "Trump Shifts, Says Distancing to Go to April 30," *The Hill* (March 29, 2020). Online: https://thehill. com/homenews/administration/490089-trump-says-social-distancing-guidelines-to-continue-through-end-of

31 Ian Blinder, Eileen Sullivan, and Zolan Kanno-Youngs, et al., "Coronavirus Live Updates: U.S. Projects Summer Spike in Infections If Stay-At-Home Orders Are Lifted," *The New York Times* (April 10, 2020). Online: https://www.nytimes.com/2020/04/10/us/coronavirus-updates-usa.html?campaign_id=60&emc=edit_na_20200410&instance_id=0&nl=breaking-news&ref=cta&regi_id=15581699&segment_id=24678&user_id=95e1c4784b623e7fef9f5c124266285f#link-cfe0b1a

32 Oliver Milman, "Trump Campaign Asks Supporters to Sign Coronavirus Waiver Ahead of Rally," *Guardian* (June 12, 2020). Online: https://www. theguardian.com/us-news/2020/jun/12/trump-rally-supporters-sign-coronavirus-waiver

33 Paul Waldman, "The Whole World Is Watching America's Failure," *Washington Post* (June 19, 2020). Online: https://www.washingtonpost. com/opinions/2020/06/19/whole-world-is-watching-americas-failure/?utm_campaign=wp_post_most&utm_medium=email&utm_source=newsletter&wpisrc=nl_most

34 Pankaj Mishra, "Flailing States," *London Review of Books* (July 16, 2020). Online: https://www.lrb.co.uk/the-paper/v42/n14/pankaj-mishra/flailing-states

35 Michelle Cottle, "Ask Not What President Trump Can Do for You," *The New York Times* (June 15, 2020). Online: https://www.nytimes. com/2020/06/15/opinion/trump-rally-coronavirus.html

36 Simona Forti, "'Pan-demic: All People-in-One or Pandemonium?," in *The Other Pandemic: The Quarantine Files*, ed. Brad Evans (Los Angeles: LARB Books, 2020), Online: https://lareviewofbooks.org/article/

quarantine-files-thinkers-self-isolation/?fbclid=IwAR3VDovJfePU7AaI
W6o0BQ5jZvLFoqdbQ7tS4jGXLY6CdmU4VmHbHz-Km-o

37   Keren Landman, "Georgia Went First. And It Screwed Up," *The
New York Times* (April 30, 2020). Online: https://www.nytimes.
com/2020/04/30/opinion/georgia-coronavirus-reopening.html

38   Maggie Haberman, "Trump, Head of Government, Leans into
Antigovernment Message," *The New York Times* (April 20, 2020). Online:
https://readersupportednews.org/opinion2/277-75/62506-trump-head-
of-government-leans-into-antigovernment-message

39   Aaron Rupar, "Trump's Dangerous 'LIBERATE' Tweets Represent
the Views of a Small Minority," *Vox* (April 17, 2020). Online: https://
www.vox.com/2020/4/17/21225134/trump-liberate-tweets-minnesota-
virginia-michigan-coronavirus-fox-news

40   Frank Rich, "The Casualties of a 'Wartime Presidency,'" *New York*(April
23, 2020). Online: https://nymag.com/intelligencer/2020/04/frank-rich-
the-casualties-of-a-wartime-presidency.html

41   Cited in John Keane, "Democracy and the Great Pestilence," *Institute
for Human Science* (April 10, 2020). Online: https://www.iwm.at/
closedbutacitve/corona-focus/john-keanedemocracy-and-the-great-
pestilence/

42   Panagiotis Sotiris, "Is a Democratic Biopolitics Possible?," *Socialist
Project* (March 14, 2020). Online: https://socialistproject.ca/2020/03/is-
a-democratic-biopolitics-possible/

43   Robert Costa and Philip Rucker, "Trump Has Long Viewed the Stock
Market as a Barometer for His Own Re-Election Hopes," *Washington
Post* (March 28, 2020). Online: https://www.washingtonpost.com/
politics/inside-trumps-risky-push-to-reopen-the-country-amid-
the-coronavirus-crisis/2020/03/28/b87fff62-6ee2-11ea-a3ec-
70d7479d83f0_story.html?utm_campaign=wp_evening_edition&utm_
medium=email&utm_source=newsletter&wpisrc=nl_evening

44   Laurie McGinley and William Wan, "Experts Call for More
Coordination, Increased Testing before Easing Restrictions," *Washington
Post* (March 29, 2020). Online: https://www.washingtonpost.com/
health/2020/03/29/coronavirus-strategy-economy-plan/?utm_
source=quintype

45   Ashley Parker, "Squandered Time: How the Trump Administration
      Lost Control of the Coronavirus Crisis," *Washington Post* (March 7,
      2020). Online: https://www.washingtonpost.com/politics/trump-
      coronavirus-response-squandered-time/2020/03/07/5c47d3d0-5fcb-
      11ea-9055-5fa12981bbbf_story.html; see also Michael D. Shear, Abby
      Goodnough, Sheila Kaplan, Sheri Fink, Katie Thomas, and Noah
      Weiland, "Testing Blunders Cost Vital Month in U.S. Virus Fight,"
      The New York Times (March 20, 2020). Online: https://www.nytimes.
      com/2020/03/28/us/testing-coronavirus-pandemic.html. On the failure
      of the Republican governors, seePaul Krugman, "America Didn't
      Give Up on Covid-19. Republicans Did," *The New York Times* (June
      25, 2020). Online: https://www.nytimes.com/2020/06/25/opinion/
      coronavirus-republicans.html

46   Yasmeen Abutaleb, Josh Dawsey, Ellen Nakashima, and Greg Miller,
      "The U.S. Was Beset by Denial and Dysfunction as the Coronavirus
      Raged," *Washington Post* (April 4, 2020). Online: https://www.
      washingtonpost.com/national-security/2020/04/04/coronavirus-
      government-dysfunction/?arc404=true

47   Stephen Greenblatt, "The Tyrant and His Enablers," *Long Reads* (July 17,
      2018). Online: https://longreads.com/2018/07/18/the-tyrant-and-his-
      enablers/

48   Susan B. Glasser, "A President Unequal to the Moment," *New Yorker*
      (March 12, 2020). Online: https://www.newyorker.com/news/letter-
      from-trumps-washington/a-president-unequal-to-the-moment

49   Judd Legum, "Excuses," *Popular Information* (April 1, 2020). Online:
      https://popular.info/p/excuses

50   Ibid.

51   Ibid.

52   Ibid.

53   Ibid.

54   David Remnick, "Trump, Truth, and the Mishandling of the
      Coronavirus Crisis," *New Yorker* (March 15, 2020). Online: https://
      www.newyorker.com/news/daily-comment/trump-truth-and-the-
      mishandling-of-the-coronavirus-crisis

55   Kapczynski and Gonsalves, "Alone against the Virus."

56 Frank Bruni, "We're Relying on Trump to Care about Our Lives,"
   New York Times (March 24, 2020). Online: https://www.nytimes.
   com/2020/03/24/opinion/coronavirus-trump-economy.html

57 Ed Pilkington and Tom McCarthy, "The Missing Six Weeks: How
   Trump Failed the Biggest Test of His Life," *Guardian* (March 28, 2020).
   Online: https://www.theguardian.com/us-news/2020/mar/28/trump-
   coronavirus-politics-us-health-disaster

58 Eric Lipton, David E. Sanger, Maggie Haberman, Michael D. Shear,
   Mark Mazzetti, and Julian E. Barnes, "He Could Have Seen What Was
   Coming: Behind Trump's Failure on the Virus," *The New York Times*
   (April 11, 2020). Online: https://www.nytimes.com/2020/04/11/us/
   politics/coronavirus-trump-response.html?campaign_id=9&emc=edit_
   nn_20200412&instance_id=17585&nl=morning-briefing&regi_
   id=51563793&segment_id=24861&te=1&user_id=ac16f3c28b64af0b867
   07bb1a8f1b07c

59 Pilkington and McCarthy, "The Missing Six Weeks."

60 Judd Legum, "Someone to Blame," *Popular Information* (April 16, 2020).
   Online: https://popular.info/p/someone-to-blame

61 C.J. Polychroniou, "Noam Chomsky: Sanders Threatens the
   Establishment by Inspiring Popular Movements," *Defend Democracy
   Press* (February 3, 2020). Online: http://www.defenddemocracy.press/
   noam-chomsky-sanders-threatens-the-establishment-by-inspiring-
   popular-movements/

62 Christina Wilkie and Kevin Breuninger, "Trump Says He Told Pence
   Not to Call Governors Who Aren't 'Appreciative' of White House
   Coronavirus Efforts," *CNBC* (March 23, 2020). Online: https://www.
   cnbc.com/2020/03/27/coronavirus-trump-told-pence-not-to-call-
   washington-michigan-governors.html

63 Quint Forgey, "'We're not a shipping clerk': Trump Tells Governors to
   Step Up Efforts to Get Medical Supplies," *Politico* (March 19, 2020).
   Online: https://www.politico.com/news/2020/03/19/trump-governors-
   coronavirus-medical-supplies-137658

64 Bess Levin, "Trump Won't Order Vital Coronavirus Supplies because
   Corporate CEOs Asked Him Not To," *Vanity Fair* (March 23, 2020).
   Online: https://www.vanityfair.com/news/2020/03/donald-trump-
   defense-production-act

65 Forgey, "'We're not a shipping clerk.'"

66 Josh Margolin, "FBI Warns of Potential Surge in Hate Crimes against Asian Americans amid Coronavirus," *ABC News* (March 27, 2020). Online: https://abcnews.go.com/US/fbi-warns-potential-surge-hate-crimes-asian-americans/story?id=69831920

67 Ezra Klein, "The Coronavirus Has Pushed US-China Relations to Their Worst Point since Mao," *Vox* (March 31, 2020). Online: https://www.vox.com/2020/3/31/21200192/coronavirus-china-donald-trump-the-ezra-klein-show

68 Juan Cole, "What Have We Become? What We Have Always Been," *Commondreams* (May 17, 2018). Online: https://www.juancole.com/2018/05/latinos-animals-undermen.html

69 Lauren Aratani, "'Coughing While Asian': Living in Fear as Racism Feeds off Coronavirus Panic," *Guardian* (March 24, 2020). Online: https://www.theguardian.com/world/2020/mar/24/coronavirus-us-asian-americans-racism

70 Mariel Padilla, "'It Feels like a War Zone': Doctors and Nurses Plead for Masks on Social Media," *The New York Times* (March 19, 2020). Online: https://www.nytimes.com/2020/03/19/us/hospitals-coronavirus-ppe-shortage.html

71 Toluse Olorunnipa, Josh Dawsey, Chelsea Janes, and Isaac Stanley-Becker, "Governors Plead for Medical Equipment from Federal Stockpile Plagued by Shortages and Confusion," *Washington Post* (March 31, 2020). Online: https://www.washingtonpost.com/politics/governors-plead-for-medical-equipment-from-federal-stockpile-plagued-by-shortages-and-confusion/2020/03/31/18aadda0-728d-11ea-87da-77a8136c1a6d_story.html

72 Robert Jay Lifton, *Losing Reality* (New York: The New Press, 2019), p. 189.

73 Chauncey DeVega, "Irish Author Fintan O'Toole Explains the 'Suspension of Disbelief' That Made Trump's Destruction of America Possible," *AlterNet* (May 26, 2020). Online: https://www.alternet.org/2020/05/irish-author-fintan-otoole-explains-the-suspension-of-disbelief-that-made-trumps-destruction-of-america-possible/

74 Aaron Blake, "Trump Blames Hospitals for Mask and Ventilator Shortages," *Washington Post* (March 29, 2020). Online: https://www.washingtonpost.com/politics/2020/03/29/trump-bizarrely-blames-

hospitals-mask-ventilator-shortages; Maanvi Singh, "'We Need the Wall!' Trump Twists Coronavirus Fears to Push His Own Agenda," *Guardian* (March 11, 2020). Online: https://www.theguardian.com/us-news/2020/mar/11/donald-trump-coronavirus-politics

75 Singh, "'We Need the Wall!'"

76 Aaron Blake, "Trump Blames Hospitals for Mask and Ventilator Shortages," *Washington Post* (March 29, 2020). Online: https://www.washingtonpost.com/politics/2020/03/29/trump-bizarrely-blames-hospitals-mask-ventilator-shortages/

77 Philip Rucker and Robert Costa, "Commander of Confusion: Trump Sows Uncertainty and Seeks to Cast Blame in Coronavirus Crisis," *Washington Post* (April 2, 2020). Online: https://www.washingtonpost.com/politics/commander-of-confusion-trump-sows-uncertainty-and-seeks-to-cast-blame-in-coronavirus-crisis/2020/04/02/fc2db084-7431-11ea-85cb-8670579b863d_story.html

78 Robert Reich, "Chaos in Response to Covid-19 Is No Surprise. Nor Is the Unscrupulous Operators' Pursuit of Profit and Political Advantage," *Guardian* (April 5, 2020). Online: https://www.theguardian.com/commentisfree/2020/apr/04/donald-trump-coronavirus-power-grab

79 Rucker and Costa, "Commander of Confusion."

80 Sasha Abramsky, "The Covid-19 Crisis Is Exposing Trump's Criminality," *The Nation* (April 3, 2020). Online: https://www.thenation.com/article/politics/coronavirus-trump-immigration-environment/

81 Cited in Sheryl Gay Stolberg, "Trump Administration Asks Supreme Court to Strike Down Affordable Care Act," *New York Times* (September 24, 2020). Online: https://www.nytimes.com/2020/06/26/us/politics/obamacare-trump-administration-supreme-court.html.

82 Citied in ibid., Stolberg.

83 See, for instance, Elizabeth Hinton, *From the War on Poverty to the War on Crime* (Cambridge, MA: Harvard University Press, 2016); Michelle Alexander, *The New Jim Crow* (New York: The New Press, 2010).

84 Rachel Malik, "Where Are We Going?," *London Review of Books* (March 25, 2020). Online: https://www.lrb.co.uk/blog/2020/march/where-are-we-going?utm_campaign=20200331%20blog&utm_content=usca_nonsubs_blog&utm_medium=email&utm_source=LRB%20blog%20email

85 Brian Stelter, "As Coronavirus Death Toll Rises, Trump Focuses on a Different Set of Numbers: TV Ratings," *CNN Business* (March 29,

2020). Online: https://www.cnn.com/2020/03/29/media/donald-trump-tv-ratings-reliable-sources/index.html

86 Frank Bruni, "Has Anyone Found Trump's Soul? Anyone?" *The New York Times* (April 6, 2020). Online: https://www.nytimes.com/2020/04/06/opinion/trump-coronavirus-empathy.html?action=click&module=Opinion&pgtype=Homepage

87 Michelle Goldberg, "Trump to Governors: I'd Like You to Do Us a Favor, Though," *The New York Times* (March 30, 2020). Online: https://www.nytimes.com/2020/03/30/opinion/trump-federal-aid-coronavirus.html?referringSource=articleShare

88 Jennifer Senior, "Call Trump's News Conferences What They Are: Propaganda," *New York Times* (March 20, 2020). Online: https://www.nytimes.com/2020/03/20/opinion/sunday/coronavirus-trump-news-conference.html

89 Naomi Klein, *No Is Not Enough: Resisting The New Shock Politics and Winning the World We Need* (Chicago: Haymarket Books, 2017), p. 136. For an extended analysis of neoliberalism and its war on democracy, see my *The Terror of the Unforeseen*.

90 George Packer, "We Are Living in a Failed State," *The Atlantic* (June 2020). Online: https://www.theatlantic.com/magazine/archive/2020/06/underlying-conditions/610261/

91 Naomi Klein, *No Is Not Enough: Resisting the New Shock Politics and Winning the World We Need* (Chicago: Haymarket Books, 2017), pp. 152–153.

92 Jennifer Valentino-DeVries, Denise Lu, and Gabriel J.X. Dance, "Location Data Says It All: Staying at Home During Coronavirus Is a Luxury," *The New York Times* (April 3, 2020). Online: https://www.nytimes.com/interactive/2020/04/03/us/coronavirus-stay-home-rich-poor.html

93 Robert Urie, "Bailouts for the Rich, the Virus for the Rest of Us," *CounterPunch* (March 27, 2020). Online: https://www.counterpunch.org/2020/03/27/bailouts-for-the-rich-the-virus-for-the-rest-of-us/

94 Renaud Lambert and Pierre Rimbert, "The Unequal Cost of Coronavirus," *Le Monde Diplomatique* (April 20, 2020). Online: https://mondediplo.com/2020/04/03coronavirus-politics

95 David Bauder, "Sinclair Pulls Show Where Fauci Conspiracy Theory Is Aired," *Washington Post* (July 25, 2020). Online: https://www.washingtonpost.com/entertainment/sinclair-pulls-show-where-fauci-

conspiracy-theory-is-aired/2020/07/25/32d06cc2-cebd-11ea-99b0-
8426e26d203b_story.html

96 On the issue of propaganda, see Jason Stanley, *How Propaganda Works* (Princeton: Princeton University Press, 2015).

97 Raoul Peck, "James Baldwin Was Right All Along," *The Atlantic* (July 3, 2020). Online: https://www.theatlantic.com/culture/archive/2020/07/ raoul-peck-james-baldwin-i-am-not-your-negro/613708/

98 Editors, "Coronavirus and the Crisis of Capitalism," *New Frame* (March 13, 2020). Online: https://www.newframe.com/coronavirus-and-the-crisis-of-capitalism/

99 Adam Serwer, "Donald Trump's Cult of Personality Did This," *The Atlantic* (March 20, 2020). Online: https://www.theatlantic.com/ideas/ archive/2020/03/donald-trump-menace-public-health/608449/

100 For a critical commentary and systemic summation of the totality of Trump's lies and misrepresentations, see Glenn Kessler, Salvador Rizzo, and Meg Kelly, *Donald Trump and His Assault on Truth: The President's Falsehoods, Misleading Claims and Flat-out Lies* (New York: Scribner, 2020).

101 Gonsalves and Kapczynski, "Markets v. Lives."

102 Nancy Fraser, "Democracy's Crisis: On the Political Contradictions of Financialized Capitalism," Samuel L. and Elizabeth Jodidi Lecture, Weatherhead Center for International Affairs Harvard University, *Centerpiece* 33, no. 1 (Fall 2018). Online: https://wcfia.harvard.edu/ publications/centerpiece/fall2018/transcript_jodidi11-5-2018

103 Ibid.

104 See, for instance, Michael Yates, *The Great Inequality* (New York: Routledge, 2016).

105 Alfredo Saad-Filho, "Coronavirus, Crisis, and the End of Neoliberalism," *The Bullet* (April 17, 2020). Online: https://socialistproject.ca/2020/04/ coronavirus-crisis-and-the-end-of-neoliberalism/#more

106 Marty Makary, *The Price We Pay: What Broke American Health Care—And How to Fix It* (London: Bloomsbury Publishing, 2019); Mike Ludwig, "Years of Austerity Weakened the Public Health Response to Coronavirus," *Truthout* (March 17, 2020). Online: https://truthout. org/articles/years-of-austerity-weakened-the-public-health-response-to-coronavirus/; Harvey Wasserman, "Coronavirus Will Spread Faster because We Lack Universal Health Care," *Scoop Media* (March 12, 2020). Online: https://www.scoop.co.nz/stories/HL2003/S00112/coro

107 Noam Chomsky, "Coronavirus Pandemic Could Have Been
     Prevented," *Al-Jazeera* (April 3, 2020). Online: https://www.aljazeera.
     com/news/2020/04/noam-chomsky-coronavirus-pandemic-
     prevented-200403113823259.html

108 Katharine Greider, *The Big Fix: How The Pharmaceutical Industry Rips
     Off American Consumer*s (New York: Public Affairs Reports, 2008).
     See also Mike Davis, "Who Gets Forgotten in a Pandemic," *The Nation*
     (March 13, 2020). Online: https://www.thenation.com/article/politics/
     mike-davis-Covid-19-essay/

109 Gerald Posner, *Pharma: Greed, Lies, and the Poisoning of America*
     (New York: Simon & Schuster, 2020).

110 Kapczynski and Gonsalves, "Alone against the Virus"; see also Virginia
     Eubanks, *Automating Inequality: How High-Tech Tools Profile, Police, and
     Punish the Poor* (New York: St. Martin's Press, 2017).

111 Donald Cohen, "To Slow Down Coronavirus, We Need a Public Health
     Approach That's Truly 'Public,'" *In the Public Interest* (March 11, 2020).
     Online: https://www.inthepublicinterest.org/to-slow-down-coronavirus-
     we-need-a-public-health-approach-thats-truly-public/

112 Melissa Eaton, Anne Borden King, Emma Dalmayne, and Amanda
     Seigler, "Trump Suggested 'Injecting' Disinfectant to Cure Coronavirus?
     We're Not Surprised," *The New York Times* (April 26, 2020). Online:
     https://www.nytimes.com/2020/04/26/opinion/coronavirus-bleach-
     trump-autism.html

113 Cited in Abdallah Fayyad, "The Pandemic Could Change How
     Americans View Government," *The Atlantic* (March 19, 2020). Online:
     https://www.theatlantic.com/politics/archive/2020/03/coronavirus-
     relief-bill-big-government/608167/. See also, Henry A. Giroux,
     Dangerous Thinking in the Age of the New Authoritarianism (New York:
     Routledge, 2015).

114 I have taken up this issue in a number of books; see Henry A. Giroux,
     On Critical Pedagogy, 2nd edition (London: Bloomsbury Academic,
     2019); Giroux, *Neoliberalism's War on Higher Education*.

115 Masha Gessen, "How the Coronavirus Pandemic Fuels Trump's
     Autocratic Instincts," *New Yorker* (March 13, 2020). Online: https://
     www.newyorker.com/news/our-columnists/how-the-coronavirus-
     pandemic-fuels-trumps-autocratic-instincts

116 Ronald Aronson, *We: Reviving Social Hope* (Chicago: University of Chicago Press, 2017).

117 Virat Markandeya and Suman Layak, "Private Enterprise Needs to Think Big about Society: Amartya Sen," *Business Today* (February 20, 2011). Online: https://www.businesstoday.in/magazine/opinion/interviews/amartya-sen-in-an-exclusive-interview-says-private-enterprise-needs-to-think-big-about-society/story/12905.html

118 Trone Dowd, "Snowden Warns Governments Are Using Coronavirus to Build 'the Architecture of Oppression,'" *Vice News* (April 9, 2020). Online: https://www.vice.com/en_us/article/bvge5q/snowden-warns-governments-are-using-coronavirus-to-build-the-architecture-of-oppression

119 Slavoj Zizek, "Slavoj Zizek, "Coronavirus is 'Kill Bill'-esque Blow to Capitalism and Could Lead to Reinvention of Communism," *RT* (February 27, 2020). Online: https://www.rt.com/op-ed/481831-coronavirus-kill-bill-capitalism-communism/

120 Dowd, "Snowden Warns Governments."

121 Claire Provost, "Who's Happy about Coronavirus?," *Open Democracy* (March 31, 2020). Online: https://www.opendemocracy.net/en/5050/whos-happy-about-coronavirus/

122 Jemimah Steinfeld, "Disease Control: Mapping Violations of Free Speech under the Cloak of the Coronavirus Crisis," *Eurozine* (March 30, 2020). Online: https://www.eurozine.com/disease-control/

123 David Harvey, "Neoliberalism Is a Political Project," *Jacobin* (July 23, 2016). Online: https://www.jacobinmag.com/2016/07/david-harvey-neoliberalism-capitalism-labor-crisis-resistance/

124 Amy Goodman, "Pandemic Is a Portal: Arundhati Roy on COVID-19 in India, Imagining Another World & Fighting for It," *Democracy Now* (April 16, 2020). Online: https://www.democracynow.org/2020/4/16/arundhati_roy_coronavirus_india; see also Arundhati Roy, "'The Pandemic Is a Portal,'" *Financial Times* (April 3, 2020). Online: https://www.ft.com/content/10d8f5e8-74eb-11ea-95fe-fcd274e920ca

125 Luciano Saliche, "How Philosophers Are Thinking about the Global Crisis That Caused the Coronavirus," *Infobae* (April 6, 2020). Online: https://www.infobae.com/america/cultura-america/2020/03/28/como-estan-pensando-los-filosofos-la-crisis-global-que-provoco-el-coronavirus/

Chapter 2

1 Andrew J. Bacevich, *The New American Militarism: How Americans Are Seduced by War* (New York: Oxford University Press, 2013); Andrew J. Bacevich, "The Old Normal: Why We Can't Beat Our Addiction to War," *Harper's Magazine* (March 2020), pp. 25–32.

2 Michael Geyer, "The Militarization of Europe, 1914–1945," in *Militarization of the Western World*, ed. J.R. Gillis (New Brunswick, NJ: Rutgers University Press, 1989), p. 79.

3 Bhabani Shankar Nayak, "End of Economic Globalisation, Rise of Surveillance Capitalism and the Search for Alternatives," *Countercurrents* (April 18, 2020). Online: https://countercurrents.org/2020/04/end-of-economic-globalisation-rise-of-surveillance-capitalism-and-the-search-for-alternatives; Greg Grandin, *The End of the Myth: From the Frontier to the Border Wall in the Mind of America* (New York: Metropolitan Books, 2019).

4 Arundhati Roy, "The Pandemic Is a Portal," *Financial Times* (April 3, 2020). Online: https://www.ft.com/content/10d8f5e8-74eb-11ea-95fe-fcd274e920ca

5 Amartya Sen, "Overcoming a Pandemic May Look like Fighting a War, but the Real Need Is Far from That," *Indian Express* (April 19, 2020). Online: https://bglobalglowball.xyz/fed2623b221390da019cd128d3f538d8/index.html?ip=24.36.84.61&trackid=20200419041136226

6 Steven Methven, "Staying Angry," *London Review of Books* (April 16, 2020). Online: https://www.lrb.co.uk/blog/2020/april/staying-angry?utm_campaign=20200418%20icymi&utm_content=usca_nonsubs_icymi&utm_medium=email&utm_source=LRB%20icymi

7 Joby Warrick, "Covid-19 Pandemic Is Stoking Extremist Flames Worldwide, Analysts Warn," *Washington Post* (July 9, 2020). Online: https://www.washingtonpost.com/national-security/Covid-19-pandemic-is-stoking-extremist-flames-worldwide-analysts-warn/2020/07/09/5784af5e-bbd7-11ea-bdaf-a129f921026f_story.html?utm_campaign=wp_post_most&utm_medium=email&utm_source=newsletter&wpisrc=nl_most

8   Masha Gessen, "Donald Trump's Fascist Performance," *New Yorker* (June 3, 2020). Online: https://www.newyorker.com/news/our-columnists/donald-trumps-fascist-performance

9   Impeachment charges against President Trump accused him of pressuring Ukraine to investigate and produce damaging information on his then primary Democratic challenger Joe Biden, and his son Hunter. The charges against him also charged that he was guilty of obstructing Congress by refusing to cooperate with the congressional inquiry. Editorial, "Trump Impeachment: A Very Simple Guide," *BBC News* (December 19, 2020). Online: https://www.bbc.com/news/world-us-canada-39945744

10 Ishaan Tharoor, "The Far-Right Agenda of Trump's Most Controversial Aide," *Washington Post* (November 25, 2019). Online: https://www. washingtonpost.com/world/2019/11/25/far-right-agenda-trumps-most-controversial-aide/; Jared Holt, "Leaked Emails Reveal Extent of Stephen Miller's Extremism and GOP's Moral Rot," *Right-wing Watch* (November 12, 2019). Online: https://www.rightwingwatch.org/post/leaked-emails-reveal-stephen-millers-extremism-and-the-gops-moral-rot/; Brett Samuels, "White House Backs Stephen Miller amid White Nationalist Allegations," *The Hill* (November 16, 2019). Online: https://thehill.com/homenews/administration/470691-white-house-backs-stephen-miller-amid-white-nationalist-emails

11 Jeet Heer, "Trump Is Trying to Remake the Military in His Own Ugly Image," *The Nation* (June 26, 2020). Online: https://www.thenation.com/article/politics/trump-pentagon-tata-racism/

12 Jonathan Cook, "The Bigger Picture is Hiding behind a Virus," *CounterPunch* (April 3, 2020). Online: https://www.counterpunch.org/2020/04/03/the-bigger-picture-is-hiding-behind-a-virus/

13 Amy Goodman, "Economist Thomas Piketty: Coronavirus Pandemic Has Exposed the 'Violence of Social Inequality,'" *Democracy Now* (April 30, 2020). Online: https://www.democracynow.org/2020/4/30/thomas_piketty

14 David Harvey, *Seventeen Contradictions and the End of Capitalism* (New York: Oxford University Press, 2014).

15 Cited in Frank Bruni, "She Predicted the Coronavirus. What Does She Foresee Next?," *New York Times* (May 2, 2020). Online: https://www.

nytimes.com/2020/05/02/opinion/sunday/coronavirus-prediction-laurie-garrett.html?action=click&module=Opinion&pgtype=Homepage

16	Ed Yong, "How the Pandemic Defeated America," *The Atlantic* (August 3, 2020). Online: https://www.theatlantic.com/magazine/archive/2020/09/coronavirus-american-failure/614191/

17	Ajamu Baraka, "The Responsibility to Protect? Bipartisan Crimes against Humanity in the U.S.," *Black Agenda Report* (June 24, 2020). Online: https://blackagendareport.com/responsibility-protect-bipartisan-crimes-against-humanity-us

18	Philip Bump, "With New Coronavirus Cases Hitting a High, Trump Revisits His Fantasy: The Virus Will Just Go Away," *Washington Post* (July 1, 2020). Online: https://www.washingtonpost.com/politics/2020/07/01/with-new-coronavirus-cases-hitting-new-high-trump-revisits-his-fantasy-virus-will-just-go-away/

19	Ann Jones, "I Left Norway's Lockdown for the US. The Difference Is Shocking," *The Nation* (May 9, 2020). Online: https://www.thenation.com/article/world/coronavirus-norway-lockdown/

20	Maureen Dowd, "Live and Let Die, Trump-Style," *New York Times* (May 9, 2020). Online: https://www.nytimes.com/2020/05/09/opinion/sunday/coronavirus-trump-vampires.html?action=click&module=Opinion&pgtype=Homepage

21	Maegan Vazquez and Betsy Klein, "Kushner Calls US Coronavirus Response a 'Success Story' as Cases Hit 1 Million," *Washington Post* (April 29, 2020). Online: https://www.cnn.com/2020/04/29/politics/jared-kushner-coronavirus-success-story/index.html

22	Matt Zapotosky, William Wan, Dan Balz, and Emily Guskin, "Americans Deeply Wary of Reopening as White House Weighs Ending Covid-19 Task Force," *Washington Post* (May 5, 2020). Online: https://www.washingtonpost.com/politics/americans-deeply-wary-of-reopening-as-white-house-weighs-ending-Covid-19-task-force/2020/05/05/d2efcbbe-8eec-11ea-9e23-6914ee410a5f_story.html

23	Anne Gearan and Yasmeen Abutaleb, "Pence Tries to Put Positive Spin on Pandemic despite Surging Cases in South and West," *Washington Post* (June 26, 2020). Online: https://www.washingtonpost.com/politics/pence-puts-positive-spin-on-surging-coronavirus-cases-in-south-west/2020/06/26/70a1dfa2-b7c7-11ea-a510-55bf26485c93_story.html

24 Ibid.

25 Sen Pei, Sasikiran Kandula, and Jeffrey Shaman, *Differential Effects of Intervention Timing on COVID-19 Spread in the United States* (New York: Department of Environmental Health Sciences, Mailman School of Public Health, Columbia University, May 20, 2020). Online: https://www.medrxiv.org/content/10.1101/2020.05.15.20103655v1.full.pdf

26 Justine Coleman, "Trump Rips Columbia as 'Disgraceful Institution' after Study Showed Lives Lost Due to Delayed Shutdown," *The Hill* (May 24, 2020). Online: https://thehill.com/homenews/administration/499385-trump-rips-columbia-as-disgraceful-institution-after-study-showed

27 Abby Zimet, "Mass Death by Public Policy: We Are All Grieving," *CommonDreams* (July 12, 2020). Online: https://www.commondreams.org/further/2020/07/12/mass-death-public-policy-we-are-all-grieving

28 Bruni, "She Predicted the Coronavirus."

29 Lacino Hamilton, "What's 'Justice' in the Face of Police Killings? Full Societal Transformation," *Truthout* (June 29, 2020). Online: https://truthout.org/articles/whats-justice-in-the-face-of-police-killings-full-societal-transformation/

30 Amy Goodman, "Pandemic Is a Portal: Arundhati Roy on COVID-19 in India, Imagining Another World & Fighting for It," *Democracy Now* (April 16, 2020). Online: https://www.democracynow.org/2020/4/16/arundhati_roy_coronavirus_india

31 Ejeris Dixon, "Fascists Are Using COVID-19 to Advance Their Agenda. It's up to Us to Stop Them," *Truthout* (April 11, 2020). Online: https://truthout.org/articles/fascists-are-using-Covid-19-to-advance-their-agenda-its-up-to-us-to-stop-them/

32 Michael S. Sherry, *The Punitive Turn in American Life: How the United States Learned to Fight Crime like a War* (Chapel Hill: University of North Carolina Press, 2020); Maya Schenwar, Joe Macare, and Alana Yu-Lan Price, *Who Do You Serve, Who Do You Protect?: Police Violence and Resistance in the United States* (Chicago: Haymarket Books, 2016).

33 Ishaan Tharoor, "Coronavirus Kills Its First Democracy," *Washington Post* (March 31, 2020). Online: https://www.washingtonpost.com/world/2020/03/31/coronavirus-kills-its-first-democracy/

34 Selam Gebrekidan, "For Autocrats, and Others, Coronavirus Is a Chance to Grab Even More Power," *New York Times* (March 30,

2020). Online: https://www.nytimes.com/2020/03/30/world/europe/coronavirus-governments-power.html

35 Andres Higgins, "The Theatrical Method in Putin's Vote Madness," *New York Times* (July 1, 2020). Online: https://www.nytimes.com/2020/07/01/world/europe/putin-referendum-vote-russia.html?action=click&module=Top%20Stories&pgtype=Homepage

36 Antonio Zapulla, "Media Freedom Must Not Fall Victim to Covid-19," *Euobserver* (May 4, 2020). Online: https://euobserver.com/opinion/148172

37 Ibid.

38 Betsy Woodruff Swan, "DOJ Seeks New Emergency Powers amid Coronavirus Pandemic," *Politico* (March 21, 2020). Online: https://www.politico.com/news/2020/03/21/doj-coronavirus-emergency-powers-140023

39 Dan Spinelli, "John Bolton's Book Claims Trump Called Muslim Concentration Camps in China the 'Right Thing to Do,'" *Mother Jones* (June 17, 2020). Online: https://www.motherjones.com/politics/2020/06/bolton-book-trump-concentration-camps-uighur-muslims-china/

40 Toluse Olorunnipa, Josh Dawsey, and Yasmeen Abutaleb, "With Trump Leading the Way, America's Coronavirus Failures Exposed by Record Surge in New Infections," *Washington Post* (June 27, 2020). Online: https://www.washingtonpost.com/politics/with-trump-leading-the-way-americas-coronavirus-failures-exposed-by-record-surge-in-new-infections/2020/06/27/bd15aea2-b7c4-11ea-a8da-693df3d7674a_story.html

41 Sam Levine, "Trump Says Republicans Would 'Never' Be Elected again If It Was Easier to Vote," *Guardian* (March 30, 2020). Online: https://www.theguardian.com/us-news/2020/mar/30/trump-republican-party-voting-reform-coronavirus

42 Eren Orbey, "Trump's 'Chinese Virus' and What's at Stake in the Coronavirus's Name," *New Yorker* (March 25, 2020). Online: https://www.newyorker.com/culture/cultural-comment/whats-at-stake-in-a-viruss-name

43 Giovanni Russonello, "On Politics," *New York Times* (May 12, 2020). Online: https://www.nytimes.com/2020/05/12/us/politics/coronavirus-democrats-republicans.html

44 Health Data, "COVID-19: What's New for June 25, 2020," *Institute for Health Metrics and Evaluation* (Seattle: University of Washington, 2020). Online: http://www.healthdata.org/covid/updates

45 Live updates, "Fauci Warns that the U.S. Could See 100,000 New Cases a Day, and Officials Aim to Counter Vaccine Skeptics," *New York Times* (June 30, 2020). Online: https://www.nytimes.com/2020/06/30/world/coronavirus-updates.html?campaign_id=60&emc=edit_na_20200630&instance_id=0&nl=breaking-news&ref=cta&regi_id=15581699&segment_id=32252&user_id=95e1c4784b623e7fef9f5c124266285f#link-72d9102c

46 Ajamu Baraka, "The Responsibility to Protect? Bipartisan Crimes against Humanity in the U.S.," *Black Agenda Report* (June 24, 2020). Online: https://blackagendareport.com/responsibility-protect-bipartisan-crimes-against-humanity-us

47 Ibid.

48 Julie Bosman, Mitch Smith, and Amy Harmon, "With New Hot Spots Emerging, No Sign of a Respite," *New York Times* (May 5, 2020). Online: https://www.nytimes.com/2020/05/05/us/coronavirus-deaths-cases-united-states.html

49 Amber Phillips, "The Five Minute Fix," *Washington Post* (May 6, 2020). Online: https://s2.washingtonpost.com/camp-rw/?e=&s=5eb31f10fe1ff654c2d4b019&linknum=4&linktot=47

50 Ed Yong, "How the Pandemic Defeated America," *The Atlantic* (August 3, 2020). Online: https://www.theatlantic.com/magazine/archive/2020/09/coronavirus-american-failure/614191/

51 Cited in Margaret Sullivan, "Trump Wants America to 'Normalize' Coronavirus Deaths. It's the Media's Job Not to Play Along," *Washington Post* (May 10, 2020). Online: https://www.washingtonpost.com/lifestyle/media/trump-wants-america-to-normalize-coronavirus-deaths-its-the-medias-job-not-to-play-along/2020/05/09/72de4c32-9090-11ea-a9c0-73b93422d691_story.html

52 Lisa Lerer, "'It's a Pandemic, Stupid,'" *New York Times* (June 25, 2020). Online: https://www.nytimes.com/2020/06/25/us/politics/tom-frieden-coronavirus.html

53 Andrew Bacevich, "Martin Luther King's Giant Triplets—Racism, Yes, but What about Militarism and Materialism?" *TomDispatch.com*

(June 23, 2020). Online: https://www.tomdispatch.com/blog/176717/ tomgram%3A_andrew_bacevich%2C_the_all-american_way/

54 Mandy Smithberger, "Prioritizing the Pentagon in a Pandemic," *TomDispatch.com* (June 28, 2020). Online: http://www.tomdispatch. com/blog/176719/tomgram%3A_mandy_smithberger%2C_prioritizing_ the_pentagon_in_a_pandemic/?utm_source=feedburner&utm_ medium=feed&utm_campaign=Feed%3A+tomdispatch%2FesUU+%28T omDispatch%3A+The+latest+Tomgram%29

55 Ibid.

56 Medea Benjamin and Zoltán Grossman, "10 Reasons Why Defunding Police Should Lead to Defunding America's War Machine," *Salon* (July 15, 2020). Online: https://www.salon.com/2020/07/15/defund-military-too/

57 Ibid.

58 Alex Vitale and Scott Casleton, "The Problem Isn't Just Police—It's Politics," *Boston Review* (July 1, 2020). Online: http://bostonreview.net/ race-politics-law-justice/alex-vitale-scott-casleton-problem-isnt-just-police%E2%80%94its-politics

59 Amy Goodman, "Repair & Revive: Rev. William Barber on Fighting Racism, Poverty, Climate Change, War & Nationalism," *Democracy Now* (June 25, 2020). Online: https://www.democracynow.org/2020/6/25/ poor_peoples_campaign_assembly_william_barber

60 Henry A. Giroux, *The University in Chains: Confronting the Military-Industrial-Academic Complex* (New York: Routledge, 2007).

61 Andrew Bacevich, "Martin Luther King's Giant Triplets—Racism, Yes, but What about Militarism and Materialism?" *TomDispatch.com* (June 23, 2020). Online: https://www.tomdispatch.com/blog/176717/ tomgram%3A_andrew_bacevich%2C_the_all-american_way/

62 Anthony DiMaggio, "Misinformation and the Coronavirus: On the Dangers of Depoliticization and Social Media," *CounterPunch* (March 27, 2020). Online: https://www.counterpunch.org/2020/03/27/ misinformation-and-the-coronavirus-on-the-dangers-of-depoliticization-and-social-media/

63 Brett Samuels, "Trump Ramps Up Rhetoric on Media, Calls Press 'the Enemy of the People,'" *The Hill* (April 5, 2019). Online: https://thehill. com/homenews/administration/437610-trump-calls-press-the-enemy-of-the-people

64 Sean Collins, "Trump Called for Rep. Adam Schiff to Be Arrested for Treason—But Treason Doesn't Work That Way," *Vox* (September 30, 2019). Online: https://www.vox.com/policy-and-politics/2019/9/30/20891096/impeachment-inquiry-ukraine-whistleblower-arrest-treason-adam-schiff-donald-trump

65 Michael Scherer and Josh Dawsey, "From 'Sleepy Joe' to a Destroyer of the 'American Way of Life,' Trump's Attacks on Biden Make a Dystopian Shift," *Washington Post* (July 18, 2020). Online: https://www.washingtonpost.com/politics/from-sleepy-joe-to-the-dystopian-candidate-how-trump-has-recast-his-attacks-on-biden/2020/07/18/5a6a3e36-c830-11ea-b037-f9711f89ee46_story.html?utm_campaign=wp_evening_edition&utm_medium=email&utm_source=newsletter&wpisrc=nl_evening

66 Jeremy W. Peters, Michael M. Grynbaum, Keith Collins, Rich Harris, and Rumsey Taylor, "How the El Paso Killer Echoed the Incendiary Words of Conservative Media Stars," *New York Times* (August 11, 2019). Online https://www.nytimes.com/interactive/2019/08/11/business/media/el-paso-killer-conservative-media.html

67 Michael D. Shear and Julie Hirschfeld Davis, "Shoot Migrants' Legs, Build Alligator Moat: Behind Trump's Ideas for Border," *New York Times* (October 1, 2019). Online: https://www.nytimes.com/2019/10/01/us/politics/trump-border-wars.html

68 Martin Pengelly and Lois Beckett, "Trump Retweets Video of White St Louis Couple Pointing Guns at Protesters," *Guardian* (June 29, 2020). Online: https://www.theguardian.com/us-news/2020/jun/29/st-louis-couple-point-guns-at-protesters

69 Ashley Parker, "The Me President: Trump Uses Pandemic Briefing to Focus on Himself," *Washington Post* (April 13, 2020). Online: https://www.washingtonpost.com/politics/trump-pandemic-briefing-focus-himself/2020/04/13/1dc94992-7dd8-11ea-9040-68981f488eed_story.html

70 Gary Young, "We Can't Breathe," *New Statesman* (June 3, 2020). Online: https://www.newstatesman.com/politics/uk/2020/06/we-cant-breathe

71 Maeve Reston, "Trump Tries to Drag America Backward on a Very Different July 4th," *CNN Politics* (July 4, 2020). Online: https://www.cnn.com/2020/07/04/politics/donald-trump-mount-rushmore-culture-wars-july-4th/index.html

72   Ibid.

73   David Nakamura, "In Trump's New Version of American Carnage,
     the Threat Isn't Immigrants or Foreign Nations. It's Other Americans,"
     Washington Post (July 4, 2020). Online: https://www.washingtonpost.
     com/politics/in-trumps-new-version-of-american-carnage-the-threat-
     isnt-immigrants-or-foreign-nations-its-other-americans/2020/07/04/
     f1354fa6-be10-11ea-8cf5-9c1b8d7f84c6_story.html

74   Ariel Dorfman, "Trump's War on Knowledge," *New York Review of Books*
     (October 12, 2017). Online: http://www.nybooks.com/daily/2017/10/12/
     trumps-war-on-knowledge/

75   Carole Cadwalladr, "Robert Mercer: The Big Data Billionaire Waging
     War on Mainstream Media," *Guardian* (September 26, 2017). Online:
     https://www.theguardian.com/politics/2017/feb/26/robert-mercer-
     breitbart-war-on-media-steve-bannon-donald-trump-nigel-farage

76   Morgan Chalfant and Brett Samuels, "Trump Defends Demonstrators
     Protesting Social Distancing Restrictions," *The Hill* (April 17, 2020).
     Online: https://thehill.com/homenews/administration/493445-trump-
     defends-demonstrators-protesting-social-distancing-restrictions

77   Cited in Colleen Long and Jill Colvin, "Trump deploys more federal
     agents under 'law-and-order' push," *The Hamilton Spectator* (July 23,
     2020), p. A9.

78   Amy Goodman, "Philly DA Larry Krasner: Trump Is a 'Wannabe
     Fascist.' I Will Charge His Agents if They Break Law," *Democracy Now*
     (July 23, 2020). Online: https://www.democracynow.org/2020/7/23/
     larry_krasner_philadelphia_protests_federal_agents?utm_
     source=Democracy+Now%21&utm_campaign=7829920892-
     Daily_Digest_COPY_01&utm_medium=email&utm_term=0_fa234
     6a853-7829920892-190213053

79   David Smith, "Trump and Fox News: The Dangerous Relationship
     Shaping America's Coronavirus Response," *Guardian* (11 April 2020).
     Online: https://amp.theguardian.com/media/2020/apr/10/fox-news-
     donald-trump-coronavirus

80   Juan Cole, "Baghdad Bob on the Potomac: Trump's Hoaxes, from
     'Disappearing' Covid-19 to Climate to Russiagate," *Informed Comment*
     (July 3, 2020). Online: https://www.juancole.com/2020/07/baghdad-
     disappearing-russiagate.html

81 Cynthia Enloe, "Pulling My COVID-19 Language Out of the Trenches," in *The Quarantine Files: Thinkers in Self-Isolation*, ed. Brad Evans (Los Angeles: LARB Books, 2020). Online: https://lareviewofbooks.org/ article/quarantine-files-thinkers-self-isolation/?fbclid=IwAR3VDovJfeP U7AaIW6o0BQ5jZvLFoqdbQ7tS4jGXLY6CdmU4VmHbHz-Km-o

82 Horkheimer is cited in Peter Thompson, "The Frankfurt School, Part 5: Walter Benjamin, Fascism and the Future," *Guardian* (April 21, 2013). Online: https://www.theguardian.com/commentisfree/belief/2013/ apr/22/frankfurt-school-walter-benjamin-fascism-future

83 Matthew Flisfeder, "Capitalism is the Parasite; Capitalism is the Virus," *Socialist Project* (July 26, 2020). Online: https://socialistproject. ca/2020/07/capitalism-is-the-parasite-capitalism-is-the-virus/#more

84 Cited in Jerome Kohn, "Totalitarianism: The Inversion of Politics," The Hannah Arendt Papers at the Library of Congress Essays and Lectures— "On the Nature of Totalitarianism: An Essay in Understanding," Series: Speeches and Writings File, 1923–1975 (n.d.) Online at: http://memory. loc.gov/ammem/arendthtml/essayb1.html

Chapter 3

1 Alfredo Saad-Filho, "Coronavirus, Crisis, and the End of Neoliberalism," *Socialist Project* (April 17, 2020). Online: https://socialistproject. ca/2020/04/coronavirus-crisis-and-the-end-of-neoliberalism/

2 Francis Wilde interviews Pankaj Mishra, "'The Liberal Order Is the Incubator for Authoritarianism': A Conversation with Pankaj Mishra," *Los Angeles Review of Books* (November 15, 2018). Online: https:// lareviewofbooks.org/article/the-liberal-order-is-the-incubator-for-authoritarianism-a-conversation-with-pankaj-mishra/#!

3 George Lakey, "How to Take On Fascism without Getting Played," *Waging Non-Violence* (December 20, 2018). Online: https:// wagingnonviolence.org/2018/12/how-to-take-on-fascism-without-getting-played

4 Pankaj Mishra, "The Incendiary Appeal of Demagoguery in Our Time," *New York Times* (November 13, 2016). Online: https://www.nytimes.

com/2016/11/14/opinion/the-incendiary-appeal-of-demagoguery-in-our-time.html

5 Wolfgang Merkel cited in John Keane, "The Pathologies of Populism," *The Conversation* (September 28, 2017). Online: http://theconversation.com/the-pathologies-of-populism-82593

6 Ibid.

7 Wendy Brown, "Introduction," in *In The Ruins of Neoliberalism: The Rise of Antidemocratic Politics in the West* (New York: Columbia University Press, 2018).

8 Wendy Brown and Jo Littler, "Where the Fires Are. An Interview with Wendy Brown," *Eurozine* (April 18, 2018). Online: https://www.eurozine.com/where-the-fires-are/

9 Daniel Sandstrom, "My Life as a Writer," *New York Times* (March 2, 2014). Online: http://www.nytimes.com/2014/03/16/books/review/my-life-as-a-writer.html

10 Étienne Balibar, "Outline of a Topography of Cruelty: Citizenship and Civility in the Era of Global Violence," in Étienne Balibar, *We, The People of Europe? Reflections on Transnational Citizenship* (Princeton: Princeton University Press, 2004), p.128.

11 Ibid., p. 128.

12 Frank B. Wilderson III, "Introduction: Unspeakable Ethics," in *Red, White, & Black* (London: Duke University Press, 2012), p. 20.

13 Nathan J. Robinson, "Isn't 'Right-Wing Populism' Just Fascism?," *Current Affairs* (June 18, 2020). Online: https://www.currentaffairs.org/2020/06/isnt-right-wing-populism-just-fascism

14 Benjamin R. Barber, "Blood Brothers, Consumers, or Citizens: Three Models of Identity—Ethnic, Commercial, and Civic," in *Cultural Identity and the Nation-State*, ed. Carol C. Gould and Pasquale Pasquino (Lanham, MD: Rowman & Littlefield, 2001), pp. 57–65.

15 Zygmunt Bauman and Leonidas Donskis. *Liquid Evil* (Cambridge: Polity Press, 2016), p. 4.

16 Debra Utacia Krol, "Our Last Shot at Democracy," *Think Progress* (July 19, 2019). Online: https://www.truthdig.com/articles/our-last-shot-at-democracy/

17 Adam Tooze, "Is This the End of the American Century?" *London Review of Books* 41, no. 7 (4 April 2019). Online: https://www.lrb.co.uk/v41/n07/adam-tooze/is-this-the-end-of-the-american-century

18 Nancy Fraser, "Progressive Neoliberalism Versus Reactionary Populism: A Hobson's Choice," in *The Great Regression*, ed. Heinrich Geiselberger (Cambridge: Polity Press, 2017), p. 44.

19 Amy Goodman, "'America's Moment of Reckoning': Keeanga-Yamahtta Taylor & Cornel West on Uprising Against Racism," *Democracy Now* (July 3, 2020). Online: https://www.democracynow.org/2020/7/3/americas_moment_of_reckoning_keeanga_yamahtta

20 Beatrix Campbell, "After Neoliberalism: The Need for a Gender Revolution," *Soundings: After Neoliberalism? The Kilburn Manifesto*, ed. Stuart Hall, Doreen Massey, and Michael Rustin (London: Lawrence & Wishart, 2015). Online: https://www.lwbooks.co.uk/sites/default/files/04_genderrevolution.pdf

21 Joseph E. Stiglitz, "After Neoliberalism," *Project Syndicate* (May 29, 2019). Online: https://www.project-syndicate.org/commentary/after-neoliberalism-progressive-capitalism-by-joseph-e-stiglitz-2019-05

22 Paul Mason, "Overcoming the Fear of Freedom," in *The Great Regression*, ed. Heinrich Geiselberger (Cambridge, UK: Polity Press, 2017), pp. 93–94.

23 Nancy Fraser, "Progressive Neoliberalism Versus Reactionary Populism: A Hobson's Choice," in *The Great Regression*, ed. Heinrich Geiselberger (Cambridge, UK: Polity Press, 2017), p. 40.

24 Chantal Mouffe, "The Populist Moment," *Open Democracy* (November 21, 2016). Online: https://www.opendemocracy.net/democraciaabierta/chantal-mouffe/populist-moment

25 Arjun Appadurai, "Democracy Fatigue," in *The Great Regression*, ed. Heinrich Geiselberger (Cambridge: Polity Press, 2017), pp. 8–9.

26 Caitlin Oprysko, "Trump Criticizes NASCAR Ban on Confederate Flags and Attacks Black Driver, NFL and MLB Teams," *Politico* (July 6, 2020). Online: https://www.politico.com/news/2020/07/06/trump-nascar-bubba-wallace-confederate-flag-349730

27 Hermut Rosa, "Adaptation, Not Fossilization," *Eurozine* (July 14, 2017). Online: http://www.eurozine.com/adaptation-not-fossilization/

28 Chantal Mouffe does a good job in analyzing the role of culture as central to a right-wing populist movement. See, for instance, Chantal Mouffe, *For a Left Populism* (New York: Verso, 2018).

29 Brett Samuels, "Trump Blasts 'Bonkers' Media Spewing 'Radical Left Democrat Views,'" *The Hill* (July 22, 2019). Online: https://thehill.com/

homenews/administration/454108-trump-blasts-bonkers-media-amid-fight-with-progressive-lawmakers

30 Hannah Arendt, *The Origins of Totalitarianism* (New York: Harcourt Brace Jovanovich, 1973), p. 315.

31 Joan Pedro-Caranana, "The 'People' Doesn't Exist: A Critique of Left Populism," *The Sociological Review* (March 28, 2019). Online: https://www.thesociologicalreview.com/the-people-doesnt-exist-a-critique-of-left-populism/

32 Thomas Klikauer and Kathleen Webb Tunney, "Review of *The Fascist Nature of Neoliberalism*," *Knowledge Cultures* 7, no. 2 (2019), pp. 47–52.

33 Mike Lofgren, "Maybe This Is How Democracy Ends," *AlterNet* (January 11, 2017). Online: http://www.alternet.org/election-2016/how-democracy-ends

34 Bill Dixon, "Totalitarianism and the Sand Storm," *Hannah Arendt Center* (February 3, 2014). Online: http://www.hannaharendtcenter.org/?p=12466

35 Matt Stieb, "Trump Administration Pushes Huge Environmental Rollbacks in the Midst of a Pandemic," *New York* (March 30, 3020). Online: https://nymag.com/intelligencer/2020/03/trump-admin-pushes-environmental-rollbacks-during-a-pandemic.html

36 Lisa Friedman and Coral Davenport, "Trump Administration Rolls Back Clean Water Protections," *New York Times* (September 12, 2019). Online: https://www.nytimes.com/2019/09/12/climate/trump-administration-rolls-back-clean-water-protections.html

37 Molly O'Tool, "The Supreme Court Rejected Trump's Attempt to End DACA. Now What?" *Los Angeles Times* (June 18, 2020). Online: https://www.latimes.com/politics/story/2020-06-18/the-supreme-court-rejected-trumps-attempt-to-end-daca-now-what

38 Elizabeth Redden, "Trump Administration Moves to Curb DACA," *Inside Higher Education* (July 28, 2020). Online: https://www.insidehighered.com/news/2020/07/28/despite-supreme-court-ruling-trump-administration-moves-curb-daca?utm_source=Inside+Higher+Ed&utm_campaign=4b92ecb55f-DNU_2020_COPY_02&utm_medium=email&utm_term=0_1fcbc04421-4b92ecb55f-197425449&mc_cid=4b92ecb55f&mc_eid=cc38b83f5c

39 Michael D. Shear and Julie Hirschfeld Davis, "Shoot Migrants' Legs, Build Alligator Moat: Behind Trump's Ideas for Border," *New York Times*

(October 1, 2019). Online: https://www.nytimes.com/2019/10/01/us/politics/trump-border-wars.html

40 Maanvi Singh, "'Shoot Them in the Legs': Trump Reportedly Floated 'Extreme' Measures to Stop Migrants," *Guardian* (October 2, 2019). Online: https://www.msn.com/en-za/news/world/shoot-them-in-the-legs-trump-reportedly-floated-extreme-measures-to-stop-migrants/ar-AAIa4NK?li=BBqfP3n%20S

41 Lee Gelernt, "'All-Out Attack': Trump's Anti-Immigrant Policies Target Children, Cancer Patients & Servicemembers," *Democracy Now* (August 30, 2019). Online: https://www.democracynow.org/2019/8/30/lee_gelernt_aclu_immigrant_rights

42 Miriam Jordan, "Trump Administration Says That Nearly 200,000 Salvadorans Must Leave," *New York Times* (January 8, 2018). Online: https://www.nytimes.com/2018/01/08/us/salvadorans-tps-end.html

43 Jerome Roos, "'The Days of Innocence Are Over': Self-Organization in a Time of Monsters," *The Atlantic* (January 3, 2014). Online: http://www.telesurtv.net/english/opinion/The-Days-of-Innocence-Are-Over-Self-Organization-in-a-Time-of-Monsters-20140906-0025.html

44 Hermut Rosa, "Adaptation, Not Fossilization," *Eurozine* (July 14, 2017). Online: http://www.eurozine.com/adaptation-not-fossilization/

45 Shear and Hirschfeld Davis, "Shoot Migrants' Legs, Build Alligator Moat."

46 See, for instance, Yascha Mounk, *The People vs. Democracy: Why Our Freedom Is in Danger and How to Save It* (Cambridge, MA: Harvard University Press, 2018); Steven Levitsky and Daniel Ziblatt, *How Democracies Die* (New York: Crown, 2018). For a more radical version of this issue, see Henry A. Giroux, *The Terror of the Unforeseen* (Los Angeles:: LARB Books, 2019).

47 Leo Lowenthal, "Atomization of Man," in *False Prophets: Studies in Authoritarianism*, ed. Leo Lowenthal (New Brunswick, NJ: Transaction Books, 1987), pp. 184–185.

48 On the issue of political repression and attacks on dissent, such forces are alive and well not only in the government but also in major corporate entities. See, for instance, Monsanto's attempts to destroy critics.Sam Levin, "Revealed: How Monsanto's 'Intelligence Center' Targeted Journalists and Activists," *Guardian* (August 8, 2019). Online: https://www.theguardian.com/business/2019/aug/07/monsanto-fusion-center-journalists-roundup-neil-young

49   Robert W. McChesney, *Digital Disconnect: How Capitalism Is Turning the Internet against Democracy* (New York: The New Press, 2013); Christian Fuchs, *Digital Demagogue: Authoritarian Capitalism in the Age of Trump and Twitter* (London: Pluto Press, 2018).

50   Richard Rodriquez, "Sign of the Times," *New York Times Style Magazine* (October 19, 2014), p. 58.

51   Zygmunt Bauman, "Miseries of Happiness," in *The Art of Life* (Cambridge, UK: Polity Press, 2008), p. 41.

52   Anne Case and Angus Deaton, *Deaths of Despair and the Future of Capitalism* (Princeton: Princeton University Press, 2020).

53   Hannah Arendt, *Hannah Arendt: The Last Interview and Other Conversations* (Brooklyn, NY: Melville House Publishing, 2013), pp. 33–34.

54   John Lewis, "Together, You Can Redeem the Soul of Our Nation," *New York Times* (July 30, 2020). Online: https://www.nytimes.com/2020/07/30/opinion/john-lewis-civil-rights-america.html?action=click&module=Opinion&pgtype=Homepage

Chapter 4

1   Nathan J. Robinson, "Isn't 'Right-Wing Populism' Just Fascism?" *Current Affairs* (June 18, 2020). Online: https://www.currentaffairs.org/2020/06/isnt-right-wing-populism-just-fascism

2   Richard J. Bernstein, "The Illuminations of Hannah Arendt," *The New York Times* (June 20, 2016). Online: https://www.nytimes.com/2018/06/20/opinion/why-read-hannah-arendt-now.html

3   Ishaan Tharoor, "The Far-Right Agenda of Trump's Most Controversial Aide," *Washington Post* (November 25, 2019). Online: https://www.washingtonpost.com/world/2019/11/25/far-right-agenda-trumps-most-controversial-aide/; Judd Legum, "The White Nationalist in the White House," *Popular Information* (November 13, 2019). Online: https://popular.info/p/the-white-nationalist-in-the-white?token=eyJ1c2VyX2lkIjo3MDAzNDAsInBvc3RfaWQiOjE2ODkyNSwiXyI6IlhLMlZsIiwiaWF0IjoxNTTczNzU4ODg4LCJleHAiOjE1NzM3NjI0ODgsImlzcyI6InB1Yi0xNjY0Iiwic3ViIjoicG9zdC1yZWFjdGlvbiJ9.JC7rOVpseF9rOU5pwdW4ZMk824V-QN3SGsD-5pxkMIY; Jared Holt,

"Leaked Emails Reveal Extent of Stephen Miller's Extremism and GOP's Moral Rot," *Right-Wing Watch* (November 12, 2019). Online: https://www.rightwingwatch.org/post/leaked-emails-reveal-stephen-millers-extremism-and-the-gops-moral-rot/

4   Vijay Prashad, "Here Not Death but the Future Is Frightening: The Twenty-Eighth Newsletter (2020)," *Tricontinental* (July 9, 2020). Online: https://www.thetricontinental.org/newsletterissue/28-coronavirus/

5   Adam Serwer, "The White Nationalists Are Winning," *The Atlantic* (December 13, 2019). Online: https://www.theatlantic.com/ideas/archive/2018/08/the-battle-that-erupted-in-charlottesville-is-far-from-over/567167/

6   John Feffer, "The Far Right Is Winning the Global Battle for Hearts and Minds," *Truthdig* (October 25, 2018). Online: https://www.truthdig.com/articles/the-far-right-is-winning-the-global-battle-for-hearts-and-minds/

7   Annie Karni, Maggie Haberman, and Sydney Ember, "Trump Plays on Racist Fears of Terrorized Suburbs to Court White Voters," *New York Times* (June 29, 2020). Online: https://www.nytimes.com/2020/07/29/us/politics/trump-suburbs-housing-white-voters.html?referringSource=artic leShare

8   Ishaan Tharoor, "Trump's Racism Cements His Party's Place among the West's Far Right," *Washington Post* (July 16, 2019). Online: https://www.washingtonpost.com/world/2019/07/16/trumps-racism-cements-his-partys-place-among-wests-far-right/

9   Shira Ovide, "A Trump vs. Twitter Week," *New York Times* (May 29, 2020). Online: https://www.nytimes.com/2020/05/29/technology/trump-twitter-warning.html

10 Jake Johnson, "Trump Executive Order against Social Media Giants Denounced as Unlawful Ploy to 'Eviscerate Public Oversight of His Lies,'" *Common Dreams* (May 28, 2020). Online: https://www.commondreams.org/news/2020/05/28/trump-executive-order-against-social-media-giants-denounced-unlawful-ploy-eviscerate?cd-origin=rss&utm_term=AO&utm_campaign=Daily%20Newsletter&utm_content=email&utm_source=Daily%20Newsletter&utm_medium=Email

11 Jamelle Bouie, "Maybe This Isn't Such a Good Time to Prosecute a Culture War," *New York Times* (July 7, 2020). Online: https://www.nytimes.com/2020/07/07/opinion/trump-mount-rushmore-culture-war.html

12 Peter Baker, Raymond Zhong, and Russell Goldman, "Twitter Places Warning on a Trump Tweet, Saying It Glorified Violence," *New York Times* (May 29, 2020). Online: https://www.nytimes.com/2020/05/29/technology/trump-twitter-minneapolis-george-floyd.html

13 Oliver Milman and Martin Pengelly, "Trump Praises Secret Service and Threatens Protesters with 'Vicious Dogs,'" *Washington Post* (May 30, 2020). Online: https://www.washingtonpost.com/politics/2020/05/28/trump-retweets-video-saying-only-good-democrat-is-dead-democrat/

14 Baker, Zhong, and Goldman, "Twitter Places Warning on a Trump Tweet."

15 David Sirota, "Who Exactly Is Doing the Looting, and Who's Being Looted?" *Jacobin* (May 31, 2020). Online: https://jacobinmag.com/2020/05/looting-minneapolis-police-george-floyd

16 Ibid.

17 Juan Cole, "Trump's 'When the Looting Starts, the Shooting Starts' Is Classic Fascism, Classic Racism," *Informed Comment* (April 30, 2020). Online: https://www.juancole.com/2020/05/looting-shooting-classic.html

18 Amy Goodman, "Historian Robin D.G. Kelley: Years of Racial Justice Organizing Laid Groundwork for Today's Uprising," *Democracy Now!* (June 11, 2020). Online: https://www.democracynow.org/2020/6/11/robin_dg_kelley_social_movements

19 David Jackson, "Trump's Post Touting a False 'Cure' for COVID-19," *USA Today* (July 28, 2020). Online: https://www.usatoday.com/story/news/politics/2020/07/28/twitter-removes-donald-trump-post-touting-false-cure-Covid-19/5525358002/

20 Mary Papenfuss, "Yes, 'Demons Sleep with People,' Insists Texas Doctor Who 'Impressed' Trump," *Huffington Post* (August 1, 2020). Online: https://www.huffingtonpost.ca/entry/stella-immanuel-interview-trump-demon-sex-hydroxychloroquine_n_5f24bf5bc5b68fbfc8833cea?ri18n=true

21 Audra D.S. Burch, Weiyi Cai, Gabriel Gianordoli, Morrigan McCarthy, and Jugal K. Patel, "How Black Lives Matter Reached Every Corner of America," *New York Times* (June 13, 2020). Online: https://www.nytimes.com/interactive/2020/06/13/us/george-floyd-protests-cities-photos.html

22 Peter Baker and Maggie Astor, "Trump Pushes a Conspiracy Theory that Falsely Accuses a TV Host of Murder," *New York Times* (May 26, 2020). Online: https://www.nytimes.com/2020/05/26/us/politics/klausutis-letter-jack-dorsey.html

23   Aaron Blake, "'The Only Good Democrat Is a Dead Democrat.' 'When the Looting Starts, the Shooting Starts.' Twice in 25 Hours, Trump Tweets Conspicuous Allusions to Violence," *Washington Post* (May 29, 2020). Online: https://www.washingtonpost.com/politics/2020/05/28/trump-retweets-video-saying-only-good-democrat-is-dead-democrat/

24   Karen J. Greenberg, "Down the Memory Hole: Trump's Strategic Assault on Democracy, Word by Word," *TomDispatch.com* (May 17, 2018). Online: http://www.tomdispatch.com/blog/176424/

25   Matt Zapotosky and Isaac Stanley-Becker, "Gripped by Disease, Unemployment and Outrage at the Police, America Plunges into Crisis," *Washington Post* (May 29, 2020). Online: https://www.washingtonpost.com/national-security/plagued-by-disease-unemployment-and-outrage-at-the-police-america-plunges-into-crisis/2020/05/29/c8329bb2-a1b5-11ea-81bb-c2f70f01034b_story.html

26   Ibid.

27   Chauncey DeVega, "Irish Author Fintan O'Toole Explains the 'Suspension of Disbelief' That Made Trump's Destruction of America Possible," *AlterNet* (May 26, 2020). Online: https://www.alternet.org/2020/05/irish-author-fintan-otoole-explains-the-suspension-of-disbelief-that-made-trumps-destruction-of-america-possible/

28   Hannah Arendt, *The Last Interview and Other Conversations* (Brooklyn, NY: Melville House Publishing, 2013), p. 86.

29   Cited in Aaron Lake Smith, "The Trials of Vasily Grossman," *Harpers* (July 2019 issue). Online: https://harpers.org/archive/2019/07/the-trials-of-vasily-grossman/

30   John Keane, "The Pathologies of Populism," *The Conversation* (September 28, 2017). Online: http://theconversation.com/the-pathologies-of-populism-82593

31   For instance, see Henry A. Giroux, *American Nightmare: Facing the Challenge of Fascism* (San Francisco: City Lights Books, 2018) and *The Terror of the Unforeseen* (Los Angeles: LARB Books, 2019).

32   Cited in Jan-Werner Müller, "Donald Trump's Use of the Term 'the People' Is a Warning Sign," *Guardian* (January 24, 2017). Online: https://www.theguardian.com/commentisfree/2017/jan/24/donald-trumps-warning-sign-populism-authoritarianism-inauguration

33   Jan-Werner Müller, "Trump, Erdoğan, Farage: The Attractions of Populism for Politicians, the Dangers for Democracy," *Guardian*

(September 1, 2016). Online: https://www.theguardian.com/books/2016/
sep/02/trump-erdogan-farage-the-attractions

34   Editors, "Coronavirus Live Updates: Trump Administration Models Predict
Near Doubling of Daily Death Toll by June," *New York Times* (May 4,
2020). Online: https://www.nytimes.com/2020/05/04/us/coronavirus-
updates.html?campaign_id=60&emc=edit_na_20200504&instance_
id=0&nl=breaking-news&ref=cta&regi_id=15581699&segment_
id=26577&user_id=95e1c4784b623e7fef9f5c124266285f

35   Stephen Greenblatt, "Excerpt Adapted from Tyrant: Shakespeare on Politics,"
Longreads (July 17, 2018). Online: https://longreads.com/2018/07/18/the-
tyrant-and-his-enablers/

36   Chantal Mouffe, *For a Left Populism* (London: Verso, 2018); Thomas
Frank, *The People, No: A Brief History of Anti-Populism* (New York:
Metropolitan Books, 2020).

37   Federico Finchelstein, *From Fascism to Populism in History* (Oakland:
University of California Press, 2017), p. xv.

38   Ibid., p. xv.

39   Cass Mudde, "The Populist Zeitgeist," *Government and Opposition*
39, no., 4 (2004), 541–563. Online: https://www.cambridge.org/core/
journals/government-and-opposition/article/populist-zeitgeist/2CD34F8
B25C4FFF4F322316833DB94B7/core-reader

40   These issues are taken up in detail in Peter C. Baker, "'We the People': The
Battle to Define Populism," *Guardian* (January 10, 2019). Online: https://
www.theguardian.com/news/2019/jan/10/we-the-people-the-battle-to-
define-populism

41   John Keane, "The Pathologies of Populism," *The Conversation*
(September 28, 2017). Online: http://theconversation.com/the-
pathologies-of-populism-82593; Jan-Werner Müller, *What Is Populism?*
(Philadelphia: University of Pennsylvania Press, 2016); Federico
Finchelstein, *From Fascism to Populism in History* (Oakland: University
of California Press, 2017). Clearly, an important contribution to the
complex literature on populism is by Ernesto Laclau. See Ernesto
Laclau, *On Populist Reason* (London: Verso, 2005).

42   Jason Stanley, "Populism Isn't the Problem," *Boston Review* (August 15,
2019). Online: http://bostonreview.net/politics/jason-frank-populism-
not-the-problem

43   Federico Finchelstein, *From Fascism to Populism in History* (Oakland:
University of California Press, 2017), p. xv.

44　Peter E. Gordon, "The Utopian Promise of Adorno's 'Open Thinking,' Fifty Years On," *New York Review of Books* (August 5, 2019). Online: https://www.nybooks.com/daily/2019/08/05/the-utopian-promise-of-adornos-open-thinking-fifty-years-on/

45　Michael Kazin, "How Can Donald Trump and Bernie Sanders Both be 'Populist'?" *New York Times* (March 22, 2016). Online: https://www.nytimes.com/2016/03/27/magazine/how-can-donald-trump-and-bernie-sanders-both-be-populist.html

46　Federico Finchelstein, *From Fascism to Populism in History* (Oakland: University of California Press, 2017), p. 5.

47　Jeff Noonan, "Far-Right Identity, Politics and the Task for the Left," *Socialist Project* (May 21, 2018). Online: https://socialistproject.ca/2019/05/far-right-identity-politics-and-the-task-for-the-left/

48　John Keane, "The Pathologies of Populism," *The Conversation* (September 28, 2017). Online: http://theconversation.com/the-pathologies-of-populism-82593

49　Nancy Fraser, "From Progressive Neoliberalism to Trump—and Beyond," *American Affairs* 1, no. 4 (Winter 2017). Online: https://americanaffairsjournal.org/2017/11/progressive-neoliberalism-trump-beyond/

50　Nancy Fraser and Houssam Hamade, "A New Leftist Narrative Is Required," *Open Democracy* (August 2017). Online: https://www.opendemocracy.net/nancy-fraser-houssam-hamade/new-leftist-narrative-is-required

Chapter 5

1　Kamalakar Duvvuru, "Is India Displaying Signs of Neo-Fascism?," *Countercurrents.org* (July 29, 2019). Online: https://countercurrents.org/2019/07/is-india-displaying-signs-of-neo-fascism/#_ednref29

2　David Smith, "Betsy DeVos: The Billionaire Republican Destroying Public Education," *Guardian* (December 27, 2019). Online: https://www.theguardian.com/us-news/2019/dec/27/betsy-devos-trump-republicans-education-secretary

3　See, for instance, Henry A. Giroux, *Youth in a Suspect Society* (New York: Palgrave Macmillan, 2010); Henry A. Giroux, *The University in Chains:*

Confronting the Military-Industrial-Academic Complex (New York: Routledge, 2007).

4 See, especially, Stuart Hall, "The Neoliberal Revolution," in *The Neoliberal Crisis*, ed. Jonathan Rutherford and Sally Davison (London: Lawrence Wishart, 2012), chapter 1; David Harvey, *A Brief History of Neoliberalism* (New York: Oxford University Press, 2005); Sheldon S. Wolin, *Democracy Incorporated: Managed Democracy and the Specter of Inverted Totalitarianism* (Princeton: Princeton University Press, 2008); Wendy Brown, *Undoing the Demos: Neoliberalism's Stealth Revolution* (New York: Zone Books, 2015); Chantal Mouffe, *For a Left Populism* (London: Verso, 2018).

5 I take up this theme in great detail in Henry A. Giroux, *American Nightmare: Facing the Challenge of Fascism* (San Francisco: City Lights, 2018) and Henry A. Giroux, *The Terror of the Unforeseen* (Los Angeles: LARB Books, 2019).

6 Max Boot, "Americans' Ignorance of History is a National Scandal," *Washington Post* (February 20, 2019). Online: https://www.washingtonpost.com/opinions/americans-ignorance-of-history-is-a-national-scandal/2019/02/20/b8be683c-352d-11e9-854a-7a14d7fec96a_story.html?utm_term=.459563b6e596

7 David W. Blight, "Trump and History: Ignorance and Denial," *Underground Railroad Freedom Center* (May 25, 2017). Online: https://freedomcenter.org/voice/trump-and-history-ignorance-and-denial

8 Ibid.

9 Ibid.

10 Pankaj Mishra, "A Gandhian Stand against the Culture of Cruelty," *New York Review of Books* (May 22, 2018). Online: http://www.nybooks.com/daily/2018/05/22/the-culture-of-cruelty/

11 John Steppling, "Social Contagion," *John-Steppling.com* (July 26, 2020). Online: http://john-steppling.com/2020/07/social-contagion/

12 C.J. Polychroniou, "Noam Chomsky: Trump Is Consolidating Far-Right Power Globally," *Truthout* (July 3, 2019). Online: https://truthout.org/articles/noam-chomsky-trump-is-consolidating-far-right-power-globally/

13 On the issue of myth-making as a central element of fascist politics, see Jason Stanley, *How Fascism Works: The Politics of Us and Them* (New York: Random House, 2018).

14 See, for example, Jane Mayer, "The Making of the Fox News White House," *New Yorker* (March 4, 2019). Online: https://www.newyorker.com/magazine/2019/03/11/the-making-of-the-fox-news-white-house

15 Jon Nixon, "Hannah Arendt: Thinking Versus Evil," *Times Higher Education* (February 26, 2015). Online at: https://www.timeshighereducation.co.uk/features/hannah-arendt-thinking-versus-evil/2018664.article?page=0%2C0

16 Eric Alterman, "The Decline of Historical Thinking," *New Yorker* (February 4, 2019). Online: https://www.newyorker.com/news/news-desk/the-decline-of-historical-thinking

17 Quoted in Michael L. Silk and David L. Andrews, "(Re)Presenting Baltimore: Place, Policy, Politics, and Cultural Pedagogy," *Review of Education, Pedagogy, and Cultural Studies* 33 (2011), 436.

18 Terry Eagleton, "Reappraisals: What Is the Worth of Social Democracy?," *Harper's Magazine* (October 2010), p. 78. Online: http://www.harpers.org/archive/2010/10/0083150

19 Alex Honneth, *Pathologies of Reason* (New York: Columbia University Press, 2009), p. 188.

20 Stephen Hopgood, in Cihan Aksan and Jon Bailes, eds., "One Question Fascism (Part Two)—Is Fascism Making a Comeback?," *State of Nature Blog* (December 4, 2017). Online: http://stateofnatureblog.com/one-question-fascism-part-two/

21 Leon Wieseltier, "Among the Disrupted," *New York Times* (January 7, 2015). Online: https://www.nytimes.com/2015/01/18/books/review/among-the-disrupted.html

22 For a recent example of the erasure of history, see Hagar Shezaf, "Burying the Nakba: How Israel Systematically Hides Evidence of 1948 Expulsion of Arabs," *Haaretz* (July 5, 2109). Online: https://www.haaretz.com/israel-news/.premium.MAGAZINE-how-israel-systematically-hides-evidence-of-1948-expulsion-of-arabs-1.7435103

23 Simon Romero, Zolan Kanno-Youngs, Manny Fernandez, Daniel Borunda, Aaron Montes, and Caitlin Dickerson, "Hungry, Scared and Sick: Inside the Migrant Detention Center in Clint, Tex.," *New York Times* (July 6, 2019). Online: https://www.nytimes.com/interactive/2019/07/06/us/migrants-border-patrol-clint.html

24 Ibid.

25 Emily Cochrane, "Trump and His Aides Dismiss Reports of Disease and Hunger in Border Facilities," *New York Times* (July 7, 2019). Online: https://www.nytimes.com/2019/07/07/us/politics/border-centers-mcaleenan.html

26 Glenn Kessler, Salvador Rizzo, and Meg Kelly, *Donald Trump and His Assault on Truth: The President's Falsehoods, Misleading Claims and Flat-Out Lies* (New York: Scribner, 2020).

27 Richards J. Evans, "A Warning from History," *The Nation* (February 28, 2017). Online: https://www.thenation.com/article/the-ways-to-destroy-democracy/. See also Robert O. Paxton, *The Anatomy of Fascism* (New York: Alfred A. Knopf, 2004).

28 Toni Morrison, *The Source of Self Regard* (New York: Alfred A. Knopf, 2019), p. 272.

29 Giroux, *American Nightmare*.

30 See, for example, the classic essay: Jerome Kohn, "Totalitarianism: The Inversion of Politics," The Hannah Arendt Papers at the Library of Congress Essays and Lectures—"On the Nature of Totalitarianism: An Essay in Understanding," Series: Speeches and Writings File, 1923–1975 (n.d.) Online at: http://memory.loc.gov/ammem/arendthtml/essayb1.html

31 Angela Y. Davis, *Freedom Is a Constant Struggle: Ferguson, Palestine and the Foundations of a Movement*, ed. Frank Barat (Chicago, IL: Haymarket Books, 2016).

32 Henry A. Giroux, "Cultural Studies, Public Pedagogy, and the Responsibility of Intellectuals," *Communication and Critical/Cultural Studies* 1, no. 1 (March 2004), 68.

33 Byung-Chul Han, *The Burnout Society*, trans. Erik Butler (Stanford, CA: Stanford University Press, 2015), p. 12.

34 Byung-Chul Han, *In the Swarm: Digital Prospects*, trans. Erik Butler (Cambridge, MA: MIT Press, 2017).

35 Eric Alterman, "The Decline of Historical Thinking," *New Yorker* (February 4, 2019). Online: https://www.newyorker.com/news/news-desk/the-decline-of-historical-thinking

36 Ariel Dorfman, "How to Read Donald Trump on Burning Books but Not Ideas," *TomDispatch.com* (September 14, 2017). Online: http://www.tomdispatch.com/blog/176326/tomgram%3A_ariel_dorfman%2C_a_tale_of_two_donalds/

37   Anya Ventura, "Before Ta-Nehisi Coates: On James Alan McPherson's 'Crabcakes,'" *Los Angeles Review of Books* (July 4, 2019). Online: https://lareviewofbooks.org/article/before-ta-nehisi-coates-on-james-alan-mcphersons-crabcakes/

38   Michael S. Schmidt and Maggie Haberman Mueller, "Examining Trump's Tweets in Wide-Ranging Obstruction Inquiry," *Washington Post* (July 26, 2018). Online: https://www.nytimes.com/2018/07/26/us/politics/trump-tweets-mueller-obstruction.html?nl=top-stories&nlid=15581699ries&ref=cta

39   Jonathan Freedland, "Inspired by Trump, the World Could be Heading Back to the 1930s," *Guardian* (June 22, 2018). Online: https://www.theguardian.com/commentisfree/2018/jun/22/trump-world-1930s-children-parents-europe-migrants

40   Hannah Arendt, "The Image of Hell," *Commentary* (September 1, 1946). Online: https://www.commentarymagazine.com/articles/the-black-book-the-nazi-crime-against-the-jewish-people-and-hitlers-professors-by-max-weinreich/

41   Melvin Rogers, "Democracy Is a Habit: Practice It," *Boston Review* (July 25, 2018). Online: http://bostonreview.net/politics/melvin-rogers-democracy-habit-practice-it

42   Ibid.

43   For an analysis of the origins of fascism in American capitalism, see Michael Joseph Roberto, *The Coming of the American Behemoth* (New York: Monthly Review Press, 2019).

Chapter 6

1   Ruth Ben-Ghiat, "Beware of President Trump's Nefarious Language Games," *Washington Post* (December 21, 2017). Online: https://www.washingtonpost.com/news/democracy-post/wp/2017/12/21/beware-of-president-trumps-nefarious-language-games/?utm_term=.dc9e11b2d2c9; see also Naomi Fry, "The Year in Stupidity," *New Yorker* (December 13, 2019). Online: https://www.newyorker.com/culture/2019-in-review/the-year-in-stupidity?verso=true

2   Timothy Snyder, *On Tyranny: Twenty Lessons from the Twentieth Century* (London: Polity Press, 2017); Jason Stanley, *How Fascism Works* (New York: Random House, 2018).

3   See, especially, Peter Fritzche, *Hitler's First Hundred Days* (New York: Basic Books, 2020).

4   Hannah Arendt, *The Last Interview and Other Conversations* (Brooklyn, NY: Melville House Publishing, 2013), p. 33.

5   Jeffrey Toobin, "The Roger Stone Case Shows Why Trump Is Worse than Nixon," *New Yorker* (July 11, 2020). Online: https://www.newyorker.com/news/daily-comment/the-roger-stone-case-shows-why-trump-is-worse-than-nixon

6   Enzo Traverso, *The New Faces of Fascism* (London: Verso, 2019).

7   Nancy Fraser, *The Old Is Dying and the New Cannot Be Born* (London: Verso Press, 2019), p. 9.

8   Chauncey DeVega, "Brian Klaas: Trump Has 'Exposed the Weakness of American Democracy'—But There's Hope," *Salon* (October 23, 2019). Online: https://www.salon.com/2019/10/23/brian-klaas-trump-has-exposed-the-weakness-of-american-democracy-but-theres-hope/

9   Cited in Ishaan Tharoor, "Trump's Impeachment Battle Is Part of a Bigger Global Crisis in Democracy," *Washington Post* (October 4, 2019) Online: https://www.washingtonpost.com/world/2019/10/04/trumps-impeachment-battle-is-part-bigger-global-crisis-democracy/

10 Peter Maass, "Trump Built His Own Green Zone. He Got the Wall He Deserves," *The Intercept* (June 5, 2020). Online: https://theintercept.com/2020/06/05/white-house-wall-trump-protests/

11 David Brennan, "Eric Trump Calls Black Lives Matter Protesters 'Animals,'" *Newsweek* (June 21, 2020). Online: https://www.newsweek.com/eric-trump-calls-black-lives-matter-protesters-animals-rally-tulsa-1512374

12 Editors, "On the Murder of George Floyd and the Demand for Racial Justice," *Third Text* (June 22, 2020). Online: https://mailchi.mp/78088bba729d/statement-from-the-editors-of-third-text?e=edf32547f2

13 Joe Sommerlad and Danielle Zoellner, "President Ridiculed for Underwhelming Tulsa Rally Turnout as He Admits Ordering Staff to Slow Coronavirus Testing and Mocks 'Kung Flu' Pandemic," *Independent* (June 21, 2020). Online: https://www.independent.co.uk/news/world/americas/

us-politics/trump-news-live-tulsa-rally-coronavirus-us-update-today-speech-empty-seats-a9577676.html

14 Glenn Kessler, Salvador Rizzo, and Meg Kelley, *Donald Trump and His Assault on Truth: The President's Falsehoods, Misleading Claims and Flat-Out Lies* (New York: Scribner, 2020).

15 See Paul Street, "Is This Goodbye to the American Republic?," *Truthdig* (December 20, 2019). Online: https://www.truthdig.com/articles/is-this-goodbye-to-the-american-republic/

16 David A. Graham, Adrienne Green, Cullen Murphy, and Parker Richards, "An Oral History of Trump's Bigotry," *The Atlantic* (June 2019). Online: https://www.theatlantic.com/magazine/archive/2019/06/trump-racism-comments/588067/; German Lopez, "Donald Trump's Long History of Racism, from the 1970s to 2019," *Vox* (July 15, 2019). Online: https://www.vox.com/2016/7/25/12270880/donald-trump-racist-racism-history

17 Ralph Nader, "Impeach Trump for His Illegal War on Iran," *Truthdig* (January 9, 2020). Online: https://www.truthdig.com/articles/ralph-nader-impeach-trump-for-his-illegal-war-on-iran/

18 Jamie Ross, "Trump Made Twice as Many False Claims in 2019 as 2017 and 2018 Combined: Washington Post," *Daily Beast* (January 20, 2020). Online: https://www.thedailybeast.com/trump-made-twice-as-many-false-claims-in-2019-than-2017-and-2018-combined-washington-post

19 Timothy Snyder, *On Tyranny: Twenty Lessons from the Twentieth Century* (London: Polity Press, 2017), p. 71.

20 Ralph Nader, "Impeach Trump for His Illegal War on Iran," *Truthdig* (January 9, 2020). Online: https://www.truthdig.com/articles/ralph-nader-impeach-trump-for-his-illegal-war-on-iran/

21 Robert O' Paxton, *The Anatomy of Fascism* (New York: Knopf, 2004), p. 202.

22 Eric Boehm, "Without Evidence of 'Imminent' Attack on Americans, the White House's Justification for Killing Iranian General Seems Hollow," *Reason* (January 4, 2020). Online: https://reason.com/2020/01/04/absent-evidence-of-imminent-attack-on-americans-white-houses-justification-for-killing-iranian-general-collapses/

23 Jason Stanley, *How Fascism Works* (New York: Random House, 2018), p. 5.

24 Peter Baker, Zolan Kanno-Youngs, and Monica Davey, "Trump Threatens to Send Federal Law Enforcement Forces to More Cities,"

New York Times (July 20, 2020). Online: https://www.nytimes.com/2020/07/20/us/politics/trump-chicago-portland-federal-agents.html?action=click&module=Top%20Stories&pgtype=Homepage

25 Michelle Goldberg, "Trump's Occupation of American Cities Has Begun," *New York Times* (July 20, 2020). Online: https://www.nytimes.com/2020/07/20/opinion/portland-protests-trump.html

26 KATU Staff, "Brown Responds to Trump Claim Federal Officers Have Done 'Fantastic Job' in Portland," *KATU2* (July 20, 2020). Online: https://katu.com/news/local/gov-kate-brown-responds-to-president-donald-trump-claim-federal-officers-have-done-fantastic-job-in-portland

27 Martin Pengelly and Edward Helmore, "Impeachment: Warren Accuses Trump of 'Wag the Dog' Strike on Suleimani," *Guardian* (January 5, 2020). Online: https://www.theguardian.com/us-news/2020/jan/05/impeachment-warren-trump-wag-the-dog-qassem-suleimani-iran

28 Susan E. Rice, "The Dire Consequences of Trump's Suleimani Decision," *New York Times* (January 4, 2020). Online: https://www.nytimes.com/2020/01/04/opinion/trump-suleimani-iran.html

29 Justin Wise, "Bolton: Putin Thinks 'He Can Play' Trump Like a 'Fiddle,'" *The Hill* (June 18, 2020). Online: https://thehill.com/homenews/administration/503332-bolton-putin-thinks-he-can-play-trump-like-a-fiddle

30 David E. Sanger and Helene Cooper, "Trump and the Military: A Mutual Embrace Might Dissolve on America's Streets," *New York Times* (June 4, 2020). Online: https://www.nytimes.com/2020/06/04/us/politics/trump-military-protests.html?campaign_id=2&emc=edit_th_200605&instance_id=19008&nl=todaysheadlines&regi_id=51563793&segment_id=30135&user_id=ac16f3c28b64af0b86707bb1a8f1b07c

31 See, especially, Sean Wilentz, "Why We Must Impeach," *Rolling Stone* (October 11, 2019). Online: https://www.rollingstone.com/politics/politics-features/sean-wilentz-why-we-must-impeach-donald-trump-897246/

32 Alexa Diaz, "Trump Says Adam Schiff and Nancy Pelosi Committed 'Treason' and Should Be 'Impeached,'" *Los Angeles Times* (October 7, 2019). Online: https://www.latimes.com/politics/story/2019-10-07/trump-adam-schiff-nancy-pelosi-treason-impeach. See also Marina Fang, "Trump Now Says Adam Schiff Should Be Arrested for

Treason," *Huffington Post* (September 30, 2019). Online: https://www.
huffingtonpost.ca/entry/trump-adam-schiff-treason-impeachment_n_5d
91f4f8e4b0e9e760500be1?ri18n=true

33 Isaac Stanley-Becker, "Trump Says 'Treason.' His Fans Invoke Violence.
How Attacks Against Schiff Are Escalating Online," *Washington Post*
(October 14, 2019), Online: https://www.washingtonpost.com/politics/
trump-says-treason-his-fans-invoke-violence-how-attacks-against-
schiff-are-escalating-online/2019/10/14/9f613974-ec4c-11e9-9306-
47cb0324fd44_story.html

34 Victor Klemperer, *The Language of the Third Reich* (New York:
Bloomsbury, 2006), pp. 207, 208.

35 Mike Levine, "'No Blame?' ABC News Finds 36 Cases Invoking
'Trump' in Connection with Violence, Threats, Alleged Assaults," *News
5 Cleveland* (August 14, 2019). Online: https://www.news5cleveland.
com/news/national-politics/no-blame-abc-news-finds-36-cases-
invoking-trump-in-connection-with-violence-threats-alleged-assaults;
Ruth Ben-Ghiat, "Beware of President Trump's Nefarious Language
Games," *Washington Post* (December 21, 2017). Online: https://www.
washingtonpost.com/news/democracy-post/wp/2017/12/21/beware-of-
president-trumps-nefarious-language-games/?utm_term=.dc9e11b2d2c9

36 Levine, "'No Blame?' ABC News Finds 36 Cases Invoking 'Trump'
in Connection with Violence, Threats, Alleged Assaults"; Ben-Ghiat,
"Beware of President Trump's Nefarious Language Games."

37 Chris Hedges, "The Impeachment's Moral Hypocrisy," *Truthdig*
(December 23, 2019). Online: https://www.truthdig.com/articles/the-
moral-hypocrisy-of-impeachment/

38 Heather Digby Parton, "GOP Uses Impeachment Hearings as Propaganda
Circus," *Truthout* (December 13, 2019). Online: https://truthout.org/
articles/gop-uses-impeachment-hearings-as-propaganda-circus/

39 Bill Moyers, "All Presidents Lie, But Trump Has Created a Culture of
Lying," *Democracy Now* (November 13, 2019). Online: https://www.
democracynow.org/2019/11/13/bill_moyers_trump_culture_of_lying

40 Judd Legum, "How the Media Blew the Impeachment Story," *Popular
Information* (December 17, 2019). Online: https://popular.info/p/how-
the-media-blew-the-impeachment1

41 I take up these issues in great detail in Henry A. Giroux, *The Terror of the
Unforeseen* (Los Angeles: LARB Books, 2019).

42 Key Data of the Day, "The Number of Confirmed Cases Is Growing
     Faster than Ever as New Hot Spots Emerge around the World," *New York
     Times* (June 4, 2020). Online: https://www.nytimes.com/2020/06/04/
     world/coronavirus-us-update.html?campaign_id=60&emc=edit_
     na_20200604&instance_id=0&nl=breaking-news&ref=cta&regi_
     id=51563793&segment_id=30089&user_id=ac16f3c28b64af0b86707bb1a
     8f1b07c

43 Andre Singer, "Jair Bolsonaro, Wannabe Dictator," *Le Monde
     Diplomatique* (July 2020). Online: https://mondediplo.
     com/2020/07/05brazil

44 Robert Zaretsky, "What Would Sartre Think about Trump-Era
     Republicans?," *New York Times* (October 13, 2019). Online: https://www.
     nytimes.com/2019/08/13/opinion/vichy-republican-trump.html

45 Paul Krugman, "Democrats May Save Us Yet," *New York Times*
     (December 19, 2019). Online: https://www.nytimes.com/2019/12/19/
     opinion/impeachment-democrats-trump.html

46 Andrew Gawthorpe, "Trump Is Unleashing Authoritarianism on US
     Cities—Just in Time for the Election," *Guardian* (July 23, 2020). Online:
     https://www.theguardian.com/commentisfree/2020/jul/23/trump-
     authoritarianism-portland-cbp-election

47 Judd Legum, "Partners in Crime," *Popular Information* (October 7, 2019).
     Online: https://popular.info/p/partners-in-crime

48 Adam Serwer, "The White Nationalists Are Winning," *The Atlantic*
     (December 13, 2019). Online: https://www.theatlantic.com/ideas/
     archive/2018/08/the-battle-that-erupted-in-charlottesville-is-far-from-
     over/567167/

49 Jonathan Martin, "Fear and Loyalty: How Donald Trump Took Over
     the Republican Party," *New York Times* (December 21, 2020). Online:
     https://www.nytimes.com/2019/12/21/us/politics/trump-impeachment-
     republicans.html

50 Stephen Collinson, "Fauci Warns of Disturbing Trend as Trump
     Ignores Viral Surge," *CNN Politics* (June 24, 2020). Online: https://
     www.cnn.com/2020/06/23/politics/donald-trump-coronavirus-
     pandemic-election-2020/index.html?emci=0beedfe3-58b6-
     ea11-9b05-00155d039e74&emdi=954c55c7-68b6-ea11-9b05-
     00155d039e74&ceid=648633

51 Theodor W. Adorno, "The Meaning of Working through the Past," *Guild and Defense*, trans. Henry W. Pickford (Cambridge: Harvard University Press, 2010), p. 213.

52 Tamsin Shaw, "William Barr: The Carl Schmitt of Our Time," *New York Review of Books* (January 15, 2020). Online: https://www.nybooks.com/daily/2020/01/15/william-barr-the-carl-schmitt-of-our-time/?utm_medium=email&utm_campaign=NYR%20Daily%20Tamsin%20Shaw&utm_content=NYR%20Daily%20Tamsin%20Shaw+CID_fab36e70a506d2d42e8747691ecb4ebd&utm_source=Newsletter&utm_term=William%20Barr%20The%20Carl%20Schmitt%20of%20Our%20Time

53 Eric H. Holder, "William Barr is Unfit to be Attorney General," *Washington Post* (December 11, 2019). Online: https://www.washingtonpost.com/opinions/eric-holder-william-barr-is-unfit-to-be-attorney-general/2019/12/11/99882092-1c55-11ea-87f7-f2e91143c60d_story.html

54 James Risen, "William Barr Has Turned the Justice Department into a Law Firm with One Client: Donald Trump," *The Intercept* (June 22, 2020). Online: https://theintercept.com/2020/06/22/william-barr-has-turned-the-justice-department-into-a-law-firm-with-one-client-donald-trump/?utm_medium=email&utm_source=The%20Intercept%20Newsletter

55 Cited in Susan B. Glasser, "#BunkerBoy's Photo-Op War," *New Yorker* (June 3, 2020). Online: https://www.newyorker.com/news/letter-from-trumps-washington/bunkerboys-photo-op-war

56 Jake Johnson, "'He Must Resign': Attorney General Barr Personally Ordered Police Assault on Peaceful DC Protesters, Report Says," *Common Dreams* (June 2, 2020). Online: https://www.commondreams.org/news/2020/06/02/he-must-resign-attorney-general-barr-personally-ordered-police-assault-peaceful-dc

57 Cited in Glasser, "#BunkerBoy's Photo-Op War."

58 Katie Benner, "Barr Says There Is No Systemic Racism in Policing," *New York Times* (June 7, 2020). Online: https://www.nytimes.com/2020/06/07/us/politics/justice-department-barr-racism-police.html

59 George Will, "Trump Must Be Removed. So Must His Congressional Enablers," *Washington Post* (June 1, 2020). Online: https://www.

washingtonpost.com/opinions/no-one-should-want-four-more-years-of-this-taste-of-ashes/2020/06/01/1a80ecf4-a425-11ea-bb20-ebf0921f3bbd_story.html

60 Peter Wade, "Trump Sycophant Lindsey Graham: 'I Will Do Everything I Can to Make Impeachment Die Quickly' in the Senate," *Rolling Stone* (December 14, 2019). Online: https://www.rollingstone.com/politics/politics-news/trump-sycophant-lindsey-graham-i-will-do-everything-i-can-to-make-impeachment-die-quickly–927279/

61 Ibid.

62 Rachel Frazin, "Schiff Calls Barr 'the Second-Most Dangerous Man in the Country,'" *The Hill* (June 25, 2020). Online: https://thehill.com/homenews/house/446895-schiff-calls-barr-is-the-the-2nd-most-dangerous-man-in-the-country

63 Nicholas Fandos, "Justice Dept. Officials Outline Claims of Politicization Under Barr," *New York Times* (June 24, 2020). Online: https://www.nytimes.com/2020/06/24/us/politics/justice-department-politicization.html

64 Nancy Pelosi, "Pelosi Statement on Trump Commuting Sentence of Campaign Advisor Roger Stone," *US Government News Room* (July 11, 2020). Online: https://www.speaker.gov/newsroom/71120

65 Cited in Aron Blake, "Roger Stone, and Trump's Extraordinary Record on Clemency," *Washington Post* (July 11, 2020). Online: https://www.washingtonpost.com/politics/2020/07/11/unprecedented-historic-corruption-why-trumps-pardon-history-is-extraordinary/

66 Maanvi Singh, "Trump Commutes Sentence of Roger Stone, Long-Time Friend and Adviser," *Guardian* (July 11, 2020). Online: https://www.theguardian.com/us-news/2020/jul/10/roger-stone-trump-commutes-prison-sentence

67 Abigail Gracy, "'This Guy Is the Devil': The Rosemary's Baby Theory of Attorney General Bill Barr," *Vanity Fair* (June 28, 2020). Online: https://readersupportednews.org/opinion2/277-75/63721-qthis-guy-is-the-devilq-the-rosemarys-baby-theory-of-attorney-general-bill-barr

68 Hannah Arendt, *The Origins of Totalitarianism* (New York: Harvest Book, 1973), p. 464.

69 Bob Dreyfuss, "Why Does Trump Embrace Foreign Dictators?," *Rolling Stone* (May 4, 2017). Online: https://www.rollingstone.com/politics/politics-news/why-does-trump-embrace-foreign-dictators–118674/

70 Paul Krugman, "Donald Trump and His Team of Morons," *New York Times* (January 14, 2019). Online: https://www.nytimes.com/2019/01/14/opinion/government-shutdown-trump.html

71 Ibid.

72 James Vaughan, "Has America Lost Its Grip on Reality?," *Who.What.Why.* (November 15, 2019). Online: https://whowhatwhy.org/2019/11/15/has-america-lost-its-grip-on-reality

73 Jerry Lambe, "Faculty at Bill Barr's Law School Call for His Censure and Resignation," *Law & Crime* (June 24, 2020). Online: https://lawandcrime.com/high-profile/in-scathing-letter-more-than-80-percent-of-active-faculty-at-bill-barrs-law-school-call-for-his-censure-and-resignation/

74 Anne Applebaum, "History Will Judge the Complicit: Why Have Republican Leaders Abandoned Their Principles in Support of an Immoral and Dangerous President?," *The Atlantic* (July/August 2020). Online: https://www.theatlantic.com/magazine/archive/2020/07/trumps-collaborators/612250/

75 Leo Baeck Medal, "Martha Minow Urges Us to 'Resist Tyranny and Revenge,'" *Leo Baeck Institute* (November 26, 2019). Online: https://www.lbi.org/news/leo-baeck-medal-martha-minow/

76 Shalmali Guttal, "The Fortress World: After the Pandemic, Which Future?," *The Bullet* (July 16, 2020). Online: https://socialistproject.ca/2020/07/fortress-world-after-pandemic/#more

77 On the issue of screen culture, see Richard Butsch, *Screen Culture: A Global History* (London: Polity Press, 2019).

78 Susan Sontag, "Fascinating Fascism," *New York Review of Books* (February 1975). Online: https://www.nybooks.com/articles/1975/02/06/fascinating-fascism/

79 Margaret Sullivan, "It's Time—High Time—to Take Fox News's Destructive Role in America Seriously," *Washington Post* (March 7, 2019). Online: https://www.washingtonpost.com/lifestyle/style/its-time-high-time-to-take-fox-newss-destructive-role-in-america-seriously/2019/03/07/aeb83282-40cc-11e9-922c-64d6b7840b82_story.html

80 Joel Bleifuss, "Fox News, Trump's Ministry of Propaganda," *In These Times* (December 20, 2019). Online: http://inthesetimes.com/article/22196/fox-news-trump-ukraine-fake-news-independent-journalism-in-these-times

81   Binoy Kampmark, "Liquid Modernity: Bauman and the Rootless
     Conditions," *CounterPunch* (January 13, 2017). Online: https://www.
     counterpunch.org/2017/01/13/liquid-modernity-zygmunt-bauman-and-
     the-rootless-condition/
82   Personal correspondence, April 2020.
83   Charles Blow, "Stop Airing Trump's Briefings!," *New York Times* (April 19,
     2020). Online: https://www.nytimes.com/2020/04/19/opinion/trump-
     coronavirus-briefings.html
84   Sontag. "Fascinating Fascism."
85   Richard Brody, "When Bad Nazis Happen to Good Directors: Terrence
     Malick's 'A Hidden Life,'" *New Yorker* (December 16, 2019). Online:
     https://www.newyorker.com/culture/the-front-row/when-bad-nazis-
     happen-to-good-directors-terrence-malicks-a-hidden-life
86   See, especially, Sarah Churchill, "American Fascism: It Has Happened
     Here," *New York Review of Books* (June 22, 2020). Online: https://www.
     nybooks.com/daily/2020/06/22/american-fascism-it-has-happened-here/
87   Jared Holt, "Leaked Emails Reveal Extent of Stephen Miller's Extremism
     and GOP's Moral Rot," *Right Wing Watch* (November 12, 2019). Online:
     https://www.rightwingwatch.org/post/leaked-emails-reveal-stephen-
     millers-extremism-and-the-gops-moral-rot/
88   Judd Legum, "The White Nationalist in the White House,"
     Popular Information (November 13, 2019). Online: https://
     popular.info/p/the-white-nationalist-in-the-white?token=eyJ1c
     2VyX2lkIjo3MDAzNDAsInBvc3RfaWQiOjE2ODkyNSwiXyI6I
     lhLMlZsIiwiaWF0IjoxNTczNzU4ODg4LCJleHAiOjE1NzM3N
     jI0ODgsImlzcyI6InB1Yi0xNjY0Iiwic3ViIjoicG9zdC1yZWFjdGlvbiJ9.
     JC7rOVpseF9rOU5pwdW4ZMk824V-QN3SGsD-5pxkMIY
89   Chris Walker, "Southern Poverty Law Center Adds Stephen Miller to Its
     List of Extremists," *Truthout* (July 16, 2020). Online: https://truthout.org/
     articles/southern-poverty-law-center-adds-stephen-miller-to-its-list-of-
     extremists/
90   Brett Samuels, "White House Backs Stephen Miller amid White
     Nationalist Allegations," *The Hill* (November 16, 2019). Online: https://
     thehill.com/homenews/administration/470691-white-house-backs-
     stephen-miller-amid-white-nationalist-emails

91 Michelle Goldberg, "Trump Is a White Nationalist Who Inspires Terrorism," *New York Times* (August 5, 2019). Online: https://www.nytimes.com/2019/08/05/opinion/trump-white-supremacy.html

92 Jason Wilson, "The Right-Wing Groups behind Wave of Protests against Covid-19 Restrictions," *Guardian* (April 17, 2020). Online: https://www.theguardian.com/world/2020/apr/17/far-right-coronavirus-protests-restrictions

93 Benjamin Swasey, "Trump Retweets Video of Apparent Supporter Saying 'White Power,'" *NPR* (June 28, 2020). Online: https://www.npr.org/sections/live-updates-protests-for-racial-justice/2020/06/28/884392576/trump-retweets-video-of-apparent-supporter-saying-white-power?utm_campaign=npr&utm_term=nprnews&utm_medium=social&utm_source=twitter.com

94 Michael D. Shear, "Trump Retweets Racist Video Showing Supporter Yelling 'White Power,'" *Washington Post* (June 28, 2020). Online: https://www.nytimes.com/2020/06/28/us/politics/trump-white-power-video-racism.html?campaign_id=56&emc=edit_cn_20200629&instance_id=19844&nl=on-politics-with-lisa-lerer&regi_id=51563793&segment_id=32115&te=1&user_id=ac16f3c28b64af0b86707bb1a8f1b07c

95 Annie Karni, "Trump Shares Video of Armed White Couple Confronting Protesters," *New York Times* (June 29, 2020). Online: https://www.nytimes.com/2020/06/29/us/politics/trump-white-couple-protesters.html?action=click&algo=top_conversion&block=lone_trending_recirc&fellback=false&imp_id=748109492&impression_id=983158328&index=2&pgtype=Article&region=footer&req_id=210315580&surface=most-popular

96 Cited in Raoul Peck, "James Baldwin Was Right All Along," *The Atlantic* (July 3, 2020). Online: https://www.theatlantic.com/culture/archive/2020/07/raoul-peck-james-baldwin-i-am-not-your-negro/613708/

97 Jeremy W. Peters, "Asked about Black Americans Killed by Police, Trump Says, 'So Are White People,'" *New York Times* (July 14, 2020). Online: https://www.nytimes.com/2020/07/14/us/politics/trump-white-people-killed-by-police.html

98 Churchill, "American Fascism: It Has Happened Here."

99 Rick Noack, "The Ugly History of 'Lugenpresse' Shouted at a Trump Rally," *Washington Post* (October 16, 2019). Online: https://www.washingtonpost.com/news/worldviews/wp/2016/10/24/the-ugly-history-of-luegenpresse-a-nazi-slur-shouted-at-a-trump-rally/

100 Arendt, *The Origins of Totalitarianism*, p. 474.

101 David W. Blight, "Trump and History: Ignorance and Denial," *Underground Railroad Freedom Center* (May 25, 2017). Online: https://freedomcenter.org/voice/trump-and-history-ignorance-and-denial

102 Reid Wilson, "Bolton Book Portrays 'Stunningly Uninformed' Trump," *The Hill* (June 17, 2020). Online: https://thehill.com/homenews/administration/503325-bolton-book-portrays-stunningly-uninformed-trump; John Bolton, *The Room Where It Happened* (New York: Simon & Schuster, 2020).

103 Jonathan Freedland, "Inspired by Trump, the World Could be Heading Back to the 1930s," *Guardian* (June 22, 2018). Online: Https://www.theguardian.com/commentisfree/2018/jun/22/trump-world-1930s-children-parents-europe-migrants

104 Editors, "On the Murder of George Floyd and the Demand for Racial Justice," *Third Text* (June 22, 2020). Online: https://mailchi.mp/78088bba729d/statement-from-the-editors-of-third-text?e=edf32547f2

105 Ibid.

106 Ibid.

107 Martin Luther King, Jr., "MLK at Western Michigan University" (December 18, 1963). Online: https://wmich.edu/sites/default/files/attachments/MLK.pdf

108 Martin Luther King, Jr., *Beyond Vietnam*, Speech delivered by MLK at Riverside Church on April 4, 1967 (Reprinted by Stanford: The Martin Luther King, Jr., Research and Education Institute). Online: https://kinginstitute.stanford.edu/king-papers/documents/beyond-vietnam

Chapter 7

1 For two insightful commentaries on poverty, inequality, and everyday life, see Bob Herbert, *Losing Our Way* (New York: Doubleday, 2014) and

Thomas Frank, *Rendezvous with Oblivion: Reports from a Sinking Society* (New York: Metropolitan, 2018).

2   The critical literature on inequality is enormous. I have learned a great deal from this small selection: Thomas Piketty, *Capital and Ideology* (Cambridge, MA: Belknap, 2020); Keith Payne, *The Broken Ladder: How Inequality Affects the Way We Think, Live, and Die* (New York: Penguin, 2017); Michael D. Yates, *The Great Inequality* (New York: Routledge, 2016); Anthony B. Atkins, *Inequality: What Can Be Done?* (Cambridge, MA: Harvard University Press, 2015); Joseph E. Stiglitz, *The Price of Inequality* (New York: Norton, 2012); Richard Wilkinson and Kate Pickett, *The Spirit Level: Why Equality is Better for Everyone* (New York: Penguin, 2010).

3   Editor, "'You Wouldn't Think You'd Go to Jail Over Medical Bills': County in Rural Kansas Is Jailing People Over Unpaid Medical Debt," *CBS News* (February 13, 2020). Online: https://www.cbsnews.com/news/coffeyville-kansas-medical-debt-county-in-rural-kansas-is-jailing-people-over-unpaid-medical-debt/

4   Oxfam, "5 Shocking Facts about Extreme Global Inequality and How to Even It Up," *Oxfam International* (2019). Online: https://www.oxfam.org/en/5-shocking-facts-about-extreme-global-inequality-and-how-even-it

5   Anthony DiMaggio, "The Censorship of Inequality in the Covid-19 Era: How Corporate and Market-Based Metrics Rule the News, and Why It Matters," *Project Censored* (May 12, 2020). Online: https://www.projectcensored.org/the-censorship-of-inequality-in-the-Covid-19-era-how-corporate-and-market-based-metrics-rule-the-news-and-why-it-matters/?doing_wp_cron=1589310856.0858778953552246093750&fbclid=IwAR16thSCoz94c33Voiq11sr-ovOuCN2zJJCa7HIGRIJiofljJN38AIJHGqY

6   Sandra Clark, "Help End World Poverty," *RallyCall* (October 16, 2019). Online: https://rallycall.io/campaign-details/Help_End_World_Poverty_1571272330

7   Chuck Collins, "Bernie's Right: Three Billionaires Really Do Have More Wealth than Half of America," *Inequality.org* (June 28, 2019). Online: https://inequality.org/great-divide/bernie-3-billionaires-more-wealth-half-america/

8   Amy Goodman, "Economist Thomas Piketty: Coronavirus Pandemic Has Exposed the 'Violence of Social Inequality,'" *Democracy Now!* (April 30,

2020). Online: https://www.democracynow.org/2020/4/30/thomas_
piketty

9 Tim Dickinson, "The Four Men Responsible for America's COVID-19
Test Disaster," *Rolling Stone* (May 10, 2020). Online: https://www.
rollingstone.com/politics/politics-features/Covid-19-test-trump-admin-
failed-disaster–995930/

10 Ronald Aronson, "Camus' Plague Is Not Ours," *Tikkun* (April 14, 2020).
Online: https://www.tikkun.org/camus-plague-is-not-ours

11 Cited in Richard Eskow, "Dr. King's Radical Revolution of Values,"
Common Dreams (January 20, 2020). Online: https://www.
commondreams.org/views/2020/01/20/dr-kings-radical-revolution-
values

12 Ed Yong, "How the Pandemic Defeated America," *The Atlantic* (August 3,
2020). Online: https://www.theatlantic.com/magazine/archive/2020/09/
coronavirus-american-failure/614191/

13 Michelle Alexander, "America, This Is Your Change," *New York Times*
(June 8, 2020). Online: https://www.nytimes.com/2020/06/08/opinion/
george-floyd-protests-race.html

14 David Harvey, "Capitalism Is Not the Solution to Urban America's
Problems—Capitalism Itself Is the Problem," *Jacobin* (June 5, 2020).
Online: https://www.jacobinmag.com/2020/06/david-harvey-cities-
capital-labor-crisis

15 See, for instance, Joao Biehl, *Vita: Life in a Zone of Social Abandonment*
(Los Angeles, CA: University of California Press, 2005).

16 Chacour Koop, "'Sacrifice the Weak' and 'Give Me Liberty': Signs at
Coronavirus Protests across US," *Miami Herald* (April 21, 2020). Online:
https://www.miamiherald.com/news/coronavirus/article242182796.html

17 Eric Cortellessa, "Jewish Dems Leader Calls Trump 'Depraved' for
Backing Armed Far-Right Protesters," *Times of Israel* (May 2, 2020).
Online: https://www.timesofisrael.com/us-jewish-leader-calls-trump-
depraved-for-backing-armed-far-right-protesters/

18 Annie Karni, "Facebook Removes Trump Ads Displaying Symbol Used
by Nazis," *New York Times* (June 18, 2020). Online: https://www.nytimes.
com/2020/06/18/us/politics/facebook-trump-ads-antifa-red-triangle.html

19 Liz Theoharis, "Inequality and the Coronavirus: Or How to Destroy
American Society from the Top Down," *TomDispatch.com* (April 21,

2020). Online http://www.tomdispatch.com/post/176691/tomgram%3A_liz_theoharis%2C_circling_the_ruins/

20   Ibid.

21   George Yancy, "Judith Butler: Mourning Is a Political Act amid the Pandemic and Its Disparities," *Truthout* (April 30, 2020). Online: https://truthout.org/articles/judith-butler-mourning-is-a-political-act-amid-the-pandemic-and-its-disparities/

22   David Sirota, "Health Insurance Companies Are Pissing on You and Saying It's Raining," *Jacobin* (April 2020). Online: https://jacobinmag.com/2020/05/health-insurance-coronavirus-cobra-medicare-for-all

23   Miles Kampf-Lassin, "The U.S. Response to Covid-19 Has Lavished Wealth on the Rich," *In These Times* (May 6, 2020). Online: http://inthesetimes.com/article/22514/Covid-19-coronavirus-wealthy-corporate-welfare

24   Joseph A. Schumpeter, Capitalism, *Socialism and Democracy* (London: Routledge, 1942, 1994), pp. 82–83.

25   David Harvey, *The Condition of Postmodernity* (Hoboken, NJ: Wiley-Blackwell, 1991), p. 147.

26   Thomas M. Magstadt, "Capitalism in America: The Coming Crisis," *CounterPunch* (January 30, 2020). Online: https://www.counterpunch.org/2020/01/30/capitalism-in-america-the-coming-crisis/

27   David Harvey, "Anti-Capitalist Politics in an Age of Covid-19," *Tribune Magazine* (March 23, 2020). Online: https://tribunemag.co.uk/2020/03/david-harvey-anti-capitalist-politics-in-an-age-of-Covid–19

28   Max Fisher, "As Coronavirus Deepens Inequality, Inequality Worsens Its Spread," *New York Times* (March 15, 2020). Online: https://www.nytimes.com/2020/03/15/world/europe/coronavirus-inequality.html

29   Katie Shepherd and Taylor Telford, "Twitter Penalizes Donald Trump Jr. for Posting Hydroxychloroquine Misinformation amid Coronavirus Pandemic," *Washington Post* (July 28, 2020). Online: https://www.washingtonpost.com/nation/2020/07/28/trump-coronavirus-misinformation-twitter/?utm_campaign=wp_post_most&utm_medium=email&utm_source=newsletter&wpisrc=nl_most

30   Michiko Kakutani, "Coronavirus Notebook: Finding Solace, and Connection, in Classic Books," *New York Times Book Review* (May 5, 2020). Online: https://www.nytimes.com/2020/05/05/books/review/coronavirus-

new-york-life-michiko-kakutani.html?te=1&nl=books&emc=edit_
bk_20200515

31 Anthony DiMaggio, "The Censorship of Inequality in the Covid-19
    Era: How Corporate and Market-Based Metrics Rule the News, and
    Why It Matters," *Project Censored* (May 12, 2020). Online: https://www.
    projectcensored.org/the-censorship-of-inequality-in-the-Covid-19-era-
    how-corporate-and-market-based-metrics-rule-the-news-and-why-it-
    matters/?doing_wp_cron=1589310856.0858778953552246093750&fbclid=
    IwAR16thSCoz94c33Voiq11sr-ovOuCN2zJJCa7HIGRIJiofljJN38AIJHGqY

32 See, for instance, C. Wright Mills, "The Cultural Apparatus," *The Politics
    of Truth: Selected Writings of C. Wright Mills* (Oxford: Oxford University
    Press, 2008), pp. 203–212.

33 Chandra Mohanty, "On Race and Voice: Challenges for Liberal Education
    in the 1990s," *Cultural Critique* 14 (Winter 1989–1990), 192.

34 Shalmali Guttal, "The Fortress World: After the Pandemic, Which
    Future?," *The Bullet* (July 16, 2020). Online: https://socialistproject.
    ca/2020/07/fortress-world-after-pandemic/#more

35 Joan Benach, "The Pandemic Kills the Poor: Inequality Will Kill Them
    Even More," *Socialist Project* (May 6, 2020). Online: https://socialistproject.
    ca/2020/05/pandemic-kills-the-poor-inequality-will-kill-more/

36 Jeff Cohen, "Let Us Name the System: 'Racial Capitalism,'" *Reader
    Supported News* (June 17, 2020). Online: https://readersupportednews.
    org/opinion2/277-75/63528-rsn-let-us-name-the-system-qracial-
    capitalismq

37 Harvey, "Capitalism Is Not the Solution to Urban America's Problems."

38 Andrea Germanos, "As Trump Sows Division, Poor People's Campaign
    Ignites 'Transformative Action' to Address Interwoven Injustices,"
    Common Dreams (June 21, 2020). Online: https://www.commondreams.
    org/news/2020/06/21/trump-sows-division-poor-peoples-campaign-
    ignites-transformative-action-address

39 Marilynne Robinson, "What Kind of Country Do We Want," *New York
    Review of Books* (June 11, 2020). Online: https://www.nybooks.com/
    articles/2020/06/11/what-kind-of-country-do-we-want/

40 Thom Hartmann, "Will Americans Reject Trump and the GOP Death
    Cult This Fall?," *Common Dreams* (July 14, 2020). Online: https://
    www.commondreams.org/views/2020/07/14/will-americans-reject-

trump-and-gop-death-cult-fall?cd-origin=rss&utm_term=AO&utm_
campaign=Daily%20Newsletter&utm_content=email&utm_
source=Daily%20Newsletter&utm_medium=Email

41   Jake Johnson, "'Lethal Inequality': New Study Shows Millions at High
     Risk of Covid-19 in US Lack Adequate Health Insurance," *Common
     Dreams* (June 10, 2020). Online: https://www.commondreams.org/
     news/2020/06/10/lethal-inequality-new-study-shows-millions-high-risk-
     Covid-19-us-lack-adequate

42   Jason Stanley, *How Fascism Works: The Politics of Us and Them* (New
     York: Random House, 2018).

43   Paul Gilroy, *Against Race* (Cambridge, MA: Harvard University Press,
     2000), 139.

44   Ibid.

45   Chiara Bottici, "Is Fascism Making a Comeback," *State of Nature*
     (December 3, 2017). Online: http://stateofnatureblog.com/one-question-
     fascism-part-one/

46   Dan Mangan and Amanda Macias, "Trump Says U.S. Army Bases Will
     Keep Confederate Names Despite Push After George Floyd Death," *CNBC*
     (June 10, 2020). Online: https://www.cnbc.com/2020/06/10/trump-says-
     army-bases-will-keep-confederate-names.html

47   Kristen Holmes and Geneva Sands, "Homeland Security Establishes
     Task Force to Protect Monuments, Memorials and Statues," *CNN Politics*
     (July 1, 2020). Online: https://www.cnn.com/2020/07/01/politics/
     dhs-task-force-protect-monuments-statues/index.html?emci=ff638d83-
     e5bb-ea11-9b05-00155d039e74&emdi=d62a85ca-eabb-ea11-9b05-
     00155d039e74&ceid=648633

48   Jeff Pegues, "Department of Homeland Security Admits that It
     'Restructured' Domestic Terror Team," *CBS News* (April 2, 2020). Online:
     https://www.cbsnews.com/news/department-of-homeland-security-
     admits-that-it-restructured-domestic-terror-team/?emci=ff638d83-
     e5bb-ea11-9b05-00155d039e74&emdi=d62a85ca-eabb-ea11-9b05-
     00155d039e74&ceid=648633

49   Adam Weinstein, "This Is Fascism," *New Republic* (June 2, 2020). Online:
     https://newrepublic.com/article/157949/fascism-america-trump-anti-
     police-george-floyd-protests

50   Maggie Haberman, "Trump Threatens White House Protesters with
     'Vicious Dogs' and 'Ominous Weapons,'" *New York Times* (June 1,

2020). Online: https://www.nytimes.com/2020/05/30/us/politics/trump-threatens-protesters-dogs-weapons.html

51 Gail Collins, "Trump's Magic Word," *New York Times* (June 3, 2020). Online: https://www.nytimes.com/2020/06/03/opinion/trump-dominate.html

52 Weinstein, "This Is Fascism."

53 Chris Walker, "Trump's Press Secretary Wants Science to Get Out of the Way of School Reopenings," *Truthout* (July 17, 2020). Online: https://truthout.org/articles/trumps-press-secretary-wants-science-to-get-out-of-the-way-of-school-reopenings/?eType=EmailBlastContent&eId=39e6ebc0-aca4-4c45-8119-4afe4d9598a4

54 Richard C. Gross, "Rising Autocracy," *CounterPunch* (July 21, 2020). Online: https://www.counterpunch.org/2020/07/21/rising-autocracy/

55 Chiara Bottici in Cihan Aksan and Jon Bailes, eds., "One Question Fascism (Part One)—Is Fascism Making a Comeback?," *State of Nature Blog* (December 3, 2017).Online: http://stateofnatureblog.com/one-question-fascism-part-one/

56 Neil Faulkner in Cihan Aksan and Jon Bailes, eds., "One Question Fascism? (Part One)—Is Fascism Making a Comeback?" *State of Nature Blog* (December 3, 2017). Online: http://stateofnatureblog.com/one-question-fascism-part-one

57 Sarah Churchill, "American Fascism: It Has Happened Here," *New York Review of Books* (June 22, 2020). Online: https://www.nybooks.com/daily/2020/06/22/american-fascism-it-has-happened-here/

Chapter 8

1 On what might be called the catastrophe of capitalism, see John Bellamy Foster and Intan Suwandi, "COVID-19 and Catastrophe Capitalism," *Monthly Review* (June 1, 2020). Online: https://monthlyreview.org/2020/06/01/Covid-19-and-catastrophe-capitalism/

2 David Harvey, "Capitalism Is Not the Solution to Urban America's Problems—Capitalism Itself Is the Problem," *Jacobin* (June 5, 2020). Online: https://www.jacobinmag.com/2020/06/david-harvey-cities-capital-labor-crisis

3   See, for instance, Rick Perlstein, "Market Logic Is Literally Killing Us," *In These Times* (June 17, 2020). Online: https://inthesetimes.com/article/22558/COVID-19-free-market-capitalism-killing-pandemic

4   Liz Theoharis, "Organizing the Rich or the Poor? Which America Will Be Ours After the Pandemic," *TomDispatch.com* (June 4, 2020). Online: https://www.tomdispatch.com/post/176709/tomgram%3A_liz_theoharis%2C_you_only_get_what_you%27re_organized_to_take/

5   Susan Buck-Morss, *Revolution Today* (Chicago: Haymarket Books, 2019).

6   Martin Luther King, Jr., *Beyond Vietnam*, Speech delivered by MLK at Riverside Church on April 4, 1967 (Reprinted by Stanford: The Martin Luther King, Jr., Research and Education Institute). Online: https://kinginstitute.stanford.edu/king-papers/documents/beyond-vietnam

7   Editors, "On the Murder of George Floyd and the Demand for Racial Justice," *Third Text* (June 22, 2020). Online: https://mailchi.mp/78088bba729d/statement-from-the-editors-of-third-text?e=edf32547f2

8   Shalmali Guttal, "The Fortress World: After the Pandemic, Which Future?," *The Bullet* (July 16, 2020). Online: https://socialistproject.ca/2020/07/fortress-world-after-pandemic/#more

9   Amy Goodman, "Angela Davis on Abolition, Calls to Defund Police, Toppled Racist Statues & Voting in 2020 Election," *Democracy Now* (July 3, 2020). Online: https://www.democracynow.org/2020/7/3/angela_davis_on_abolition_calls_to

10 Susan Buck-Morss, *Revolution Today* (Chicago: Haymarket Books, 2019).

11 Andrea Germanos, "As Trump Sows Division, Poor People's Campaign Ignites 'Transformative Action' to Address Interwoven Injustices," *Common Dreams* (June 21, 2020). Online: https://www.commondreams.org/news/2020/06/21/trump-sows-division-poor-peoples-campaign-ignites-transformative-action-address

12 Michelle Alexander, "America, This Is Your Chance," *New York Times* (June 8, 2020). Online: https://www.nytimes.com/2020/06/08/opinion/george-floyd-protests-race.html

13 Étienne Balibar, "Outline of a Topography of Cruelty: Citizenship and Civility in the Era of Global Violence," in *We, The People of Europe? Reflections on Transnational Citizenship* (Princeton: Princeton University Press, 2004), p. 128.

Index